VOGUE® KNITTING
DESIGNER KNITS

VOGUE® KNITTING
DESIGNER KNITS

DKNY • Calvin Klein • Adrienne Vittadini • Perry Ellis

Missoni • Joan Vass • Cynthia Rowley

Todd Oldham • Michael Simon • Betty Jackson • Anna Sui

Edited by Trisha Malcolm

THE BUTTERICK® PUBLISHING COMPANY
NEW YORK

THE BUTTERICK® PUBLISHING COMPANY
161 Avenue of the Americas
New York, New York 10013

Editor-in-Chief
Trisha Malcolm

Editor
Annemarie McNamara

Managing Editor
Daryl Brower

Designer Liaison
Rae Ann Scandroli

Yarn Editor
Ruth Tobacco

Yarn Coordinator
Veronica Manno

Technical Illustration Editor
Lila P. Chin

Copy Editor
Jacquelyn Smyth

Editorial Coordinator
Kathleen Kelly

Photo Archivist
Sherry Onna Handlin

Art Director, Butterick® Company, Inc
Joe Vior

Book Designer
Christine Lipert

Page Layout
Ben Ostasiewski

Project Directors
Martha Moran
Caroline Politi

Production Managers
Lillian Esposito
Winnie Hinish

Publishing Consultant
Mike Shatzkin

Executive Vice President and Publisher, Butterick® Company, Inc
Art Joinnides

President and CEO, Butterick® Company, Inc
Jay H. Stein

Manufactured by Quebecor in the United States of America

1 3 5 7 9 10 8 6 4 2

Library of Congress Catalog Card Number: 97-077513

ISBN: 1-57389-009-X

Introduction

Since the inception of the "modern" *Vogue Knitting* magazine in 1982, one of the most popular features has always been the selection of designer patterns presented in each issue. Over the years, the editors have developed very unique working relationships with the major knitwear designers, allowing *Vogue Knitting* to bring the best of designer handknit fashion to you, our readers. This collection pays homage to the talent, innovation and expertise of the designers featured—the classic minimalism of Calvin Klein, Adrienne Vittadini, Joan Vass and Perry Ellis...the refined whimsical style of Michael Simon, Betty Jackson, Todd Oldham and Cynthia Rowley...the sporty attitude of DKNY...the vibrant, harmonious colorwork of the Missonis.

From beginning to end, this book has been a wonderful experience for the editors. Once the seed was planted and the idea grew, many hours were spent researching past issues to gather together this crème de la crème selection of designer knits. We endeavored to select classic, timeless designs that have as much appeal now as when they first appeared, and will continue to have as the years go by.

Searching through our archives for the photographs was certainly an enjoyable process. Often the original view shown in *Vogue Knitting* was chosen, while other times, a different view was selected to better show the features of the sweater.

Unearthing comparable substitute yarns was an exciting challenge. Sometimes we were lucky—a yarn, or its twin under a different name—was still available. Other times we were less fortunate, but persevered until we could find the perfect substitute in the latest yarns available today. We can assure you deep in the closets at *Vogue Knitting* there is a box containing enough test swatches for the sweaters in this book to make a very cozy afghan!

Both the original and substitute yarns are listed where appropriate—even though a yarn may no longer be available, we're sure some still exists in the collection of a knitter somewhere.

We hope you enjoy the variety and quality of these incredible designer knits, and that this collection will inspire you to take up your needles and create your own designer classic.

We endeavored to select classic, timeless designs that have as much appeal now as when they first appeared...

Table of Contents

● Introduction 5

● Before You Begin 8
  Yarn Selection
  Gauge
  Reading Patterns
  Following Charts
  Knitting Terms and Abbreviations
  Needle Chart

● Adrienne Vittadini 10
  Zigzag and Bobble Pullover 12
  Argyle Cardigan 15
  Floral Pattern Pullover 18
  Cable and Garter Pullover 22
  Diamond Cable Turtleneck 25
  Cabled Cardigan 28
  Fur-Trimmed Cabled Cardigan 31
  Allover Leaf-Rib Pullover 34

● DKNY 36
  Enchanted Forest 38
  Entrelac Pullover 44
  Interlocking Cable Tunic 47
  Cable and Leaf Motif V-Neck Pullover 50
  Openwork Cable Cardigan 53
  Counterpane Pullover 56
  Flared Cable Tunic 60

● Missoni 62
  Man's Cardigan 64
  Hooded Cardigan 67
  Sawtooth Cardigan 70
  One-Piece T-Shirt Pullover 73
  Flame Stitch Cardigan 76
  Summer Cardigan 79
  Funnel-Neck Short Pullover 82

● Calvin Klein 84
  Fitted Cable Sweater 86
  Stitchwork Cardigan 89
  Cable V-Neck 92
  Cable Cardigan 95
  Cable Turtleneck 98

● Perry Ellis 100
  Bubble Sweater 102
  Stitchwork Turtleneck 105
  Cable Dart Cardigan 108
  Zebra Print Pullover 111
  Man's Aran 114
  Fair Isle Crew Neck 117
  Short Top 120

● Joan Vass 122
  Eyelash Turtleneck 124
  Cropped Hooded Sweater 126
  Diagonal V-Front Sweater 128
  Tank Top 130
  Family Cable Pullovers 132

● The Innovators 136
  Gingerbread Cookie Cardigan *Michael Simon* 138
  Aran Pullover and Matching Hat *Cynthia Rowley* 142
  Aran and Bobble Cardigan *Anna Sui* 145
  Pony Print Pullover *Betty Jackson* 148
  Rose Tunic *Betty Jackson* 152
  Cropped Striped Pullover *Todd Oldham* 156

● Resources 158

● Acknowledgements 160

Before You Begin

This book was designed as an anthology of patterns. For more precise technical information and explanation, refer to Vogue Knitting—The Ultimate Knitting Book *(New York: Pantheon Books). See page 159 for ordering information.*

YARN SELECTION

Some of the yarns, or colors, used in the original designer patterns are no longer available. We have provided substitute yarns readily available in the U.S. and Canada at the time of printing. The Resources on page 158 lists addresses of yarn distributors—contact them for the name of a retailer in your area or for mail order information.

If you wish to substitute a yarn, check the gauge carefully to ensure the finished garment will knit to the correct measurements. To facilitate yarn substitution, *Vogue Knitting* grades yarn by the standard stitch gauge obtained in stockinette stitch. There is a grading number in the Materials section of each pattern. Look for a substitute yarn that falls into the same category—the suggested gauge on the ball band should be comparable to that on the Yarn Symbols Chart (right).

After successfully gauge-swatching in a substitute yarn, you'll need to determine yarn requirements. First, find the total length of the original yarn in the pattern (multiply number of balls by yards/meters per ball). Divide this figure by the new yards/meters per ball (listed on the ball band). Round up to the next whole number. The answer is the number of balls required.

GAUGE

Always knit a gauge swatch before beginning to ensure a successful project. Normally, gauge is measured over a four-inch (10cm) square. Using the needles and yarn suggested, cast on enough stitches to knit a square at least this size. Gauge is usually given in stockinette stitch, but if the pattern calls for a specific stitch, work this stitch for the swatch. Measure stitches carefully with a ruler or gauge tool. If the swatch is smaller than the stated gauge (more stitches per inch/cm), try larger needles. If it is larger (fewer stitches per inch/cm), use smaller needles. Experiment with needle size until the gauge exactly matches the one given before proceeding.

If a pattern calls for knitting in the round, this may tighten the gauge, so if the gauge was measured on a flat swatch, take another reading after beginning the project.

YARN SYMBOLS

The following symbols 1- 6 represent a range of stitch gauges. Note that these symbols correspond to the standard gauge in stockinette stitch.

① **FINE WEIGHT**
(29-32 stitches per 4"/10cm)
Includes baby and fingering yarns, and some of the heavier crochet cottons.

② **LIGHTWEIGHT**
(25-28 stitches per 4"/10cm)
Includes sport yarn, sock yarn, UK 4-ply and lightweight DK yarns.

③ **MEDIUM WEIGHT**
(21-24 stitches per 4"/10cm)
Includes DK and worsted, the most commonly used knitting yarns.

④ **MEDIUM-HEAVY WEIGHT**
(17-20 stitches per 4"/10cm)
Also called heavy worsted or Aran.

⑤ **BULKY WEIGHT**
(13-16 stitches per 4"/10cm)
Also called chunky. Includes heavier Icelandic yarns.

⑥ **EXTRA-BULKY WEIGHT**
(9-12 stitches per 4"/10cm)
The heaviest yarns available.

READING PATTERNS

Each pattern is rated for technical ability. Choose a pattern that fits within your experience range. Read all instructions thoroughly before starting to knit a gauge swatch and again before beginning a project. Familiarize yourself with all abbreviations (see Knitting Terms and Abbreviations, opposite). Refer to the *Vogue Knitting* book for clear explanations of any stitches or techniques you may not be familiar with.

Generally, patterns are written in several sizes. The smallest appears first, and figures for larger sizes are given in parentheses. Where only one figure appears, it applies to all sizes. Highlight numbers pertaining to your size before beginning.

Knitted measurements are the dimensions of the garment after all the pieces have been sewn together. Usually, three measurements are given: finished chest; finished length; and, sleeve width at upper arm. The finished chest measurement is the width around the entire sweater at the underarm. For cardigans, the width is determined with the front bands buttoned. Finished length is measured from the highest point of the shoulder to the bottom of the ribbing. Sleeve width is measured at the upper arm, after all increases have been worked and before any cap shaping takes place.

Schematics are a valuable tool for determining size selection and proper fit. Schematics are scale drawings showing the dimensions of the finished knitted pieces.

Work figures given inside brackets the number of times stated afterward. Directions immediately following an asterisk are to be repeated the given number of times. If the instructions call for working

KNITTING TERMS AND ABBREVIATIONS

approx approximately

beg begin(ning)

bind off Used to finish an edge and keep stitches from unraveling. Lift the first stitch over the second, the second over the third, etc. (UK: cast off)

cast on A foundation row of stitches placed on the needle in order to begin knitting.

CC contrast color

ch chain(s)

cm centimeter(s)

cont continu(e)(ing)

dc double crochet (UK: tr-treble)

dec decrease(ing)—Reduce the stitches in a row (knit 2 together).

dpn double pointed needle(s)

foll follow(s)(ing)

g gram(s)

garter stitch Knit every row. Circular knitting: knit one round, then purl one round.

hdc half-double crochet (UK: htr-half treble)

inc increase(ing)—Add stitches in a row (knit into the front and back of a stitch).

k knit

k2tog knit 2 stitches together

lp(s) loops(s)

LH left hand

m meter(s)

M1 make one stitch—With the needle tip, lift the strand between the last stitch worked and next stitch on the left-hand needle and knit into the back of it. One stitch has been added.

MC main color

mm millimeter(s)

oz ounce(s)

p purl

p2tog purl 2 stitches together

pat pattern

pick up and knit (purl) Knit (or purl) into the loops along an edge.

pm place markers—Place or attach a loop of contrast yarn or purchased stitch marker as indicated.

rem remain(s)(ing)

rep repeat

rev St st reverse Stockinette stitch—Purl right-side rows, knit wrong-side rows. Circular knitting: purl all rounds. (UK: reverse stocking stitch)

rnd(s) round(s)

RH right hand

RS right side(s)

sc single crochet (UK: dc - double crochet)

sk skip

SKP Slip 1, knit 1, pass slip stitch over knit 1.

sl slip—An unworked stitch made by passing a stitch from the left-hand to the right-hand needle as if to purl.

sl st slip stitch (UK: single crochet)

SSK slip, slip, knit—Slip next 2 stitches knitwise, one at a time, to right-hand needle. Insert tip of left-hand needle into fronts of these stitches from left to right. Knit them together. One stitch has been decreased.

st(s) stitch(es)

St st Stockinette stitch—Knit right-side rows, purl wrong-side rows. Circular knitting: knit all rounds. (UK: stocking stitch)

tbl through back of loop

tog together

WS wrong side(s)

wyif with yarn in front

wyib with yarn in back

work even Continue in pattern without increasing or decreasing. (UK: work straight)

yd yard(s)

yo yarn over—Make a new stitch by wrapping the yarn over the right-hand needle. (UK: yfwd, yon, yrn)

* repeat directions following * as many times as indicated.

[ ] Repeat directions inside brackets as many times as indicated.

---

even, work in the same pattern stitch without increasing or decreasing.

FOLLOWING CHARTS

Charts are a convenient way to follow colorwork, lace, cable and other stitch patterns. *Vogue Knitting* stitch charts utilize the universal language of "symbolcraft." Each symbolcraft symbol represents the stitch as it appears on the right side of the work. For example, the symbol for the knit stitch is a vertical line and the symbol for a purl stitch is a horizontal one. On right-side rows, work the stitches as they appear on the chart—knitting the vertical lines and purling the horizontal ones. When reading wrong-side rows, work the opposite of what is shown; that is, purl the vertical lines and knit the horizontal ones.

Each square on a chart represents one stitch and each horizontal row of squares equals a row or round. When knitting back and forth on straight needles, right-side rows (RS) are read right to left, wrong-side rows (WS) are read from left to right; bottom to top. When knitting in rounds on circular needles, read charts from right to left on every round, repeating any stitch and row repeats as directed in the pattern. Posting a self-adhesive note under the working row is an easy way to keep track on a chart.

Sometimes, only a single repeat of the pattern is charted. Heavy lines drawn through the entire chart indicate a repeat. The lines are the equivalent of an asterisk (*) or brackets [] used in written instructions.

KNITTING NEEDLES		
US	METRIC	UK
0	2mm	14
1	2.25mm	13
	2.5mm	
2	2.75mm	12
	3mm	11
3	3.25mm	10
4	3.5mm	
5	3.75mm	9
	4mm	8
6		
7	4.5mm	7
8	5mm	6
9	5.5mm	5
10	6mm	4
10½	6.5mm	3
	7mm	2
	7.5mm	1
11	8mm	0
13	9mm	00
15	10mm	000

Adrienne Vittadini

DESIGNING KNITWEAR IS Adrienne Vittadini's "great love." Her wonderfully simple, beautifully colored sweaters were an instant hit, and have since served as the undeniable foundation of her entire collection. Alluring textures, sensual shapes, and intense colors are the signature of Vittadini's designs. Her unique vision makes its impact through well-defined contrasts: Ribs and cables are intertwined or contrasted with stockinette; richly textured sweaters are made sleek and fitted; intense colors and intricate patterns play off her simple silhouettes.

With a European heritage, an American upbringing, and an Italian sensibility, this award-winning designer brings to her collection a global vision and intuitive style that results in sophisticated fashion with a feminine edge. Vittadini designs appeal to the needs of active women worldwide—with an easy blend of stylish knitwear to take a woman from home to office and beyond.

While her designs and color choices often appear intuitive, Vittadini entered her profession with an impressive background and a degree in fine arts. After working in Italy as a freelance designer, she came to New York in the early '70s,

Photo courtesy of Adrienne Vittadini Enterprises, Inc.

Alluring textures, sensual shapes, and intense colors are the signature of Vittadini's designs.

then opened her own business in 1979 with her manager-husband Gianluigi Vittadini. The Vittadinis have since built a multi-million dollar company with design lines ranging from sweaters and yarns to fragrance, eyewear, luggage, shoes, swimwear, cosmetics, wallpaper and, most recently, home accessories.

Vittadini takes an active roll in all aspects of knit design and production, including the development of her line of exclusive handknitting yarns, which coordinate with her ready-to-wear collection. She travels extensively, visiting cities around the world to fuel her intellect and to stay on top of today's trends. Her design house holds a vast reference and fabric library to inspire new print and pattern ideas.

A finely tuned instinct for what women need and desire has been a critical component of Vittadini's remarkable success. She has earned her long-standing reputation as a fashion leader by designing clothes that are comfortable and practical, yet streamlined and casually elegant. The following sweaters were selected for their very special and very Vittadini style—timeless, distinctive, and always in fashion.

Rolled edges give this lavish, oversized pattern stitch pullover casual appeal. With fanciful bobbles and geometrics, the pullover has enormous vitality of surface pattern and line on a grand scale. The Zigzag and Bobble Pullover first appeared in the Fall/Winter '84, then the Fall '92 issue of *Vogue Knitting*.

Zigzag and Bobble Pullover

FOR EXPERIENCED KNITTERS

SIZES
To fit 32-34 (36-38, 40)"/81-86 (91-96, 101)cm bust. Directions are for smallest size with larger sizes in parentheses. If there is only one set of figures it applies to all sizes.

KNITTED MEASUREMENTS
● Bust at underarm 42 (45, 47)"/106 (112, 120)cm.
● Length 24 (24½, 25)"/61 (62, 63.5)cm.
● Sleeve width at upper arm 18 (19, 20)"/45 (47, 49)cm.

MATERIALS
● 4 3½oz/100g balls (each approx 190yd/173m) of Patons *Ballybrae* (wool 4) in #200 off-white (A)
● 3 balls in #277 brown tweed (B)
● Size 8 (5mm) circular needle 24"/60cm long OR SIZE TO OBTAIN GAUGE

Note
The original color used for this sweater is no longer available. A comparable color substitute has been made, which is available at the time of printing.

GAUGE
19 sts and 24 rows to 4"/10cm over St st using size 8 (5mm) needle.
18 sts to 4"/10cm over chart pat.
FOR PERFECT FIT, TAKE TIME TO CHECK GAUGES.

Notes
1 When changing colors, twist yarns on WS to prevent holes.
2 Due to nature of chart pat, pieces will pull in slightly at side edges. Be sure to block carefully to finished measurements.

BACK
With A, cast on 95 (101, 107) sts. Work back and forth as with straight needles in St st for 4"/10cm, end with a p row.
Beg Pats: Row 1 (RS) With A, k2; *with B, [k1, p1, k1] in next st, turn, p3, turn, k3, turn, p3, turn, k3tog—called make bobble (MB); with A, k5; rep from *, end MB, k2A. With A only, p 1 row, k 1 row, p 1 row. Sl sts to other end of needle.
Row 5 (WS) With B, purl.
Row 6 With B, purl.
Row 7 With B, knit. With A, k 1 row, p 1 row, k 1 row. Sl sts to other end of needle.
Row 11 (RS) With B, knit.
Row 12 With B, knit.
Row 13 With B, purl. With A, p 1 row, k 1 row, p 1 row. Sl sts to other end of needle.
Row 17 (WS) With B, purl.
Row 18 With B, purl.
Row 19 With B, knit.
Rows 20-31 Beg chosen size as

indicated on chart, work 12 rows foll chart. With B, k 2 rows, p 1 row. Sl sts to other end of needle.
Row 35 (RS) With A, knit. With A, p 1 row, k 1 row. With B, p 2 rows, k 1 row. Sl sts to other end of needle.
Row 41 (WS) With A, purl.
Row 42 With A, knit.
Row 43 With A, purl. Rep rows 1-43 for pats once more, then rep rows 1-16 once, then rep row 1 once. With A only, work in St st until back measures 24 (24½, 25)"/61 (62, 63.5)cm from beg, or desired length.

Shoulder shaping
Bind off 26 (29, 32) sts at beg of next 2 rows. Bind off rem 43 sts.

FRONT
Work as for back until front measures 21½ (22, 22½)"/54.5 (55.5, 57)cm from beg, end with a WS row.

Neck shaping
Next row (RS) Work 36 (39, 42) sts, join 2nd ball of yarn and bind off center 23 sts for neck, work to end. Working both sides at once, bind off 3 sts from each neck edge twice, then dec 1 st at each neck edge every other row 4 times—26 (29, 32) sts each side. Work even until same length as back to shoulder. Bind off sts each side for shoulders.

SLEEVES
With A, cast on 39 (41, 43) sts. Work back and forth in St st for 4"/10cm, inc 1 st each end every 4th row 9 (12, 15)

times, then every 6th row 12 (10, 8) times, and AT SAME TIME, when 4"/10cm of St st has been worked, rep pat rows 1-43 as on back twice. After all incs and pats have been worked and there are 81 (85, 89) sts, with A only, work even if necessary in St st until sleeve measures 18½"/47cm from beg, or desired sleeve length. Bind off all sts.

FINISHING
Block pieces to measurements. Sew shoulder seams.

Neckband
With RS facing and A, pick up and k43 sts along back of neck, 11 sts along left front neck, 23 sts along center front neck, 11 sts along right front neck—88

sts. Join and work in rnds of St st (k every rnd) for 3"/7.5cm. Bind off all sts. Place markers on front and back 9 (9½, 10)"/22.5 (23.5, 24.5)cm down from shoulder seam for armholes. Sew top of sleeves between markers. Sew side and sleeve seams. ●

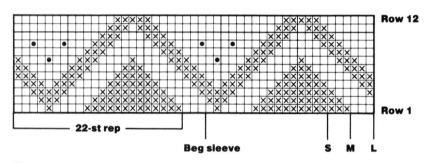

Row 12

Row 1

⊢ 22-st rep ⊣

Beg sleeve

S M L

☐ **St st with off white (A)**

☒ **Rev St st with brown tweed (B)**

⊡ **Bobble st with brown tweed (B)**

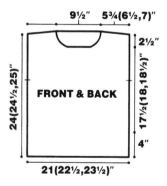

9½"   5¾(6½,7)"

2½"

24(24½,25)"

17½(18,18½)"

FRONT & BACK

4"

21(22½,23½)"

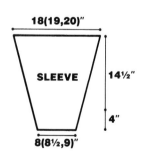

18(19,20)"

SLEEVE

14½"

4"

8(8½,9)"

Argyle Cardigan

A lithe body line, an unstudied air, and a decisive drama of color and pattern—such is the artistry of Adrienne Vittadini. This oversized argyle pattern cardigan is worked in a symphony of color, with blue sleeves, purple and green on the front, and fuschia on the back. The sweater features drop shoulders, V-neck and pockets. Shown in size 36. The Argyle Cardigan first appeared in the Fall/Winter '86 issue of *Vogue Knitting*.

Argyle Cardigan

FOR INTERMEDIATE KNITTERS

SIZES
To fit 32 (34, 36, 38)"/81 (86, 91, 96)cm bust. Directions are for smallest size with larger sizes in parentheses. If there is only one set of figures it applies to all sizes.

KNITTED MEASUREMENTS
● Bust measurement at underarm (buttoned) 42 (44, 46, 48)"/105 (109, 114, 119)cm.
● Length 27½ (28½, 29½, 30½)"/68.5 (71, 74, 76.5)cm.
● Sleeve width at upper arm 19 (20, 21, 22)"/48 (50, 52, 54)cm.

MATERIALS
Original Yarn
● 8 (8, 9, 9) 1¾oz/50g balls (each approx 142yd/130m) of Busse *Softino* (wool/alpaca 4) in #8876 brown (MC)
● 3 (3, 3, 4) balls each in #4894 fuchsia (A) and #5854 blue (D)
● 2 balls each in #6898 green (B) and #5856 purple (C)
● 1 ball each in #8864 gold (E) and #7877 black (F)
Substitute Yarn
● 8 (8, 9, 9) 1¾oz/50g balls (each approx 140yd/130m) of Tahki *Sable* (wool/angora 4) in #1638 reddish brown (MC)
● 3 (3, 3, 4) balls each in #1624 dark coral (A) and #1634 blue (D)
● 2 balls each in #1633 green (B) and #1636 purple (C)
● 1 ball each in #1620 yellow

heather (E) and #1608 black (F)
● One pair each sizes 7 and 9 (4.5 and 5.5mm) needles OR SIZE TO OBTAIN GAUGE
● Size 7 (4.5mm) circular needle 36"/90cm long
● Five ¾"/20mm buttons
● Stitch holders and markers
● Bobbins
● Shoulder pads (optional)
Note
The original yarn used for this sweater is no longer available. A comparable substitute has been made, which is available at the time of printing. Check gauge of substitute yarns very carefully before beginning.

GAUGE
17 sts and 26 rows to 4"/10cm over St st using size 9 (5.5mm) needles. FOR PERFECT FIT, TAKE TIME TO CHECK GAUGE.

Notes
1 When changing colors, twist yarns on WS to prevent holes. Use a separate bobbin for each large block of color.
2 Block pieces to measurements.
3 Diagonal lines between diamonds are worked in duplicate st after pieces are complete.

BACK
With smaller needles and MC, cast on 89 (93, 97, 101) sts. Work in k1, p1 rib for 1"/2.5cm. Change to larger needles.

Work in St st with MC and A as foll:
Beg chart: Row 1 (RS) Beg with 4th (2nd, 32nd, 30th) st, work to end of chart, then work 32-st rep of chart 1 (1, 2, 3) times, then work first 28 (30, 32, 2) sts once more. Cont to work chart, working rows 1-64 twice, then rows 1-44 (50, 58, 64) once more—piece measures approx 27½ (28½, 29½, 30½)"/68.5 (71, 74, 76.5)cm from beg. Bind off.

Pocket linings (make 2)
With larger needles and MC, cast on 23 sts. Work in St st for 7½/19cm. Sl sts to holder.

LEFT FRONT
With smaller needles and MC, cast on 43 (45, 47, 49) sts. Work in k1, p1 rib for 1"/2.5cm. Change to larger needles. Work in chart pat with MC and B as foll:
Row 1 (RS) Beg with 27th (29th, 31st, 1st) st, work to end of chart, then work 32-st rep 1 (1, 1, 0) times, then work first 5 (9, 13, 17) sts. Cont in pat until piece measures 8½"/21cm from beg.

Pocket joining
Next row (RS) Work 7 (9, 11, 13) sts, sl next 21 sts to holder for pocket opening, work to end.
Next row Work 14 sts, with RS of 1 lining facing WS of front, p next st tog with first st of lining, p across sts of lining to last st, p last st of lining tog with next st of front, work to end. Cont in pat on all sts until piece measures 11½"/29cm from beg.

Neck shaping

Next row (RS) Work to last 2 sts, k2tog. Cont in this way to dec 1 st at neck edge (working dec sts into pat) every 4th row 9 (11, 11, 10) times more, every 6th row 4 (3, 3, 5) times—29 (30, 32, 33) sts. Work even until same length as back. Bind off.

RIGHT FRONT

Work to correspond to left front, using MC and C for chart pat, reversing pocket joining and neck shaping and reversing chart pat by beg with 27th (23rd, 19th, 15th) st of chart.

SLEEVES

With smaller needles and MC, cast on 43 (45, 47, 49) sts. Work in k1, p1 rib for 1"/2.5cm. Change to larger needles. Work in chart pat with MC and D as foll:
Row 1 (RS) Beg with 3rd (2nd, 1st,

32nd) st work to end of chart, then work 32-st rep 0 (0, 0, 1) time, then work first 13 (14, 15, 16) sts once. Cont in pat, inc 1 st each end (working inc sts into pat) every 4th row 5 (8, 11, 14) times, every 6th row 14 (12, 10, 8) times—81 (85, 89, 93) sts. Work even until piece measures 18"/45cm from beg. Bind off.

FINISHING

Block pieces. Sew shoulder seams.

Front band

Place markers for buttonholes along right front edge with the first ½"/1.5cm from lower edge and last ½"/1.5cm below first neck dec, others spaced evenly between. With RS facing, circular needle and MC, pick up and k275 (277, 279, 281) sts evenly along right front edge, back neck edge and left

front edge. Work back and forth as with straight needles in k1, p1 rib, working buttonholes after 1 row opposite markers by k2tog, yo for each buttonhole. Work yo into rib on next row. Rib until band measures 1"/2.5cm. Bind off knitwise. Place markers 9½ (10, 10½, 11)"/24 (25, 26, 27)cm down from shoulders on front and back for armholes. Sew top of sleeves to front and back between markers. Sew side and sleeve seams.

Pocketbands

Sl 21 sts from holder to smaller needles to work first row from RS. With MC, work in k1, p1 rib for 1"/2.5cm. Bind off in rib. Sew sides of band to front. Sew pocket linings to inside of fronts. Work diagonal lines in E and F in duplicate st foll chart. ●

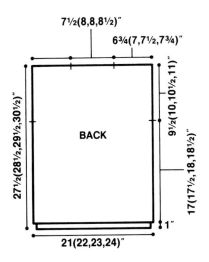

7½(8,8,8½)"
6¾(7,7½,7¾)"
BACK
27½(28½,29½,30½)"
9½(10,10½,11)"
17(17½,18,18½)"
1"
21(22,23,24)"

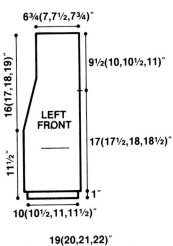

6¾(7,7½,7¾)"
16(17,18,19)"
LEFT FRONT
11½"
9½(10,10½,11)"
17(17½,18,18½)"
1"
10(10½,11,11½)"

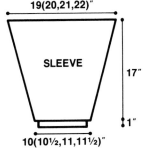

19(20,21,22)"
SLEEVE
17"
1"
10(10½,11,11½)"

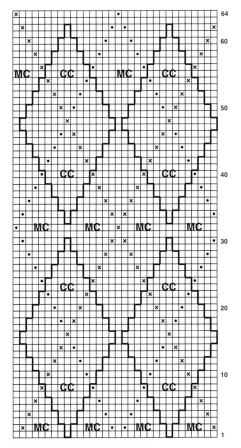

64
60
MC   CC   MC   CC
50
CC   CC
40
MC   MC   MC   MC
30
CC   CC
20
CC   CC
10
MC   MC   MC   MC
1

COLOR KEY FOR DUPLICATE STITCH

⊡ black
⊠ yellow heather

A d r i e n n e   V i t t a d i n i

A classic Vittadini pullover becomes the backdrop for her Hungarian folk-art inspired colorwork pattern of stylized flowers and embroidered French knots. With angled armholes and crew neck, this sweater combines modern ease with understated elegance. Shown in size 32-34. The Floral Pattern Pullover first appeared in the Fall '87 issue of *Vogue Knitting*.

Floral Pattern Pullover

FOR EXPERIENCED KNITTERS

SIZES

To fit 32-34 (36, 38, 40)"/81-86 (91, 96, 101)cm bust. Directions are for smallest size with larger sizes in parentheses. If there is only one set of figures it applies to all sizes.

KNITTED MEASUREMENTS

● Bust at underarm 38½ (41, 42, 44½)"/97 (102, 106, 111)cm.
● Length 26 (27, 27½, 28)"/65.5 (68, 69, 70.5)cm.
● Sleeve width at upper arm 18 (18, 19, 19)"/45 (45, 47, 47)cm.

MATERIALS
Original Yarn
● 13 (14, 14, 15) 1¾oz/50g balls (each approx 98yd/90m) of Nomotta/Leisure Arts *Alpha* (cotton 3) in #75300 ecru (MC)
● 5 balls in #75319 black (CC)
Substitute Yarn
● 11 (11, 11, 12) 1¾oz/50g balls (each approx 125yd/115m) of Lang/Berroco *Fiorina* (cotton 3) in #1594 ecru (MC)
● 5 balls in #1504 black (CC)
● One pair each sizes 3 and 5 (3.25 and 3.75mm) needles OR SIZE TO OBTAIN GAUGE
● Stitch markers and bobbins
Note
The original yarn used for this sweater is no longer available. A comparable substitute has been made, which is available at the time of printing. Check gauge of substitute yarns very carefully before beginning.

GAUGE

22 sts and 32 rows to 4"/10cm over St st using size 5 (3.75mm) needles.
23 sts and 32 rows to 4"/10cm over colorwork pat using size 5 (3.75mm) needles. FOR PERFECT FIT, TAKE TIME TO CHECK GAUGES.

Notes

1 Use a separate bobbin of yarn for each block of color. When changing colors, twist yarns on WS to prevent holes in work.
2 When working chart #2, work rows 1-140, then beg again with row 1.

BACK

With smaller needles and MC, cast on 111 (117, 121, 127) sts. Work in k1, p1 rib for ½"/1.5cm. Change to larger needles. Beg and end as indicated, work 38 rows of chart #1.
Beg chart #2: Row 1 (RS) K2 (5, 7, 10) MC, place marker (pm), work row 1 of chart #2 over 107 sts, pm, k2 (5, 7, 10) MC. Cont in this way to work chart over 107 sts and St st with MC over sts outside markers until piece measures 17 (18, 18, 18½)"/43 (45.5, 45.5, 47)cm from beg, end with a WS row.

Armhole shaping

Dec 1 st each end every other row 3 (4, 4, 5) times—105 (109, 113, 117) sts. Cont in pat until armhole measures 9 (9, 9½, 9½)"/22.5 (22.5, 23.5, 23.5)cm. Bind off.

FRONT

Work as for back until armhole mea-
sures 6½ (6½, 7, 7)"/16 (16, 17, 17)cm, end with a WS row.

Neck shaping

Next row (RS) Work 44 (45, 47, 48) sts, join 2nd ball of yarn and bind off center 17 (19, 19, 21) sts, work to end. Working both sides at once, dec 1 st at each neck edge every row 5 times, every other row 5 times. When same length as back, bind off rem 34 (35, 37, 38) sts each side for shoulders.

SLEEVES

With smaller needles and MC, cast on 48 (48, 50, 50) sts. Work in k1, p1 rib for ½"/1.5cm. Change to larger needles.
Beg chart #1: Row 1 (RS) Inc 1 st in first st, beg with the 7th (7th, 6th, 6th) st of chart, work to rep line, then work 35-st rep once, work next 6 (6, 7, 7) sts of chart, inc 1 st in last st. Cont to work 38 rows of chart, AT SAME TIME, inc 1 st each end every 6th row (working inc sts into pat) 6 times more—62 (62, 64, 64) sts.
Beg chart #2: Row 1 (RS) K20 (20, 21, 21) MC, pm, work first 22 sts only of chart #2, pm, k20 (20, 21, 21) MC. Cont to work chart over center 22 sts and St st with MC over sts outside markers, AT SAME TIME, inc 1 st each end every 6th row (working inc sts with MC) 6 (10, 8, 10) times, then every 4th row 13 (9, 12, 10) times—100 (100, 104, 104) sts. Work even until piece measures 17 (18,18,18½)"/43 (45.5, 45.5, 47)cm from beg, end with same chart row as back to armhole.

Cap shaping

Dec 1 st each end every other row 3 (4, 4, 5) times. Bind off rem 94 (92, 96, 94) sts.

FINISHING

Block pieces. Sew left shoulder seam.

Neckband

With RS facing, smaller needles and MC, beg at right shoulder, pick up and k104 (108, 108, 112) sts around entire neck edge. Work in k1, p1 rib for ½"/1.5cm. Bind off in rib. Sew right shoulder seam including neckband. Sew top of sleeve to straight edge of armhole, then sew dec armhole sts of front and back to dec sts of sleeve. Sew side and sleeve seams. Work french knots randomly in St st sections of floral pats. ●

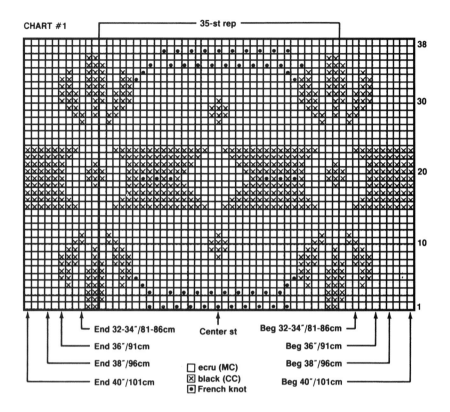

CHART #1

35-st rep

End 32-34"/81-86cm

End 36"/91cm

End 38"/96cm

End 40"/101cm

Center st

Beg 32-34"/81-86cm

Beg 36"/91cm

Beg 38"/96cm

Beg 40"/101cm

☐ ecru (MC)
☒ black (CC)
⊙ French knot

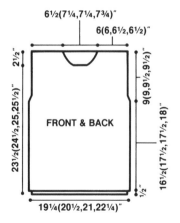

6½(7¼,7¼,7¾)"

6(6,6½,6½)"

2½"

9(9,9½,9½)"

23½(24½,25,25½)"

FRONT & BACK

16½(17½,17½,18)"

½"

19¼(20½,21,22¼)"

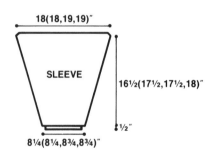

18(18,19,19)"

SLEEVE

16½(17½,17½,18)"

½"

8¼(8¼,8¾,8¾)"

140

130

120

110

100

90

80

70

60

50

40

30

20

10

1

107 sts

☐ ecru (MC)
☒ black (CC)

A versatile, can't-live-without wardrobe builder, this relaxed garter stitch pullover with cables is knit in a neutral, go-with-everything tone. The pullover is slightly oversized with square armholes and a relaxed round neck. Shown in size Medium. The Cable and Garter Pullover first appeared in the Spring/Summer '94 issue of *Vogue Knitting*.

Cable and Garter Pullover

FOR INTERMEDIATE KNITTERS

SIZES
To fit Small (Medium, Large). Directions are for smallest size with larger sizes in parentheses. If there is only one figure it applies to all sizes.

KNITTED MEASUREMENTS
● Bust at underarm 42 (44, 46)"/106.5 (112, 117)cm.
● Length 20 (21, 22)"/51 (53.5, 56)cm.
● Sleeve width at upper arm 17 (18, 19)"/43.5 (46, 48.5)cm.

MATERIALS
● 11 (12, 13) 1¾oz/50g balls (each approx 113yd/103m) of Adrienne Vittadini Yarns *Gabriella* (silk/linen 4) in #400 bark
● One pair size 6 (4mm) needles OR SIZE TO OBTAIN GAUGE
● Size 6 (4mm) circular needle 16"/40cm long
● Cable needle (cn) and stitch markers

GAUGE
20 sts and 32 rows to 4"/10cm over garter st with size 6 (4mm) needles. FOR PERFECT FIT, TAKE TIME TO CHECK GAUGE.

STITCH GLOSSARY
2-st Front Purl Cross Sl 1 to cn, hold to *front* of work, p1, k1 from cn.
2-st Back Purl Cross Sl 1 to cn, hold to *back* of work, k1, p1 from cn.
6-st Front Cable Sl 3 sts to cn, hold to *front* of work, k3, k3 from cn.
6-st Back Cable Sl 3 sts to cn, hold to *back* of work, k3, k3 from cn.

BACK
Cast on 114 (118, 126) sts.
Row 1 (WS) *K2, p2; rep from *, end k2. Work 2 more rows in rib, inc 17 (19, 17) sts evenly across last row—131 (137, 143) sts.
Beg pats: Next row (RS) K6 (6, 7), place marker (pm), *p2, k1, pm, work 23 sts of row 1 of chart #2, pm, k1, p2, pm, ** k16 (19, 21), pm, * rep from * to * once, then work from * to ** once, end k6 (6, 7).
Next row (WS) K6 (6, 7), *k2, p1, work row 2 of chart #2, p1, k2, ** k16 (19, 21), * rep from * to * once, then work from * to ** once, end k6 (6, 7).
Beg chart #1: Next row K6 (6, 7), *work 3 sts of row 1 of chart #1, work 23 sts of row 3 of chart #2, work 3 sts of row 5 of chart #1, ** k16 (19, 21), pm, * rep from * to * once, then work from * to ** once, end K6 (6, 7). Cont pats, working 8-row rep of chart #1, working through row 12 of chart #2,

then rep rows 1-12, and working all other sts in garter st. When piece measures 10 (10½, 11)"/25.5 (27, 28)cm from beg, end with a WS row.

Armhole shaping
Bind off 4 sts at beg of next 2 rows. Dec 1 st each side every other row once— 121 (127, 133) sts. Work even until armhole measures 8 (8½, 9)"/20.5 (21.5, 23)cm, end with a WS row.

Neck and shoulder shaping
Next row (RS) Work 43 (46, 49) sts, join 2nd ball of yarn and bind off 35 sts, work to end. Working both sides at once, bind off from each neck edge 4 sts once, 3 sts twice, AT SAME TIME, when armhole is 8½ (9, 9½)"/21.5 (23, 24.5)cm, bind off 5 sts at beg of next 12 rows, 3 (6, 9) sts at beg of next 2 rows.

FRONT
Work as for back until armhole measures 6½ (7, 7½)"/16.5 (18, 19)cm, end with a WS row.

Shoulder and neck shaping
Next row (RS) Work 51 (54, 57) sts, join 2nd ball of yarn and bind off 19 sts, work to end. Working both sides at once, work 1 row even. Dec 1 st at each neck edge every row 18 times as foll: On RS rows, work to last 5 sts, k2tog, k3. On right side of neck, k3, ssk, work to end. On WS rows, work to last 5 sts, k2tog, p3. On left side, p3, k2tog, work to end. AT SAME TIME, when armhole measures same as back, shape shoulders as for back.

SLEEVES

Cast on 54 (58, 62) sts. Work rib as for back, inc 11 (9, 7) sts evenly across last row—65 (67, 69) sts.

Beg pats: Next row (RS) K18 (19, 20), pm, p2, k1, pm, work 23 sts of row 1 of chart #2, pm, k1, p2, pm, k18 (19, 20).

Next row K18 (19, 20), pm, k2, p1, pm, work row 2 of chart #2, pm, p1, k2, pm, k18 (19, 20).

Beg chart #1: Next row K18 (19, 20), work 3 sts of row 1 of chart #1, work row 3 of chart #2, work 3 sts of row 5 of chart #1, k18 (19, 20). Cont pats, working 8-row rep of chart #1, working through row 12 of chart #2, then cont to rep rows 1-12 and working all other sts in garter st, AT SAME TIME, inc 1 st each side (working inc sts into garter st) every 8th row 6 (14, 18) times, every 10th row 8 (2, 0) times—93 (99, 105) sts. Work even until sleeve measures 16½ (17, 17½)"/42 (43.5, 44.5)cm from beg, end with a WS row.

Cap shaping

Bind off 4 sts at beg of next 2 rows, dec 1 st at beg of next 2 rows, bind off 10 sts at beg of next 4 rows. Bind off rem sts.

FINISHING

Block pieces. Sew both shoulder seams.

Rolled neck

With RS facing and circular needle, pick up and k100 sts evenly around neck edge. Place marker, join and work in St st (k every rnd) for 2"/5cm. Bind off. Set in sleeves, easing cap to fit. Sew side and sleeve seams. ●

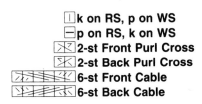

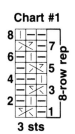

Chart #1

3 sts

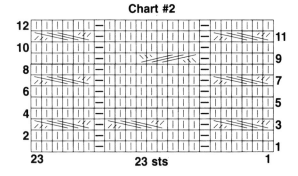

Chart #2

23   23 sts   1

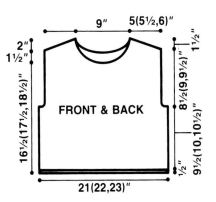

9"   5(5½,6)"

2"
1½"

16½(17½,18½)"

FRONT & BACK

8½(9,9½)"

1½"

½"   9½(10,10½)"

21(22,23)"

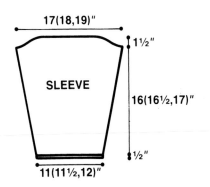

17(18,19)"

1½"

SLEEVE

16(16½,17)"

½"

11(11½,12)"

Diamond Cable Turtleneck

Diamonds are forever in this oversized diamond intarsia and Aran pattern pullover with angled armholes and turtleneck. A traditional pattern of cable stitches is cleverly plotted in glowing color blocks. Tweedy wool yarns impart depth and texture. Shown in size Medium. The Diamond Cable Turtleneck first appeared in the Fall '90 issue of *Vogue Knitting*.

Diamond Cable Turtleneck

FOR EXPERIENCED KNITTERS

SIZES
To fit Small (Medium, Large). Directions are for smallest size with larger sizes in parentheses. If there is only one figure it applies to all sizes.

KNITTED MEASUREMENTS
- Bust at underarm 42½ (45½, 48½)"/108 (114, 120)cm.
- Length 28 (28½, 29)"/71 (72, 73)cm.
- Sleeve width at upper arm 19 (19, 20)"/48 (48, 50)cm.

MATERIALS
Original Yarn
- 3 (3, 4) 3½oz/100g balls (each approx 194yd/178m) of Tahki *Donegal Tweed* (wool 4) in #839 dark olive (A)
- 2 (2, 3) balls each in #826 purple (B) and #837 gold (C)
- 2 balls in #840 red (D)
- 2 3½oz/100g balls (each approx 175yd/160m) of Tahki *Designer Homespun Tweed* (wool 4) in #204 blue (E)

Substitute Yarn
- 3 (3, 4) 3½oz/100g balls (each approx 194yd/178m) of Tahki *Donegal Tweed* (wool 4) in #894 olive (A)
- 2 (2, 3) balls each in #826 purple (B) and #837 gold (C)
- 2 balls in #840 red (D)
- 2 balls in #882 blue (E)
- One pair each sizes 5 and 6 (3.75 and 4mm) needles OR SIZE

TO OBTAIN GAUGE
- Size 5 (3.75mm) circular needle 16"/40cm long
- Cable needle (cn) and bobbins
- Stitch markers

Note
The original colors and/or yarns used for this sweater are no longer available. A comparable substitute has been made, which is available at the time of printing. Check gauge of substitute yarns very carefully before beginning.

GAUGE
18 sts and 26 rows to 4"/10cm over moss st using size 6 (4mm) needles. 22 sts and 26 rows to 4"/10cm over chart pats using size 6 (4mm) needles. FOR PERFECT FIT, TAKE TIME TO CHECK GAUGES.

STITCH GLOSSARY
Moss St
Row 1 *K1, p1; rep from * to end.
Rows 2 and 4 K the knit sts and p the purl sts.
Row 3 *P1, k1; rep from * to end.
Rep rows 1-4 for moss st.
Right Twist Skip next st on LH needle and k 2nd st in *back* of first st, then k first st.
2-st Right Purl Cable Sl 1 st to cn and hold to *back* of work, k1, p1 from cn.
2-st Left Purl Cable Sl 1 st to cn and hold to *front* of work, p1, k1 from cn.
3-st Right Purl Cable Sl 1 st to cn and hold to *back* of work, k2, p1 from cn.
3-st Left Purl Cable Sl 2 sts to cn and hold to *front* of work, p1, k2 from cn.
4-st Right Cable Sl 2 sts to cn and hold to *back* of work, k2, k2 from cn.
4-st Left Cable Sl 2 sts to cn and hold to *front* of work, k2, k2 from cn.
6-st Left Cable Sl 3 sts to cn and hold to *front* of work, k3, k3 from cn.

Notes on working chart
Pat #1 = 6 sts and 6 rows
Pat #2 = 6 sts and 8 rows
Pat #3 = 2 sts and 2 rows
Pat #4 = 16 sts and 20 rows
Pat #5 = 7 sts and 24 rows

Notes
1 When working second half of chart, set up individual pats by working from right to left.
2 Each diamond consists of 39 sts at widest point and 40 rows. Colors are changed every other row as shown on cable chart.
3 Place markers between pats for ease in working.
4 See schematic drawings for placement of colors for diamonds. Diamond colors are given for back. See front instructions to set up colors on front. On small areas where no color is given, work as desired.
5 Use a separate bobbin for each block of color. When working first st in new color, k st on RS and p st on WS for an even color change.

BACK
With smaller needles and A, cast on 122 (128, 134) sts. Work in k2, p2 rib for 1½"/5cm, dec 7 sts evenly across last row—115 (121, 127) sts. Change to larger needles. Mark center

st to correspond with center st on cable chart. Set up diamond colorwork as foll: (WS) P17 (20, 23)C, 1A, 39E, 1C, 39B, 1D, 17 (20, 23)A.

Next row Work moss st and cable chart as foll: Work 6 (9, 12) sts in moss st, beg with row 1, work cable chart from st 1 to st 56, beg with pat #3, work pats in reverse as foll: pat #3, p1, pat #4, p1, pat #3, p1, k4, p1, pat #2, p1, k4, p1, pat #1, p1, work 6 (9, 12) sts in moss st. Cont in pats as established until piece measures 18½ (19, 19)"/47 (48, 48)cm from beg, end with a WS row.

Armhole shaping

Bind off 3 (3, 4) sts at beg of next 2 rows. Dec 1 st each side every other row 3 (4, 4) times—103 (107, 111) sts. Work even in pats until armhole measures 9½ (9½, 10)"/24 (24, 25)cm. Bind off.

FRONT

Rib as for back. Set up diamond colorwork as foll: (WS) P17 (20, 23)A, 1D, 39B, 1C, 39E, 1A, 17 (20, 23)C. Cont to work as for back until armhole measures 6½ (6½, 7)"/16.5 (16.5, 17.5)cm, end with a RS row.

Neck shaping

Next row (WS) Work 41 (43, 43) sts, join 2nd ball of yarn and bind off 21 (21, 25) sts, work to end. Working both sides at once, bind off from each neck edge 3 sts once, 2 sts once, dec 1 st every other row 6 times—30 (32, 32) sts each side. When same length as back, bind off rem 30 (32, 32) sts each side.

SLEEVES

With smaller needles and A, cast on 60 (60, 64) sts. Work in k2, p2 rib for 1½"/5cm, dec 1 st on last row—59 (59, 63) sts. Change to larger needles. Mark center st to correspond with center st on cable chart. Set up diamond colorwork as foll: (WS) P29 (29, 31)E, 1C, 29 (29, 31)B.

Next row Sleeve set up: Work row 1 of cable chart. Beg with st 23 (23, 21), work to st 56, then beg with pat #3, work in reverse as foll: pat #3, p1, pat #4, p1, pat #3, p1, end k2 (2, 4). Cont in pats as established, inc 1 st each side (working inc sts into chart pat) every 4th row 22 (22, 20) times, then every 6th row 1 (1, 3) times—105 (105, 109) sts. Work even in pats until piece measures 17 (17, 17½)"/42.5 (42.5, 44)cm from beg, end with a WS row.

Cap shaping

Bind off 3 (3, 4) sts at beg of next 2 rows. Dec 1 st each side every other row 3 (4, 4) times. Bind off rem 93 (91, 93) sts.

FINISHING

Block pieces. Sew shoulder seams.

Turtleneck

With RS facing, circular needle and A, pick up and k112 (112, 116) sts around neck edge. Join and work in k2, p2 rib for 9½"/24cm. Bind off in rib. Sew top of sleeve to straight edge of armhole, then sew dec armhole sts of front and back to dec sts of sleeve. Sew side and sleeve seams. ●

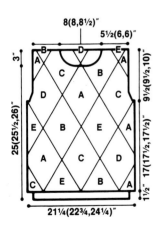

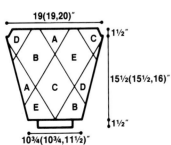

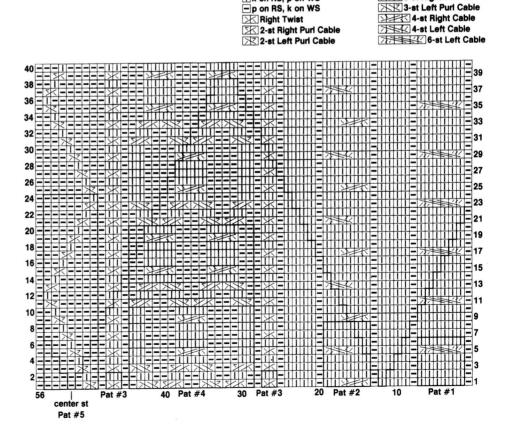

	k on RS, p on WS		3-st Right Purl Cable
	p on RS, k on WS		3-st Left Purl Cable
	Right Twist		4-st Right Cable
	2-st Right Purl Cable		4-st Left Cable
	2-st Left Purl Cable		6-st Left Cable

Understated elegance best describes this mock shawl collar cabled cardigan. The oversized cardigan features full-fashioning detail and roomy ease—with angled armholes, side slits and patch pockets. Shown in size Medium. The Cabled Cardigan first appeared in the Winter '95 issue of *Vogue Knitting*.

Cabled Cardigan

FOR INTERMEDIATE KNITTERS

SIZES
To fit Small (Medium, Large). Directions are for smallest size with larger sizes in parentheses. If there is only one figure it applies to all sizes.

KNITTED MEASUREMENTS
● Bust at underarm (closed) 44 (50, 55½)"/111.5 (127, 141)cm.
● Length 28 (29, 30)"/71.5 (73.5, 76)cm.
● Sleeve width at upper arm 14 (14, 15)"/35.5 (35.5, 38)cm.

MATERIALS
● 22 (23, 24) 1¾oz/50g balls (each approx 96yd/86m) of Adrienne Vittadini/JCA *Daniella* (wool/cashmere 4) in #465 cream
● One pair each sizes 6 and 8 (4 and 5mm) needles OR SIZE TO OBTAIN GAUGE
● Cable needle (cn)
● Stitch holders

GAUGE
19 sts and 26 rows to 4"/10cm over cable pat using size 8 (5mm) needles. FOR PERFECT FIT, TAKE TIME TO CHECK GAUGE.

STITCH GLOSSARY
Cable Pat (multiple of 14 sts)
Row 1 (RS) *K10, sl 2 sts to cn and hold to *back*, k2, k2 from cn (4-st BC); rep from * to end.
Rows 2-10 Work in St st.
Row 11 *K3, 4-st BC, k7; rep from * to end.
Rows 12-20 Work in St st.
Rep rows 1-20 for cable pat.

BACK
With smaller needles, cast on 97 (111, 125) sts. Work in k1, p1 rib for ¾"/2cm. Change to larger needles.
Next (inc) row (RS) [K1, p1] 3 times, m1, k to last 6 sts, m1, [p1, k1] 3 times. Work 3 rows even, keeping first and last 6 sts in rib and rem sts in St st. Rep inc row. Rep last 4 rows twice more. P next row on WS, dec 1 st in center of row—104 (118, 132) sts.
Beg cable pat: Row 1 (RS) K3, work 14-st rep of cable pat 7 (8, 9) times, k3. Cont in pat as established until piece measures 19 (20, 20½)"/48.5 (50.5, 52) from beg, end with a WS row.

Armhole shaping
Bind off 4 (4, 5) sts at beg of next 2 rows. Work 6 rows even.
Next row (RS) K3, k2tog, work to last 5 sts, SKP, k3. Work 5 rows even. Rep last 6 rows 3 (4, 4) times more—88

(100, 112) sts. Work even until armhole measures 8 (8, 8½)"/20.5 (20.5, 21.5)cm, end with a WS row.

Shoulder shaping
Bind off 9 (11, 13) sts at beg of next 6 rows. Bind off rem 34 sts for back neck.

LEFT FRONT
With smaller needles, cast on 60 (68, 74) sts. Work in rib and incs at side edge only (beg of RS rows) as for back—64 (72, 78) sts. Change to larger needles.
Beg cable pat: Row 1 (RS) Work 14-st rep 4 (5, 5) times, work first 8 (2, 8) sts of pat once more. Cont in cable pat as established until same length as back to armhole. Shape armhole at side edge as for back—56 (63, 68) sts. Work even until same length as back to shoulder. Shape shoulder at side edge as for back, inc 1 (0, 1) st on last row—30 sts. Work even on rem sts for 3½"/9cm for back collar. Place sts on a holder.

RIGHT FRONT
Work to correspond to left front, reversing shaping and cable pat placement.

SLEEVES
With smaller needles, cast on 56 sts. Work in k1, p1 rib for ¾"/2cm. Change to larger needles.
Beg cable pat: Row 1 (RS) Work 14-st rep 4 times. Cont in cable pat as established, inc 1 st each side (working inc sts into pat) every 16th

(16th, 10th) row 5 (5, 8) times—66 (66, 72) sts. Work even until piece measures 14½"/37cm from beg, end with a WS row.

Cap shaping

Bind off 4 sts at beg of next 2 rows.
Next row (RS) K3, k3tog, work to last 6 sts, SK2P (sl 1, k2tog, psso), k3. Work 1 row even. Rep last 2 rows 6 (6, 7) times more.
Next row (RS) K3, k2tog, work to last 5 sts, SKP, k3. Work 1 row even. Rep last 2 rows 4 (4, 5) times more. Bind off rem 20 sts.

POCKETS (make 2)

With larger needles, cast on 25 sts. Work in St st for 2 rows, inc 1 st each side of next row, then every other row twice more—31 sts. Cont in St st until 10 rows have been worked from beg.
Beg cable pat: Row 1 (RS) Work 14-st rep twice, k3. Cont in pat as established until piece measures 6½"/16.5cm from beg. Change to smaller needles and work in k1, p1 rib for ¾"/2cm. Bind off in rib.

FINISHING

Block pieces to measurements. Sew shoulder seams. Sew sides of collar along back neck. Weave sts tog at center back neck. Sew pockets to fronts with cast-on edge just above rib and 3"/7.5cm from side edge. Set in sleeves. Sew side and sleeve seams. ●

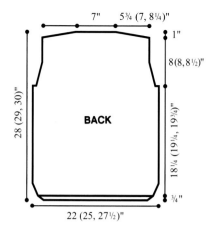

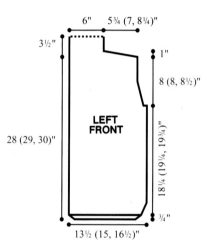

Adrienne Vittadini

Fur-Trimmed Cabled Cardigan

An elegant cabled cardigan with a luxurious difference—dramatic faux-fur cuffs and collar. Perfect for dressier occasions, the standard-fitting cardigan has set-in sleeves, round neck, and foldback frontbands. The faux-fur trim can be omitted if a more casual look is desired. Shown in size 36. The Fur-Trimmed Cabled Cardigan first appeared in the Winter '93 issue of *Vogue Knitting*.

Fur-Trimmed Cabled Cardigan

FOR INTERMEDIATE KNITTERS

SIZES
To fit 32 (34, 36, 38)"/81 (86, 91, 96, 101)cm bust. Directions are for smallest size with larger sizes in parentheses. If there is only one figure it applies to all sizes.

KNITTED MEASUREMENTS
● Bust at underarm (buttoned) 37¼ (40¾, 42, 45)"/94.5 (103.5, 106.5, 114.5)cm.
● Length 23½ (24, 25½, 26)"/60 (61, 64.5, 66)cm.
● Sleeve width at upper arm 13 (14, 15, 16)"/33 (35.5, 38, 40.5)cm.

MATERIALS
● 16 (16, 17, 17) 1¾oz/50g balls (each approx 121yd/110m) of Baruffa/Lane Borgosesia *Maratona*® (wool 4) in #2408 dark brown
● One pair each sizes 2 and 4 (2.75 and 3.5mm) needles OR SIZE TO OBTAIN GAUGE
● ¼yd/.25m dark brown faux fur
● Six 1"/25mm buttons
● Cable needle (cn)
● Stitch markers
Note
The original color used for this sweater is no longer available. A comparable color substitute has been made, which is available at the time of printing.

GAUGE
28 sts and 38 rows to 4"/10cm over charts #1, #2 and #3 using size 4 (3.5mm) needles. (**Note** To work a gauge swatch, cast on 30 sts. K1 (selvage st), work 4 sts of chart #1, 12 sts of chart #3, 4 sts of chart #1, 4 sts of chart #2, 4 sts of chart #1, k1 (selvage st). Cont in pats, k first and last st for selvage sts for 38 rows.) FOR PERFECT FIT, TAKE TIME TO CHECK GAUGE.

STITCH GLOSSARY
P1 b Purl 1 in the row below.
K3tog Knit 3 sts together.
SK2P Sl 1 st, k2tog, pass sl st over.
4-st Front Cable Sl 2 sts to cn and hold to *front* of work, k2, k2 from cn.
6-st Back Cable Sl 3 sts to cn and hold to *back* of work, k3, k3 from cn.
6-st Front Cable Sl 3 sts to cn and hold to *front* of work, k3, k3 from cn.

BACK
With smaller needles, cast on 134 (142, 150, 158) sts. Work in k1, p1 rib for 1¾"/4.5cm, end with a WS row. Change to larger needles.
Beg charts: Row 1 (RS) K1 (5, 3, 1), work sts 0 (0, 7-12, 1-12) of chart #3, [work 4 sts of chart #1, 4 sts of chart #2, 4 sts of chart #1, 12 sts of chart #3] 5 times, work 4 sts of chart #1, 4 sts of chart #2, 4 sts of chart #1, work sts 0 (0, 1-6, 1-12) of chart #3, k1 (5, 3, 1). Cont to work in chart pats as established, keeping first and last sts in St st until piece measures 3"/7.5cm from beg, end with a WS row.

Waist shaping
Cont in pat, dec 1 st each side every 4th row 7 (7, 8, 8) times—120 (128, 134, 142) sts. Work even for 1½"/4cm more. Inc 1 st each side every 8th row 4 (5, 5,

6) times, working inc sts into pat—128 (138, 144, 154) sts. Work even until piece measures 15½ (15½, 16½, 16½)"/39.5 (39.5, 42, 42)cm from beg, end with a WS row.

Armhole shaping
Bind off 2 sts at beg of next 2 rows. Work 2 rows.
Full-fashioned dec row (RS) K2, k3tog, work to last 5 sts, SK2P, k2. Work 3 rows. Rep last 4 rows 5 (5, 5, 7) times—100 (110, 116, 118) sts. Work even in pats until armhole measures 7 (7½, 8, 8½)"/18 (19, 20.5, 21.5)cm, end with a WS row.

Neck shaping
Next row Work 30 (35, 38, 39) sts, join 2nd ball of yarn, bind off 40 sts, work to end. Working both sides at once, bind off from each neck edge 4 sts once. Work even until armhole measures 8 (8½, 9, 9½)"/20.5 (21.5, 23, 24)cm. Bind off rem 26 (31, 34, 35) sts each side for shoulders.

LEFT FRONT
With smaller needles, cast on 74 (78, 82, 86) sts.
Row 1 (RS) Work in k1, p1 rib over 67 (71, 75, 79) sts, sl 1, k6.
Row 2 (WS) P7, work in k1, p1 rib to end. Cont to work as established until piece measures 1¾"/4.5cm, end with a WS row. Change to larger needles.
Beg charts: Row 1 (RS) K1 (5, 3, 1) sts, work sts 0 (0, 7-12, 1-12) of chart #3, [work 4 sts of chart #1, 4 sts of chart #2, 4 sts of chart #1, 12 sts chart #3] twice, work 4 sts of chart #1, place marker

(pm), k6, sl 1, k6 for band.

Next row P13 for band, sl marker. Work row 2 of pats as established, p1 (5, 3, 1). Cont to work as established, keeping 13 sts for band and first sts in St st until piece measures same length as back to waist shaping. Work waist dec at side edge only (beg of RS row) as for back—67 (71, 74, 78) sts. Work 1½"/4cm even. Work waist inc at side edge only as for back—71 (76, 79, 84) sts. When same length as back to armhole, shape armhole as for back at side edge only—57 (62, 65, 66) sts. Work even until armhole measures 5 (5½, 6, 6½)"/12.5 (14, 15, 16½)cm, end with a RS row.

Neck shaping

Next row (WS) Bind off 13 sts, work to end. Bind off from neck edge 5 sts once, 4 sts once, 3 sts once, 2 sts twice, dec 1 st at neck edge every other row twice—26 (31, 34, 35) sts. When same length as back to shoulder, bind off. Place markers for 6 buttons along front band with first 1"/2.5cm from lower edge and last ½"/1.5cm from beg of neck shaping and 4 evenly between.

RIGHT FRONT

Work to correspond to left front, reversing band and pat placement and all shaping. Work buttonholes opposite markers on front placket as foll: (RS) K3, join 2nd strand of yarn and k3, sl 1, k3, join 3rd strand of yarn and work to end. Cont as established for 3 more rows.

Next row Work across row with one strand of yarn to join.

SLEEVES

With smaller needles, cast on 70 (76, 76, 78) sts. Work in k1, p1 rib for 1¾"/4.5cm, end with a WS row. Change to larger needles.

Beg charts: Row 1 K1 (0, 0, 1), work 4 sts of chart #2 for 0 (1, 1, 1) time, [work 4 sts of chart #1, 12 sts of chart #3, 4 sts of chart #1, 4 sts of chart #2] twice, work 4 sts of chart #1, 12 sts of chart #3, 4 sts of chart #1, 4 sts of chart #2 for 0 (1, 1, 0) time, k1 (0, 0, 1). Cont to work pats as established, AT SAME TIME, inc 1 st

each side (working inc sts into pats as foll: 4 sts of chart #2, 4 sts of chart #1, 12 sts of chart #3, rem sts in St st) every 12 (12, 10, 8) rows 11 (11, 14, 17) times—92 (98, 104, 112) sts. Work even in pat until piece measures 17½"/44.5cm from beg, end with a WS row.

Cap shaping

Bind off 2 sts at beg of next 2 rows. Work 2 rows. Work full-fashioned dec row same as for back every 4th row 6 (6, 8, 8) times, then every other row 5 (6, 5, 6) times—44 (46, 48, 52) sts. Bind off.

FINISHING

Block pieces. Sew shoulder seams.

Collar

From RS, with smaller needles and beg after 13 sts of placket, pick up and k146 sts evenly spaced around neck edge. Work in St st for 1"/2.5cm. K 1 row on WS for turning ridge. Cont in St st for 1"/2.5cm more. Bind off. Fold collar in half to WS. Sew in place. Fold band in half to WS and sew in place. Sew around buttonholes through both layers. Set in sleeves. Sew side and sleeve seams. Sew on buttons.

Faux-fur trim

From faux fur, cut a 7" X 24"/18cm X 61cm piece for collar and 2 pieces each 7" X 13 (14, 14, 14½)"/18cm X 33 (35.5, 35.5, 37)cm for cuffs. Fold collar in half lengthwise, RS tog. Sew short ends and long raw edges with a ½"/1.5cm seam, leaving an opening for turning. Trim pile from seam allowances. Turn collar to RS, slipstitch opening closed. With tapestry needle, work out any pile from stitched seam. Fold cuff in half crosswise, RS tog. Sew ends with a ½"/1.5cm seam to form a loop. Fold cuff in half lengthwise, RS tog. Sew raw edges in a ½"/1.5cm seam, leaving an opening for turning. Complete as for collar. Tack collar and cuffs in place. ●

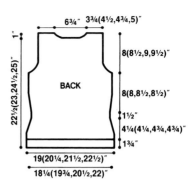

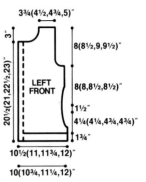

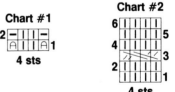

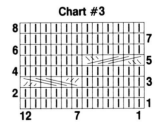

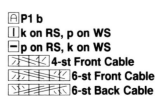

This versatile openwork pullover trailed with vines of ribbed leaves and eyelets is worked in crisp white cotton for a refreshing spring to summer look. The sporty yet feminine pullover is loose-fitting with angled armholes and crew neck. Shown in size Small/Medium. The Allover Leaf-Rib Pullover first appeared in the Spring/Summer '91 issue of *Vogue Knitting*.

Allover Leaf-Rib Pullover

FOR EXPERIENCED KNITTERS

SIZES
To fit Small/Medium (Large). Directions are for smaller size with larger size in parentheses. If there is only one figure it applies to both sizes.

KNITTED MEASUREMENTS
● Bust at underarm 40 (45)"/101 (113)cm.
● Length 26 (27)"/65 (68)cm.
● Sleeve width at upper arm 18 (19)"/45 (48)cm.

MATERIALS
Original Yarn
● 15 (17) 1¾oz/50g balls (each approx 139yd/127m) of Lane Borgosesia *Colle* (cotton 3) in #1 white
Substitute Yarn
● 11 (13) 1¾oz/50g balls (each approx 192yd/178m) of Sesia/Lane Borgosesia *Sesia Baby* (cotton 3) in #51 white
● One pair size 4 (3.5mm) needles OR SIZE TO OBTAIN GAUGE
● Size 4 (3.5mm) circular needle 16"/40cm long
● Stitch markers and cable needle (cn)
Note
The original yarn used for this sweater is no longer available. A comparable substitute has been made, which is available at the time of printing. Check gauge of substitute yarns very carefully before beginning.

GAUGE
44 sts to 5"/12.5cm and 32 rows to 4"/10cm over ribbed leaf pat using size 4 (3.5mm) needles. FOR PERFECT FIT, TAKE TIME TO CHECK GAUGE. (**Note** To work gauge swatch, cast on 44 sts. Work leaf pat for 32 rows. Bind off. Piece measures approx 5"/12.5cm X 4"/10cm, slightly stretched.)

STITCH GLOSSARY
Inc 2 Knit, purl, knit into st.
Right Double Dec (R2dec) (over 4 sts) Sl p st to RH needle, sl k st to cn and hold to *front* of work, sl next p st to RH needle, sl k st from cn back to LH needle, sl 2 p sts back to LH needle, p2tog, k2tog.
Left Double Dec (L2dec) (over 4 sts) Wyib, sl k st to RH needle knitwise, sl p st to cn and hold to *back* of work, sl next k st to RH needle knitwise, sl p st from cn back to LH needle. Leaving 2 k sts on RH needle, ssk, p next 2 sts on LH needle tog.
Ribbed Leaf Pat (multiple of 22 sts)
Rows 1, 3, 5 and 7 (RS) K1, p1, yo twice, [k1, p1] twice, k1, R2dec, [p1, k1] 5 times, p1.
Row 2 and all WS rows Rib, working double yo as 2 sts.
Rows 9, 11, 13 and 15 [K1, p1] 6 times, L2dec, [k1, p1] twice, k1, yo twice, p1.
Row 16 Rep row 2. Rep rows 1-16 for ribbed leaf pat.

BACK
Cast on 154 (172) sts. Work in k1, p1 rib for 7 rows.
Preparation row (WS) Rib 14, place marker (pm), *inc 2, [p1, k1] 6 times, p1, inc 2, p1, k1, p1; rep from * 6 (7) times more, pm, rib 14-182 (204) sts.
Beg leaf pat: Row 1 (RS) Rib first 14 sts, sl marker, work 22-st rep of pat 7 (8) times, sl marker, rib 14. Cont in pats until piece measures 17 (17½)"/42.5 (44)cm from beg.

Armhole shaping
Dec 1 st each side every row 14 times —154 (176) sts. Cont in pats until armhole measures 8 (8½)"/20 (21.5)cm, end with a WS row.

Neck shaping
Work 57 (66) sts, join 2nd ball of yarn and bind off 40 (44) sts, work to end. Working both sides at once, bind off from each neck edge 5 sts twice, 3 sts once. Bind off rem 44 (53) sts each side.

FRONT
Work as for back until armhole measures 5½ (6)"/13.5 (15)cm, end with a WS row.

Neck shaping
(Note: Work full-fashioned neck decs on RS rows as foll: On left neck edge, work to last 4 sts, k2tog, k2. On right neck edge, k2, ssk, work to end.)
Next row (RS) Work 60 (69) sts, join 2nd ball of yarn and bind off 34 (38) sts, work to end. Working both sides at once, bind off from each neck edge 4 sts once, dec 1 st each side (using full-fashioned decs) every other row 12 times. When same length as back, bind off rem 44 (53) sts each side.

SLEEVES
Cast on 58 (66) sts. Rib as for back.
Preparation row (WS) Rib 2 (6), pm, *[k1, p1] twice, inc 2, [p1, k1] 4 times, p1, inc 2, p1, k1, p1; rep from * twice more, pm, rib 2 (6)—70 (78) sts.
Beg leaf pat: Row 1 (RS) Rib 2 (6), sl marker, work 22-st rep of pat 3

times, sl marker, rib 2 (6). Cont in pats, inc 1 st each side (working inc sts into leaf pat) [every 4th row once, every 2nd row once] 22 times—158 (166) sts. Work even in pat until piece measures 18 (18½)"/45 (46.5)cm from beg.

Cap shaping
Dec 1 st each side every row 14 times. Bind off rem 130 (138) sts.

FINISHING
Block pieces. Sew shoulder seams.

Neckband
With RS facing and circular needle, beg at right shoulder, pick up and k142 (148) sts evenly around neck edge. Join. Work in k1, p1 rib for 1"/2.5cm. Bind off in rib. Sew top of sleeves to straight edge of armholes. Sew dec armhole sts of front and back to dec sts of sleeve. Sew side and sleeve seams. ●

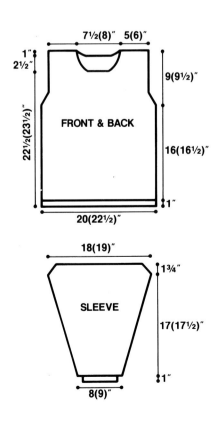

DKNY

SHAPING AND SUBTLE COLOR are the key ingredients of sweater designs by DKNY. Not only do the sweaters feel good to wear, they flatter the figure, accenting the best parts while de-emphasizing the others. Textured knits meld with the body, simple silhouettes drape casually in relaxed and easy shaping, and little details, like picot edgings and lacy stitches add feminine appeal. As for color, the choices are usually versatile neutrals like ivory and black, occasionally alternating with navy, taupe, brown, and grey.

Donna Karan, the force behind DKNY, was literally born into fashion. Her father was a custom tailor, her mother a showroom model and fashion sales rep, so it was only natural that Karan designed her first collection while still in high school. Following her second year at Parson's School of Design, Karan was hired by Anne Klein for a summer job. She subsequently spent three years there as Associate Designer, then was named successor after Klein's death in 1974. As chief designer at Anne Klein, Karan was honored with three Coty Awards as well as elected into its prestigious Hall of Fame.

Photo courtesy of DKNY

Comfort, ease, and sensuality in versatile, day-into-evening styles are the essence of DKNY designs.

In 1984, together with husband, sculptor Stephen Weiss, Karan launched her own company—Donna Karan New York (DKNY)—and debuted her first collection. The ensuing enthusiastic responses from both the press and retailers guaranteed her career as a fashion leader. Since then, DKNY has evolved into an international fashion empire, with Donna Karan being named Designer of the Year by The Council of Fashion Designers of America an unprecedented six times.

Karan credits her feminine instincts for the success of her company. Her designs mirror her own wardrobe needs as well as those of her friends and family. As a working mother, she understands the fashion demands of busy women, who long for comfortable clothes that are modern yet classic, stylish yet individual. Comfort, ease, and sensuality in versatile, day-into-evening styles are the essence of DKNY designs. The following sweaters were chosen for their unbeatable DKNY style—timeless fashions to reach for again and again.

Cabled trees, a slipstitch fence and other textural stitches combine with a moss-stitch sky to create this roomy oversized cardigan. It features set-in sleeves and a face-framing, ribbed polo collar. The Enchanted Forest cardigan first appeared in the Fall '92 issue of *Vogue Knitting*.

Enchanted Forest

FOR EXPERIENCED KNITTERS

SIZES
The body of the cardigan is one size fits all, with size variations in the sleeve length.

KNITTED MEASUREMENTS
● Bust at underarm (buttoned) 58¼"/148cm.
● Length 26¼"/66.5cm.
● Sleeve width at upper arm 19"/48.5cm.

MATERIALS
Original Yarn
● 26 1¾oz/50g balls (each approx 120yd/110m) of Baruffa/Lane Borgosesia *Folk Mohair* (mohair/wool/acrylic 4) in #25558 oatmeal
Substitute Yarn
● 24 1¾oz/50g balls (each approx 132yd/120m) of Baruffa/Lane Borgosesia *7 Settembre* (wool 3) in #3155 oatmeal
● One pair each sizes 5 and 9 (3.75 and 5.5mm) needles OR SIZE TO OBTAIN GAUGE
● Seven 1"/25mm buttons
● Cable needle (cn)
● Crochet hook for working V-st
● Stitch markers

Note
The original yarn used for this sweater is no longer available. A comparable substitute has been made, which is available at the time of printing. Check gauge of substitute yarns very carefully before beginning.

GAUGE
18 sts and 22 rows to 4"/10cm over moss st with 2 strands of yarn held tog using size 9 (5.5mm) needles.
FOR PERFECT FIT, TAKE TIME TO CHECK GAUGE.

STITCH GLOSSARY
Moss St (over even # of sts)
Row 1 (RS) *K1, p1; rep from * to end.
Rows 2 and 4 K the knit sts and p the purl sts.
Row 3 *P1, k1; rep from * to end. Rep rows 1-4 for moss st.
Twisted St K1 tbl on RS, p1 tbl on WS.
Small Bobble K in front, back and front of st (3 sts in one st), turn, p3, turn, k3tog.
Large Bobble K in [front, back] twice and front of st (5 sts in one st), turn, p5, turn, ssk, k1, k2tog, turn, p3, turn, sl 2, k1, pass 2 sl sts over k st.
Float St Sl 2 sts wyif, bring yarn to back, return 2 sl sts to LH needle and k2.
Right Twist (RT) K2tog but do not sl sts from needle, k first st again, sl both sts from LH needle.
2-st Back Purl Cross Sl 1 st to cn and hold to *back* of work, k1, p1 from cn.
2-st Front Purl Cross Sl 1 st to cn and hold to *front* of work, p1, k1 from cn.
2-st Back Purl Twist Sl 1 st to cn and hold to *back* of work, k1 tbl, p1 from cn.
2-st Front Purl Twist Sl 1 st to cn and hold to *front* of work, p1, k1 tbl from cn.
Sl 3 Sl 3 wyib, bring yarn to front.
3-st Back Purl Twist Sl 1 st to cn and hold to *back* of work, RT, p1 from cn.
3-st Front Purl Twist Sl 2 sts to cn and hold to *front* of work, p1, RT from cn.

3-st Back Purl Cross Sl 1 st to cn and hold to *back* of work, k2, p1 from cn.
3-st Front Purl Cross Sl 2 sts to cn and hold to *front* of work, p1, k2 from cn.
4-st Back Cable Sl 2 sts to cn and hold to *back* of work, k2, k2 from cn.
4-st Front Cable Sl 2 sts to cn and hold to *front* of work, k2, k2 from cn.
4-st Back Purl Cross Sl 2 sts to cn and hold to *back* of work, k2, p2 from cn.
4-st Front Purl Cross Sl 2 sts to cn and hold to *front* of work, p2, k2 from cn.
V-St (over 7 sts and 3 rows): Work 2 rows in St st.
Next row (RS) Insert crochet hook from front to back into center of 4th st on LH needle 2 rows below, pull yarn through to front and draw up a lp, sl lp to LH needle and k it tog with next st on LH needle tbl, k5, pull up lp in same st as before and k it tog with next st tbl.
Note
Use 2 strands of yarn held together throughout.

LEFT FRONT
With smaller needles and 2 strands held tog, cast on 75 sts. Work in k1, p1 rib for 1½"/4cm, dec 12 sts evenly across last WS row—63 sts. Change to larger needles and work chart for left front through row 82.

Armhole shaping
Next row (RS) Bind off 3 sts (armhole edge), work to end. Cont to work chart, bind off from armhole edge 3 sts once more, 2 sts twice, dec 1 st once—52 sts. Cont to work chart through row 119.

Neck and shoulder shaping

Next row (WS) Bind off 4 sts (neck edge), work to end. Cont in chart, bind off from neck edge 3 sts twice, 2 sts twice—38 sts. Work chart through row 132.

Next row (RS) Bind off 12 sts for shoulder, work to end. Bind off 13 sts from shoulder edge twice.

RIGHT FRONT

Work rib to correspond to left front—63 sts. Change to larger needles and work chart for right front, inc 1 st at end of row 19—64 sts. Cont to work chart through row 83.

Armhole shaping

Next row (WS) Bind off 3 sts (armhole edge), work to end. Cont to work chart, bind off from armhole edge 3 sts once more, 2 sts twice, dec 1 st once—53 sts. Cont to work chart through row 120.

Neck and shoulder shaping

Next row (RS) Bind off 4 sts (neck edge), work to end. Cont in chart, bind off from neck edge 3 sts twice, 2 sts twice, dec 1 st once—38 sts. Work even in chart through row 133.

Next row (WS) Bind off 12 sts for shoulder, work to end. Bind off 13 sts from shoulder edge twice.

BACK

With smaller needles and 2 strands held tog, cast on 153 sts. Work in k1, p1 rib for 1½"/4cm, dec 21 sts evenly spaced across last WS row—132 sts. Change to larger needles.

Beg chart B: Row 1 K1, work 4-st rep of chart B for 32 times across row, end with st 2, k1. Cont to work 4 rows of chart B, keeping first and last st in St st.

Beg charts: Row 5 Beg with first st of left front chart, work 61 sts of chart, cont to work 4-st rep of chart B as established. Work through row 18.

Row 19 Beg with first st of left front chart, work to st 62, place marker (pm), work next 7 sts of chart C, pm, beg with st 2 work 63 sts of right front

chart, omitting inc in last st. Cont in pat as established through row 50. (Note: After row 26, there will be 133 sts.)

Row 51 (RS) Work 62 sts of left front chart, sl marker, work row 51 of chart D, sl marker, work 63 sts of right front chart. Cont in pats as established through row 82.

Armhole shaping

Cont to work in left and right front charts as established and work center 8 sts in moss st, AT SAME TIME, bind off for armholes 3 sts at beg of next 4 rows, 2 sts at beg of next 4 rows, dec 1 st each side once—111 sts. Cont in pats through row 114.

Row 115 Work 47 sts of left front chart, pm, work 17 sts of chart E, pm, work last 47 sts of right front chart. Cont to work as established, omitting neck shaping and working in moss st, until all 12 rows of chart E have been worked. Cont in moss st for 2 rows.

Neck and shoulder shaping

Next row (RS) Work 43 sts, join 2nd ball of yarn and bind off center 25 sts, work to end. Working both sides at once, bind off from each neck edge 3 sts once, 2 sts once, AT SAME TIME, when same length as front to shoulder, bind off from each shoulder edge 12 sts once, 13 sts twice.

SLEEVES

With smaller needles and 2 strands held together, cast on 49 sts. Work in k1, p1 rib for 1½"/4cm, inc 5 sts evenly across last WS row—54 sts. Change to larger needles and work

in moss st, inc 1 st each side (working inc sts into moss st) every 4th row 16 (13, 10) times, every 6th row 0 (3, 6) times—86 sts. Work even until piece measures 13¾ (14¾, 15¾)"/35 (37.5, 40)cm from beg.

Cap shaping

Bind off 4 sts at beg of next 2 rows, 3 sts at beg of next 2 rows, 2 sts at beg of next 4 rows, dec 1 st each side every other row 5 times. Bind off rem 54 sts.

FINISHING

Block pieces. Sew shoulder seams.

Left front band

With RS facing, smaller needles and 2 strands held together, beg at neck, pick up and k131 sts along straight edge of left front. Work in k1, p1 rib for 1¼"/3cm. Bind off in rib. Place markers on band for 7 buttons, with first ½"/1.5cm from lower edge and last ¾"/2cm from neck edge and 5 spaced evenly between.

Right front band

Work as for left front band, working buttonholes opposite markers as folls: K2tog, yo.

Collar

With RS facing, smaller needles and 2 strands held together, beg at right front neck, pick up and k103 sts evenly around neck edge, including top of bands. Work in k1, p1 rib for 5"/12.5cm. Bind off in rib. Set in sleeves. Sew side and sleeve seams. Sew on buttons. ●

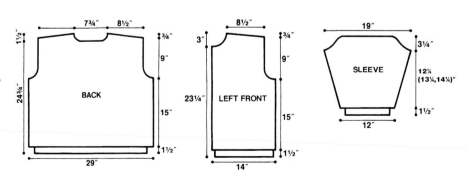

Chart A

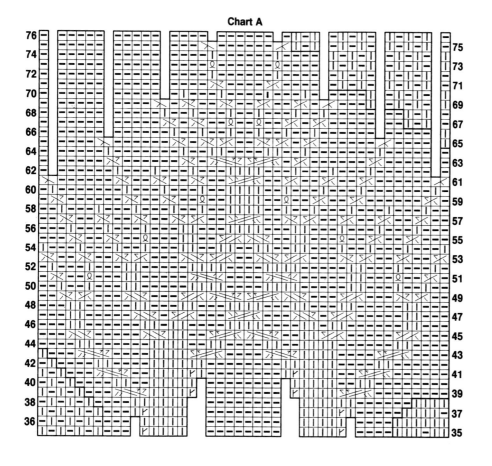

Chart E

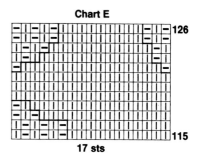

17 sts

Chart C

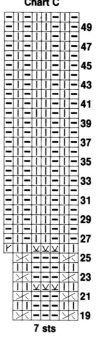

7 sts

Chart B

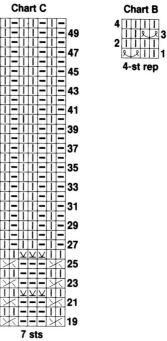

4-st rep

Chart D

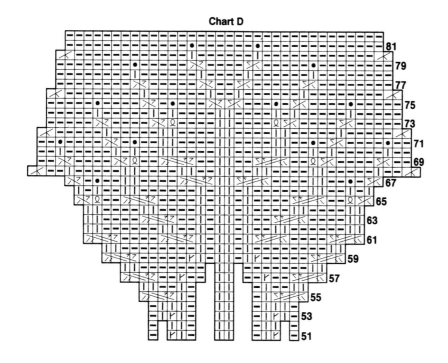

	k on RS, p on WS
	p on RS, k on WS
	twisted st
	small bobble
	large bobble
	m1
	float st
	k2tog
	ssk
	RT
	2-st Back Purl Cross
	2-st Front Purl Cross
	2-st Back Purl Twist
	2-st Front Purl Twist
	sl 3
	3-st Back Purl Cross
	3-st Front Purl Cross
	3-st Back Purl Twist
	3-st Front Purl Twist
	4-st Back Cable
	4-st Front Cable
	4-st Back Purl Cross
	4-st Front Purl Cross
	V-st

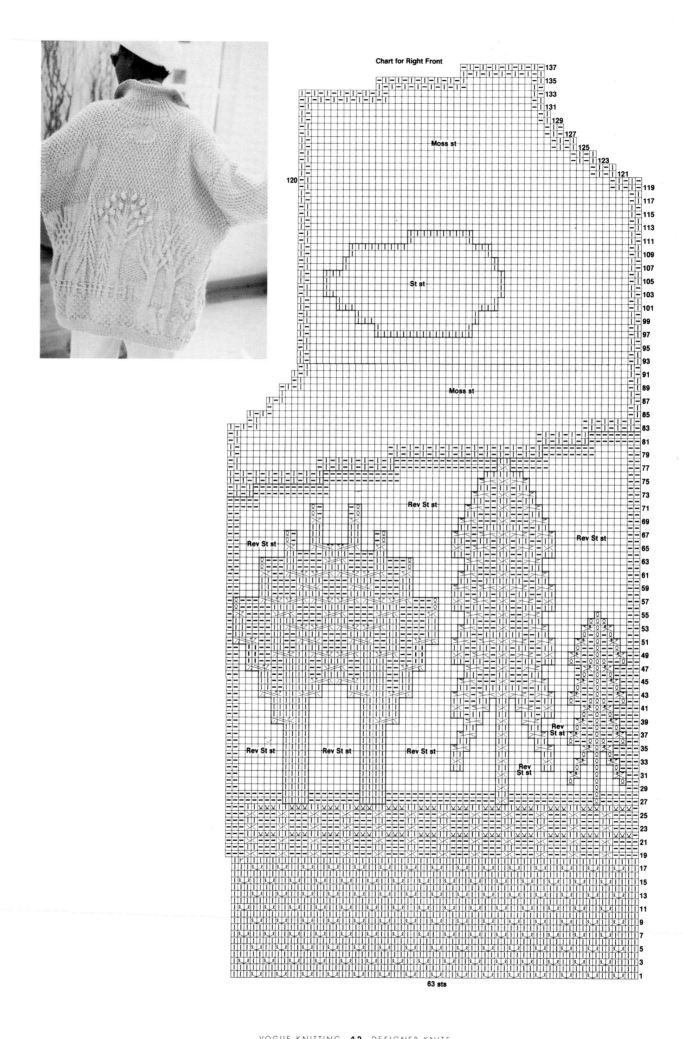

Chart for Right Front

Moss st

137
135
133
131
129
127
125
123
121

120
119
117
115
113
111
109
107
105
103
101
99
97
95
93
91
89
87
85
83
81
79
77
75
73
71
69
67
65
63
61
59
57
55
53
51
49
47
45
43
41
39
37
35
33
31
29
27
25
23
21
19
17
15
13
11
9
7
5
3
1

St st

Moss st

Rev St st

Rev St st

Rev St st

Rev St st

Rev St st

Rev St st

Rev
St st

Rev
St st

63 sts

Chart for Left Front

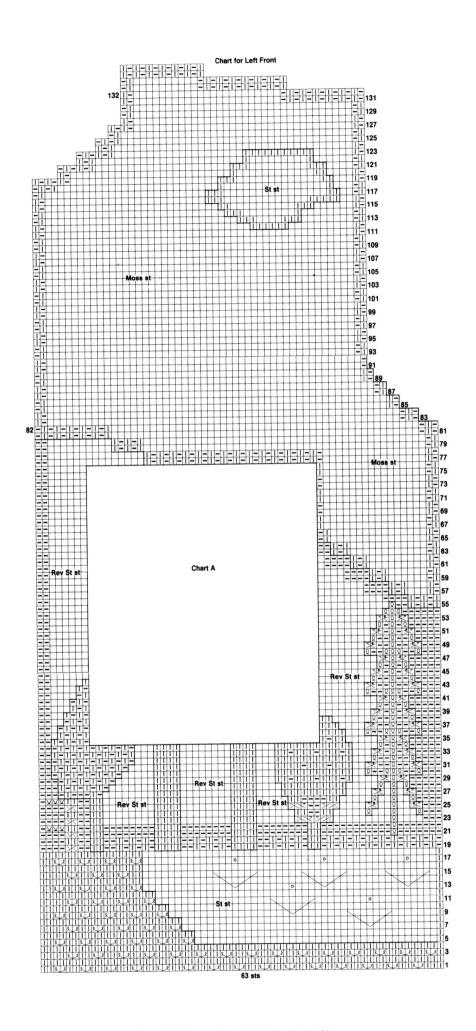

St st

Moss st

Moss st

Rev St st

Chart A

Rev St st

Rev St st

Rev St st

Rev St st

St st

63 sts

132 131
129
127
125
123
121
119
117
115
113
111
109
107
105
103
101
99
97
95
93
91
89
87
85
83
82 81
79
77
75
73
71
69
67
65
63
61
59
57
55
53
51
49
47
45
43
41
39
37
35
33
31
29
27
25
23
21
19
17
15
13
11
9
7
5
3
1

Entrelac stitching enlivens this oversized, relaxed fitting basketweave-look pullover with drop shoulders and turtleneck—subtle, sophisticated stitchery. Shown in size Large. The Entrelac Pullover first appeared in the Winter '91 issue of *Vogue Knitting*.

Entrelac Pullover

FOR EXPERIENCED KNITTERS

SIZE
To fit Small (Large). Directions are for smaller size with larger size in parentheses. If there is only one figure it applies to both sizes.

KNITTED MEASUREMENTS
● Bust at underarm 42 (56)"/106.5 (142)cm.
● Length 28½"/72.5cm.
● Sleeve width at upper arm 17¾"/45cm.

MATERIALS
● 11 (13) 3½oz/100g balls (each approx 127yd/117m) of Classic Elite *Montera* (wool/llama 4) in #3816 natural
● One pair each sizes 5 and 7 (3.75 and 4.5mm) needles OR SIZE TO OBTAIN GAUGE
● Size 5 (3.75mm) circular needle 16"/40cm long

GAUGE
(**Note** To work gauge swatch, cast on 20 sts. Work steps 1, 2, 3 and step 2 bind off of entrelac pat.)
20 sts to 7"/17.5cm over entrelac pat using size 7 (4.5mm) needles. Steps 1, 2, 3 and step 2 bind off of entrelac pat equals 5½"/14cm (length). FOR PERFECT FIT, TAKE TIME TO CHECK GAUGE.

STITCH GLOSSARY
Entrelac Pat (multiple of 10 sts)
Notes
1 Each rectangle is 10 sts and 20 rows.
2 When picking up sts on WS, push RH needle from RS to WS and purl.
3 After first repeat of step 2, sts will be picked up along side edge of rectangle instead of triangle.
4 All binding off is done when step 2 or 3 is complete.
Preparation Step 1 *K2, turn, p2, turn, k3, turn, p3. Cont in this manner working one more st every RS row until 10 sts have been worked. Leave on RH needle—one triangle complete. Rep from * across row.
Step 2 (WS) Inc 1 st by purling in the front and back of first st, p2tog, turn, k3, turn, inc 1 in first st, p1, p2tog, turn, k4. Cont in this manner, inc 1 st in first st, with 1 more p st between, then p2tog on every WS row until 10 sts are on RH needle. Leave sts on RH needle. **With WS facing, pick up and p10 sts along side edge of first triangle, sl last picked up st back to LH needle and p2tog with first st of next triangle,

*turn, k10, turn, p9, p2tog with first st of next triangle; rep from * until 10 sts of triangle have been worked. Leave on RH needle. Rep from ** across row. On side edge of last triangle, pick up and p9 sts, turn, k9, turn, p7, p2tog, turn, k8. Cont in this manner, p2tog at end of every WS row until 1 st rem. Turn.
Step 3 (RS) K1 and pick up and k9 sts along edge of first half-rectangle, k1 from first rectangle, sl last st picked up over it, *turn, p10, turn, k9, sl 1, k1 from rectangle, psso; rep from * until all 10 sts from first rectangle have been worked and there are 10 sts on RH needle. Leave on RH needle. Pick up and k10 sts along side edge of next rectangle. Rep from * as for last rectangle across row. Rep steps 2 and 3 for entrelac pat.

Bind off (Note: Use either bind-off method depending on last step worked.)
Step 2 bind off Beg step 2 and end on k6 row, turn.
Next row (WS) P2tog, p3, p2tog, turn, k5, turn, p2tog, p2, p2tog, turn, k4, turn, p2tog, p1, p2tog, turn, k3, turn, p2tog twice, turn, k2, turn, p2tog—1 st rem. *Pick up and p10 sts, turn, k11, turn, p2tog, p8, p2tog, turn, k10, turn, cont in this manner, dec 1 st at each side, end p3 tog—1 st rem. Rep from *, end last triangle as foll: on side edge, pick up and p9 sts, turn, k10, turn, p2 tog at beg and end of row. Cont in this manner, end p3 tog.
Step 3 bind off Beg step 3 by pick-

ing up sts and end on p10, turn.
Next row (RS) Sl 1, k1, psso at beg of every RS, AT SAME TIME, cont to work dec at end of row as per step 3. End last rep with sl 1, k2tog, psso.

BACK

With smaller needles, cast on 85 (117) sts. Work in k1, p1 rib for 2"/5cm, dec 25 (37) sts evenly across last WS row—60 (80) sts. Change to larger needles. Beg with preparation step 1, work entrelac pat across row. Cont in pat as established until piece measures 28½"/72.5cm from beg. Work bind off on all sts.

FRONT

Work as for back until piece measures 27"/68.5cm from beg.

Neck shaping

Next row (RS) Work 20 (30) sts, join 2nd ball of yarn and work bind off over next 20 sts, work to end. Working both sides at once, cont until same length as back. Work bind off on 20 (30) sts each side.

SLEEVES

With smaller needles, cast on 45 sts. Work in k1, p1 rib for 2"/5cm, dec 15 sts evenly across last WS row—30 sts. Change to larger needles. Beg with preparation step 1, work entrelac pat across row. Cont in pat as established through step 3.

Beg sleeve inc Work first half-rectangle of step 2 as established, AT SAME TIME, inc 1 st in last st of RS rows every 4th row until 10 sts of rectangle have been made. Turn; k10. Turn, p9, k2tog (1 from RH needle with 1 from LH needle), turn, k10, turn, p9, k2tog (1 st from RH needle, 1 st from LH needle). Cont to work step 2 from ** to last half rectangle. Work 10 sts of rectangle as a full rectangle until all sts have been worked. Leave on RH needle. Cont to work step 2 across row until last half-rectangle. Work as

established, only p2tog every 4th row instead of every other row, end with 5 sts.

Step 3 (RS) Inc 1 st in first st, turn, p1, inc 1 st in last st, turn, inc 1 st in first st, k1, sl 1, k1, psso, turn, p3, inc 1 st in last st, turn.

Next row Inc 1 st in first st, k3, sl 1, k1, psso, turn, p5, inc 1 st in last st. Turn. Inc 1 st in first st, k5, sl 1, k1, psso, turn. P8, inc 1 st in last st. Turn, inc into first st, k7, sl 1, k1, psso—10 sts on RH needle. Leave aside. Cont to work step 3 across row. Cont in this manner, inc 1 st in first st of every RS row and last st of every WS row until 5 sts of half-rectangle have been worked. Cont to work step 3 across row. On last half-rectangle, pick up 5 sts along edge, work 5 sts as for full rectangle, only k2tog every 4th row instead of every other row, until 1 st rem and 20 rows have been worked.

Next step 2 Pick up 9 sts across long edge of first half-rectangle and work step 2 across row.

Next step 3 Inc 1 st in first st, turn, p2, turn, inc 1 st in first st, sl 1, k1, psso, turn, p2, inc in last st, turn. Cont to inc 1 st in first st of every RS row and in last st every 4th row on WS rows, AT SAME TIME, work rectangle with 1 st more every other row until 10 sts are on needle, then cont to work as for full rectangle. Cont in step 3 across row to last rectangle. Pick up and k10 sts on side edge of last rectangle, turn, p10, turn, k8, k2tog, turn, p9, turn, k9, turn, cont to work rectangle, k2tog every 4th row on RS until 5 sts rem and 20 rows have been worked.

Next step 2 Inc 1 st in first st, turn, k1, inc 1 st in last st, turn, inc 1 st in first st, p1, p2tog, turn, k3, inc 1 st in last st, cont to work as established, inc 1 st in first st on WS rows and every last st on RS rows until 5 sts of half-rectangle have been worked and 10 sts are on RH needle. Cont to work step 2 across row until last rectangle. Pick up 5 sts along side edge of last

rectangle, work on 5 sts, p2tog every 4th row on WS until 1 st rem.

Next step 3 Pick up 9 sts across side edge and work step 3 with full rectangles across row. Work even on 50 sts until piece measures 18"/45.5cm from beg. Work bind off on all sts.

FINISHING

Block pieces. Sew shoulder seams.

Turtleneck

With RS facing and circular needle, beg at right shoulder, pick up and k105 sts evenly around neck edge. Join. Work in k1, p1 rib for 8"/20.5cm. Bind off in rib. Place markers 8¾"/22cm down from shoulders on front and back for armholes. Sew tops of sleeves between markers. Sew side and sleeve seams. ●

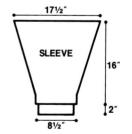

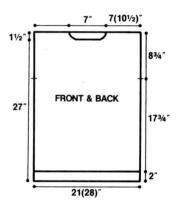

Interlocking Cable Tunic

An all-over cable trellis design blooms in winter white on this cozy, oversized pullover with seed st, square armholes and a rib turtleneck. Shown in size Large. The Interlocking Cable Tunic first appeared in the Fall '93 issue of *Vogue Knitting*.

Interlocking Cable Tunic

FOR EXPERIENCED KNITTERS

SIZES
To fit Small/Medium (Large). Directions are for smaller size with larger size in parentheses. If there is only one figure it applies to both sizes.

KNITTED MEASUREMENTS
- Bust at underarm 48 (52)"/122 (132)cm.
- Length 29 (30)"/74 (76)cm.
- Sleeve width at upper arm 19 (20)"/48 (51)cm.

MATERIALS
- 26 (27) 1¾oz/50g balls (each approx 115yd/105m) of Classic Elite *Inca Alpaca* (alpaca 4) in #1116 natural
- One pair size 7 (4.5mm) needles OR SIZE TO OBTAIN GAUGE
- Cable needle (cn)

GAUGE
20 sts and 28 rows to 4"/10cm over St st using size 7 (4.5mm) needles. 30 sts and 30 rows to 4"/10cm over chart pat using size 7 (4.5mm) needles. FOR PERFECT FIT, TAKE TIME TO CHECK GAUGES.

Note
Omit 8-st Front or Back Cable Twist at side edges of front and back.

STITCH GLOSSARY
Double Seed St
Row 1 (RS) *K1, p1; rep from *.
Row 2 K the knit sts and p the purl sts.
Row 3 P the knit sts and k the purl sts.
Row 4 Rep row 2. Rep rows 1-4 for double seed st.
5-st Front Cross Sl 4 sts to cn and hold to *front* of work, p1, k4 from cn.
5-st Back Cross Sl 1 st to cn and hold to *back* of work, k4, p1 from cn.
8-st Front Cable Sl 4 sts to cn and hold to *front* of work, k4, k4 from cn.
8-st Back Cable Sl 4 sts to cn and hold to *back* of work, k4, k4 from cn.
10-st Front Cross Sl 5 sts to cn and hold to *front* of work, p1, k4, k4, p1 from cn.

BACK
With size 7 (4.5mm) needles, cast on 171 (187) sts. Work in k1, p1 rib for 1"/2.5cm, inc 7 sts evenly across last RS row—178 (194) sts.
Beg chart: Row 1 (WS) P1 (selvage), beg with st 0 (16) of chart, and working chart from left to right, work through st 0 (1), work 32-st rep 5 times, work sts 32-17 of chart, p1 (selvage).
Row 2 K1 (selvage), work sts 17-32 of chart, work 32-st rep 5 times, work sts 0 (1-16) of chart, k1 (selvage). Cont to work in chart pat as established, keeping first and last st in St st until piece measures 18½ (19)"/47 (48.5)cm from beg, end with a WS row.

Armhole shaping
Cont in pat, bind off 11 sts at beg of next 2 rows—156 (172) sts (selvage sts eliminated). Work even until armhole measures 9½ (10)"/24 (25.5)cm, end with a WS row.

Shoulder shaping
Bind off 16 (19) sts at beg of next 4 rows, 16 (18) sts at beg of next 2 rows. Bind off rem 60 sts.

FRONT
Work as for back until armhole measures 8 (8½)"/20.5 (21.5)cm.

Neck shaping
Next row (RS) Work across 56 (64) sts, join 2nd ball of yarn and bind off 44 sts, work to end. Working both sides at once, bind off from each neck edge 2 sts 4 times, AT SAME TIME, when same length as back to shoulder, shape shoulders as for back.

SLEEVES
With size 7 (4.5mm) needles, cast on 58 (60) sts. Work in k1, p1 rib for ¾"/2cm, inc 8 (6) sts evenly across last RS row—66 sts.

Beg chart: Row 1 (WS) P1 (selvage), beg with st 32, work 32-st rep of chart twice, p1 (selvage). Cont in chart pat, keeping first and last sts in St st, AT SAME TIME, inc 1 st each side (inside selvage sts) every other row 17 (23) times, every 4th row 22 (20) times—144 (152) sts, working inc sts into chart pat.

When piece measures 19 (19½)"/48.5 (49.5)cm from beg, bind off.

FINISHING
Block pieces. Sew left shoulder seam.

Collar
With RS facing, and size 7 (4.5mm)

needles, pick up and k123 (127) sts around neck edge. Work in k1, p1 rib for 9"/23cm. Bind off loosely in rib. Sew right shoulder seam, including collar. Sew straight edge of sleeve to armhole. Sew bound-off sts of armhole to side edge of sleeve. Sew side and sleeve seams. ●

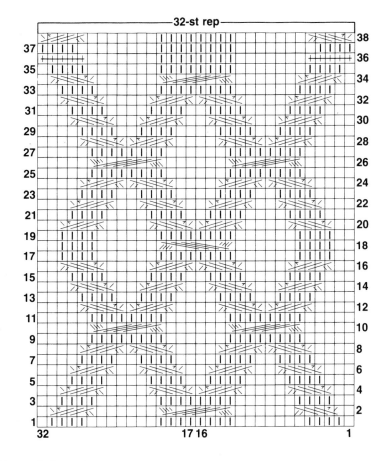

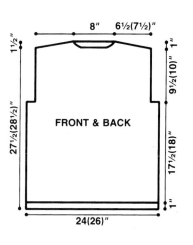

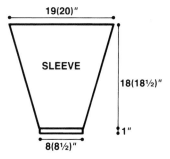

☐ Double seed st
Ⅰ k on RS, p on WS
⬚ 5-st Back Cross
⬚ 5-st Front Cross

⬚ 8-st Back Cable
⬚ 8-st Front Cable
⬚ 10-st Front Cross

This roomy pullover sports spiralling cabled vines and embossed leaves on a seed stitch ground. Very oversized, it features square armholes and a deep, ribbed V-neck. The Cable and Leaf Motif V-Neck Pullover first appeared in the Fall '91 issue of *Vogue Knitting*.

Cable and Leaf Motif V-Neck Pullover

FOR EXPERIENCED KNITTERS

SIZES
One size. To fit 34-44"/86-112cm bust. (Note: For smaller sizes, shorten sleeves to fit.)

KNITTED MEASUREMENTS
● Bust at underarm 60"/152.5cm.
● Length 26"/66cm.
● Sleeve width at upper arm 20"/51cm.

MATERIALS
● 14 3½oz/100g balls (each approx 138yd/124m) of Manos del Uruguay/ Simpson Southwick *700 Tex* (wool 5) in #21 banana
● One pair each sizes 6 and 8 (4 and 5mm) needles OR SIZE TO OBTAIN GAUGE
● Size 5 (3.75mm) circular needle 24"/60cm long
● Cable needle (cn) and stitch markers

GAUGE
16 sts and 28 rows to 4"/10cm over seed st using size 8 (5mm) needles. FOR PERFECT FIT, TAKE TIME TO CHECK GAUGE.

Notes
1 To avoid striping in this variegated yarn, use two balls of yarn and alternate between two balls approx. every 4 rows.
2 Take care to set up first row of seed st and chart #2 correctly.
3 For ease in working pats use markers to separate cables and leaf pats.

STITCH GLOSSARY
3-st Front Cross Sl 1 to cn and hold to front, k1, p1; k1 from cn.
4-st Front Cross Sl 3 to cn and hold to front, work 1 seed st, k3 from cn.
4-st Back Cross Sl 1 to cn and hold to back, k3, work 1 seed st from cn.
4-st Front Cross Inc Sl 3 to cn and hold to front, k and p into front and back of next st, k3 from cn.
4-st Back Cross Inc Sl 1 to cn and hold to back, k3, k and p into front and back of st from cn.
6-st Back Cable Sl 3 to cn and hold to back, k3, k3 from cn.
10-st Front Cable Sl 5 to cn and hold to front, k5, k5 from cn.
10-st Back Cable Sl 5 to cn and hold to back, k5, k5 from cn.
14-st Back Cable Sl 7 to cn and hold to back, k7, k7 from cn.
Seed St (over even # of sts)
Row 1 *K1, p1; rep from * to end.
Row 2 *P1, k1; rep from * to end. Rep rows 1 and 2 for seed st.

BACK
With smaller needles, cast on 125 sts.
Beg chart #1: Preparation row (WS) Reading charts from left to right, work last st of chart, then work 4-st rep of chart 31 times. Work rows 1-4 of chart #1 until piece measures 2"/5cm from beg, end with a RS row, inc 3 sts evenly across—128 sts. Change to larger needles.
Beg chart pats: Row 1 (WS) Work 12 sts seed st, reading chart from right to left work 29 sts of chart #2, work 12 sts seed st, work 22 sts of chart #3, work 12 sts seed st, reading chart from left to right work 29 sts of chart #2, work 12 sts seed st. Cont as estab-lished, working rows of chart #2 as foll: 1-72 once, then rep rows 25-72 once, then work rows 73-115, AT SAME TIME, when piece measures 16"/40.5cm from beg, work armhole shaping as foll:

Armhole shaping
Bind off 7 sts at beg of next 2 rows—114 sts. Cont to work as established until piece measures 26"/66cm from beg. Bind off.

FRONT
Work as for back until piece measures 13½"/34.5cm from beg.

V-neck shaping
Work 62 sts, dec 1 st, join 2nd ball of yarn and dec 1 st, work to end. Working both sides at once, dec 1 st from each neck edge every other row 10 times more, then every 6th row 10 times, until piece measures same length as back to armhole, shape armhole as for back. When same length as back to shoulder, bind off 36 sts each side for shoulders.

SLEEVES
With smaller needles, cast on 45 sts.
Beg chart #1: Preparation row (WS) Reading chart from left to right, work last st of chart, then work 4-st rep of chart 11 times. Cont to work rows 1-4 of chart until piece measures 2"/5cm from beg, inc 7 sts evenly across last RS row—52 sts. Change to larger needles.
Beg chart #4: Row 1 (WS) Work 19 seed st, work 14 sts of chart #4, work 19 seed st. Cont to work as established, AT SAME TIME, inc 1 st each side (working inc sts into seed st) every 6th row 14

times, then every 8th row twice—84 sts. Work even until piece measures 18¾"/47.5cm from beg. Bind off.

FINISHING
Block pieces. Sew shoulder seams.

Neckband
With RS facing and circular needle, beg at right shoulder and pick up and K34 sts evenly across back neck, 70 sts along left front neck, place marker (pm) 1 st at center front neck, pm, 70 sts along right front neck—175 sts. Join. Work in k1, p1 rib to 2 sts before marker: k2tog, sl marker, k1, sl marker, ssk, work in k1, p1 rib to end. Cont in rib, working decs outside of markers every rnd, for 1¼"/3cm. Bind off, working decs on bind off row. Sew tops of sleeves to straight edge of armholes, then sew last 1¾"/4.5cm at top of sleeve to bound-off arm-hole sts. Sew side and sleeve seams. ●

Chart #2

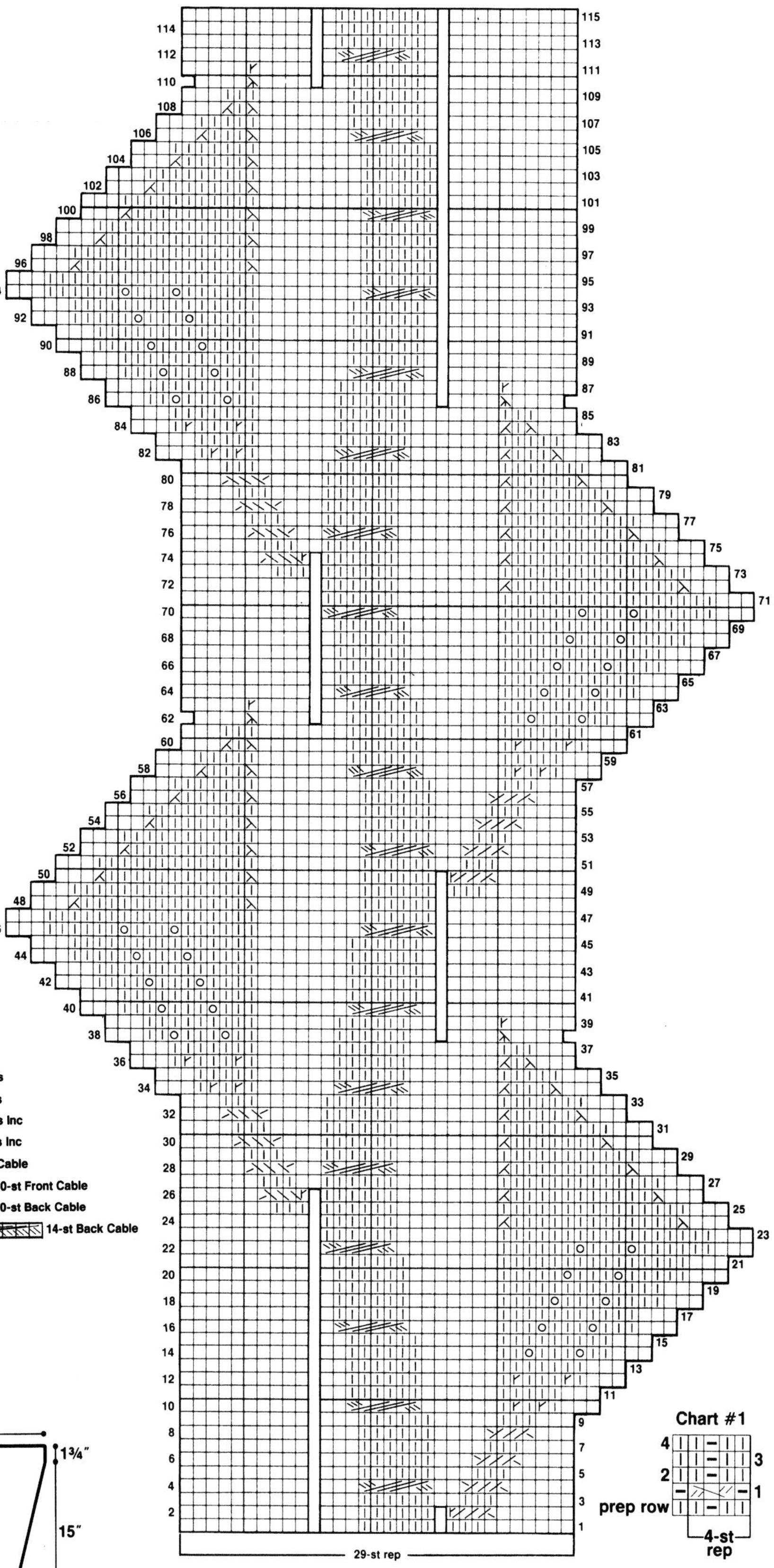

Chart #3
22 sts 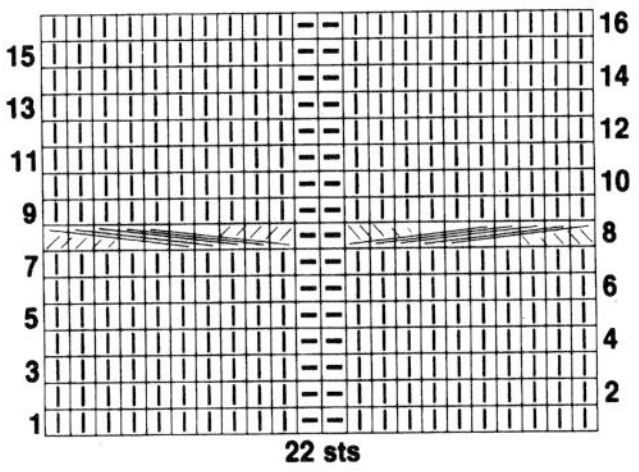

Chart #4
14 sts

Chart #1
4-st rep
prep row

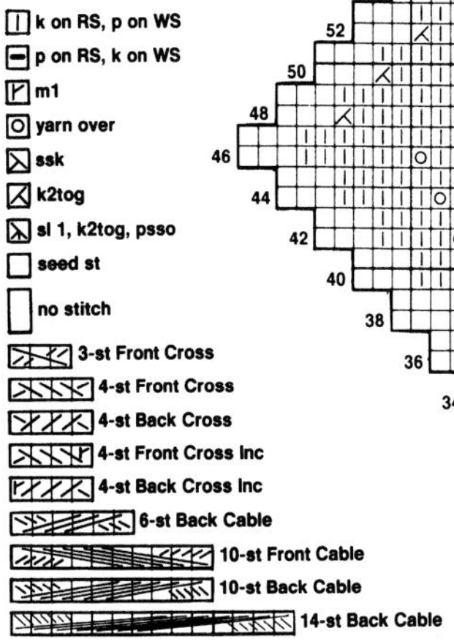

	k on RS, p on WS
-	p on RS, k on WS
	m1
O	yarn over
	ssk
	k2tog
	sl 1, k2tog, psso
	seed st
	no stitch
	3-st Front Cross
	4-st Front Cross
	4-st Back Cross
	4-st Front Cross Inc
	4-st Back Cross Inc
	6-st Back Cable
	10-st Front Cable
	10-st Back Cable
	14-st Back Cable

29-st rep

Note: When working chart #2 from left to right, work 4-st front cross as 4-st back cross; 4-st back cross as 4-st front cross.

FRONT & BACK
9" 8¾"
12½"
13½"
10"
14"
2"
30"

SLEEVE
20"
1¾"
15"
2"
12½"

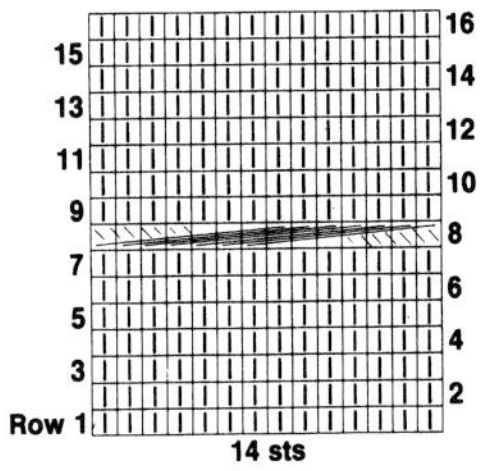

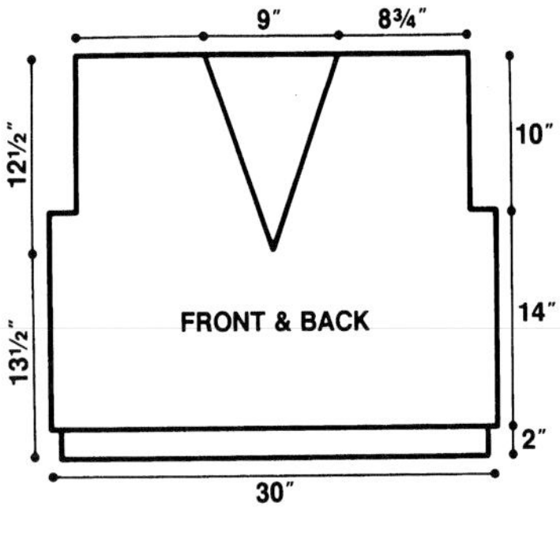

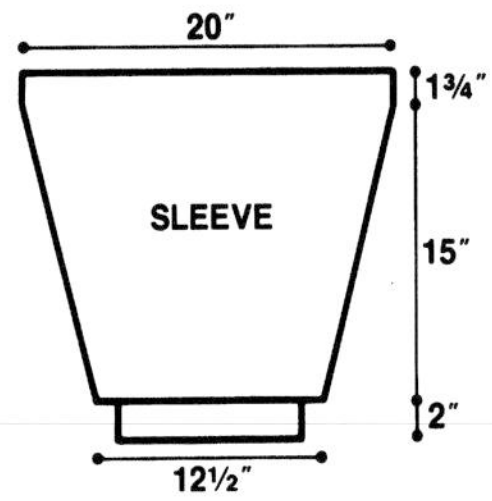

Openwork Cable Cardigan

This roomy, oversized V-neck cardigan with drop shoulders and set-in pockets has the potential to be a year-round favorite. Openwork keeps the texture light, while cables give it a rich dimension. Shown in size Medium. The Openwork Cable Cardigan first appeared in the Spring/Summer '94 issue of *Vogue Knitting*.

Openwork Cable Cardigan

FOR EXPERIENCED KNITTERS

SIZES
To fit Small (Medium, Large). Directions are for smallest size with larger sizes in parentheses. If there is only one figure it applies to all sizes.

KNITTED MEASUREMENTS
● Bust at underarm (buttoned) 47 (49, 51)"/119.5 (124.5, 129.5)cm.
● Length 26 (27, 28)"/66 (68.5, 71)cm.
● Sleeve width at upper arm 17 (18, 19)"/ 43 (45.5, 48)cm.

MATERIALS
● 8 (9, 9) 3½oz/100g balls (each approx 181yd/164m) of Classic Elite *Rain* (cotton/linen/rayon/silk 4) in natural #5562
● One pair size 7 (4.5mm) needles OR SIZE TO OBTAIN GAUGE
● Size 7 (4.5mm) circular needle 24"/60cm long
● Stitch markers and holders
● Six 1"/2.5cm buttons

GAUGE
20 sts and 27 rows to 4"/10cm over St st with size 7 (4.5mm) needles.
FOR PERFECT FIT, TAKE TIME TO CHECK GAUGE.

STITCH GLOSSARY
Zigzag Lace Panel (17 sts)
Rows 1, 3, 5 and 7 (RS) P2, k2, yo, k2tog, ssk, k2, yo, k2, yo, k2tog, k1, p2.
Rows 2, 4, 6 and 8 K2, p2, yo, p2tog, p5, p1, yo, p2tog, p1, k2.
Rows 9, 11, 13 and 15 P2, k2, yo, k2tog, k1, yo, k2, k2tog, k1, yo, k2tog, k1, p2.
Rows 10, 12, 14 and 16 K2, p2, yo, p2tog, p5, p1, yo, p2tog, p1, k2.
Rep rows 1-16 for zigzag lace pat.

4-st Openwork Pat (4 sts)
Row 1 (RS) Yo, ssk, yo, ssk.
Rows 2 and 4 P4.
Row 3 K2tog, yo, k2tog, yo.

8-st Back Cable Pat (8 sts)
Row 1 (RS) K8.
Row 2 P8.
Row 3 Sl 4 sts to cn, hold to *back* of work, k4, k4 from cn.
Rows 4-12 K the knit sts and p the purl sts.
Row 13 Rep row 3. Rep rows 4-13 for 8-st back cable pat.

BACK
Cast on 114 (120, 126) sts. Work in k1, p1 rib for 1"/2.5cm, inc 6 sts evenly across last row—120 (126, 132) sts.
Beg pats: Next row (RS) Beg with row 1 of each pat, p4, place marker

(pm), work 8-st back cable pat, pm, *p3 (4, 5), pm, work 4-st openwork pat, pm, p3 (4, 5) pm, work 8-st back cable pat, pm, work zigzag lace pat, pm, work 8-st back cable pat, pm, * rep between *'s once, p3 (4, 5), pm, work 4-st openwork pat, pm, p3 (4, 5), pm, work 8-st back cable pat, pm, p4. Work even in pats as established, keeping all other sts in rev St st, until piece measures 16½ (17, 17½)"/42 (43.5, 44.5)cm from beg, end with a WS row.

Armhole shaping
Bind off 3 sts at beg of next 2 rows—114 (120, 126) sts. Work even until armhole measures 8½ (9, 9½)"/21.5 (23, 24)cm, end with a WS row.

Shoulder shaping
Bind off 14 (16, 16) sts at beg of next 2 rows, 15 (15, 16) sts at beg of next 4 rows. Bind off rem 26 (28, 30) sts for neck.

Pocket linings (make 2)
Cast on 26 sts and work in St st for 5"/13cm. Place sts on holder.

LEFT FRONT
Cast on 54 (56, 58) sts. Work k1, p1 rib as for back, inc 6 sts evenly across last row—60 (62, 64) sts.
Beg pats: Next row (RS) Beg with row 1 of each pat, p4, pm, work 8-st back cable pat, pm, p3 (4, 5), pm, work 4-st openwork pat, pm, p3 (4, 5), work 8-st back cable pat, pm, work zigzag lace pat, pm, work 8-

st back cable pat, pm, p5 (center front edge). Work even in pats as established, keeping all other sts in rev St st, until piece measures 7"/18cm from beg, end with a WS row.

Pocket joining

Next row (RS) Work 21 (23, 25) sts, place next 26 sts on holder and, with k side facing, k26 sts of pocket lining from holder, work to end. Work even until piece measures 14 (15, 16)"/35.5 (38, 40.5)cm from beg, end with a WS row.

V-neck shaping

Next row (RS) Work in pat to last 4 sts, p2tog, p2. Cont to dec 1 st at neck edge every 4th row 6 times, every 6th row 6 times as foll: Keeping 2 purl sts at neck edge as selvage, cont to p2tog through center front purl sts, then work k2tog through 8-st back cable sts, then work rem decs leaving zigzag pat intact, AT SAME TIME, when piece measures same as back to armhole, shape armhole as for back. When armhole measures same as back to shoulder, shape shoulder as for back.

RIGHT FRONT

Cast on, rib and inc as for left front.
Beg pats: Next row (RS) Beg with row 1 of each pat, p5 (center front), pm, work 8-st back cable pat, pm, work zigzag lace pat, pm, work 8-st back cable pat, pm, p3 (4, 5), pm, work 4-st openwork pat, pm, p3 (4, 5), work 8-st back cable pat, pm, p4. Work even in pats as established and reverse placement of pocket lining as foll: Work 13 sts, place next 26 sts on holder and, with k side facing, k26 sts of pocket lining from holder, work to end. Reverse V-neck, armhole and shoulder shaping.

SLEEVES

Cast on 54 sts and rib as for back, inc 8 sts evenly across last row —62 sts.

Beg pats: Next row (RS) Beg with row 1 of each pat, work zigzag lace panel, work 8-st back cable pat, pm, p4, pm, work 4-st openwork pat, pm, p4, pm, work 8-st back cable pat, pm, work zigzag lace pat. Cont in pats as established, working all other sts in rev St st, AT SAME TIME, inc 1 st each side (working inc sts into rev St st) every 4th row 10 (16, 20) times, every 6th row 11 (8, 6) times—104 (110, 114) sts. When piece measures 16½ (17, 17½)"/42 (43.5, 44.5)cm from beg, end with a WS row.

Cap shaping

Bind off 3 sts at beg of next 2 rows, 20 sts at beg of next 2 rows. Bind off rem 58 (64, 68) sts.

FINISHING

Block pieces. Sew shoulder seams.

Pocket edging

With RS facing, k26 sts from holder and work in k1, p1 rib for 1"/2.5cm. Bind off. Sew sides of edging to front. Sew pocket linings to WS of fronts.

Buttonband

With RS facing, beg at center back neck edge and pick up and k156 (164, 172) sts evenly to lower edge of left front. Work in k1, p1 rib for 1"/2.5cm. Bind off. Place 6 markers on band, the first at beg of neck shaping, the last 1"/2.5cm from lower edge and 4 others spaced evenly between.

Buttonhole band

Work as for buttonband for ½"/1.5cm. Make buttonholes by binding off 2 sts opposite markers. On next row, cast on 2 sts over bound-off sts of previous row. Complete as for buttonband. Sew bands at center back neck. Set in sleeves, easing cap to fit. Sew side and sleeve seams. Sew on buttons. ●

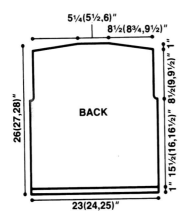

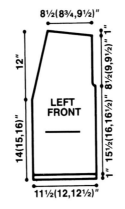

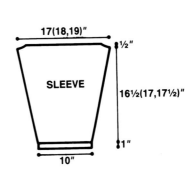

An innovative update of an heirloom coverlet pattern produces this arresting lacy pullover. Both challenging and interesting to knit, its eighteen patchwork pieces unite in a swingy, tent shape. Very oversized, the pullover features angled armholes, round neck and scalloped crochet edging. The Counterpane Pullover first appeared in the Spring/Summer '91 issue of *Vogue Knitting*.

Counterpane Pullover

FOR EXPERIENCED KNITTERS

SIZES
One size. To fit 34-42"/86-106cm.

KNITTED MEASUREMENTS
● Bust at underarm 5½"/140cm.
● Length 28½"/72.5cm.
● Sleeve width at upper arm 18"/45cm.

MATERIALS
Original Yarn
● 15 1¾oz/50g balls (each approx 136yd/122m) of Classic Elite *Willough* (silk/cotton 4) in #3616 natural
Substitute Yarn
● 12 1¾oz/50g balls (each approx 183yd/169m) of Classic Elite *Simple Cotton* (cotton 4) in #6616 natural
● One pair size 6 (4mm) needles OR SIZE TO OBTAIN GAUGE
● Size F (4mm) crochet hook
● Stitch markers and cable needle (cn)

Note
The original yarn used for this sweater is no longer available. A comparable substitute has been made, which is available at the time of printing. Check gauge of substitute yarns very carefully before beginning.

GAUGE
45 sts (including 2 selvage sts) to 9½"/24cm and 36 rows to 5"/12.5cm over chart for Panel 2 using size 6 (4mm) needles. FOR PERFECT FIT, TAKE TIME TO CHECK GAUGE.

STITCH GLOSSARY
Make 1 (m1) Insert LH needle from front to back under horizontal strand between last st worked and next st on LH needle, forming loop on LH needle, k in back loop of this st.
4-st Back Cable Sl 2 sts to cn and hold to *back* of work, k2, k2 from cn.
Inc 1 K into front and back of lp.
Inc to 5 (K1, yo, k1, yo, k1) in one st.
Dec 2 On RS, sl 2 sts as if knitting them tog, k1, pass sl sts over k st. On WS, p3tog.
Right Purl Cross Sl 1 st to cn and hold to *back* of work, k1, p1 from cn.
Left Purl Cross Sl 1 st to cn and hold to *front* of work, p1, k1 from cn.
Right Twist Skip next st on LH needle and k 2nd st in front of skipped st, k skipped st, sl both sts from LH needle.

Notes
1 It is helpful to mark RS of each piece.
2 For ease in assembling, label each completed panel or square.

BACK
Panel 1
Cast on 22 sts.
Next row (RS) Work chart A over 16 sts, then chart B over 6 sts. Cont in pats until piece measures 17"/43cm from beg, end with a RS row.

Armhole shaping
Next row (WS) Dec 1 st (armhole edge), work to end. Then dec 1 st at same edge every row 20 times more. Fasten off last st.
Panel 2
Cast on 45 sts.
Next row (RS) Work first st of chart for panel 2, then work 12-st rep 3 times, work last 8 sts of chart. Cont in pats until piece measures 26"/66cm from beg, end with a WS row.

Neck and shoulder shaping
Bind off 6 sts (neck edge), dec 1 st at same edge every row 4 times, every other row 3 times, AT SAME TIME, bind off from shoulder edge (beg of WS rows) 4 sts 8 times.
Panel 3
Cast on 16 sts. Work chart A over 16 sts. Cont in pats until piece measures 26"/66cm from beg. Bind off.
Panel 4
Cast on 45 sts.
Next row (RS) Work first 7 sts of chart for panel 4, then work 12-st rep 3 times, work last 2 sts of chart. Cont in pat until same length as panel 2 to neck and shoulder shaping. Work as for panel 2 reversing neck and shoulder shaping.
Panel 5
Cast on 22 sts.
Next row (RS) Work chart C over 6 sts, then chart A over 16 sts. Cont in pats until same length as panel 1 to armhole. Work as for panel 1, reversing armhole shaping.

FRONT
Panel 6

Cast on 25 sts.

Next row (RS) Work chart A over 16 sts, then chart D over 9 sts. Cont in pats until piece measures 17"/43cm from beg, end with a RS row.

Armhole shaping

Next row Dec 1 st (armhole edge), work to end. Dec 1 st at same edge every row 16 times more, dec 2 sts every row 3 times. K2tog. Fasten off last st.

Panel 7

Work as for panel 2 for 36 rows. Bind off.

Panel 8

Cast on 7 sts.

Next row (RS) Work 7-st chart for panel 8. Cont in pat until piece measures 24½"/62.5cm from beg. Bind off.

Panel 9

Work as for panel 4 for 36 rows. Bind off.

Panel 10

Cast on 25 sts.

Next row (RS) Work chart E over 9 sts, chart A over 16 sts. Cont in pats until same length as panel 6 to armhole. Work as for panel 6 reversing armhole shaping.

Squares 11, 12, 13, 14

Cast on 3 sts. Work square chart. Bind off rem 3 sts.

Panel 15

Work as for panel 2 for 8 rows.

Neck and shoulder shaping

Bind off 6 sts from neck edge (beg of RS row), then dec 1 st every row 4 times, every other row 3 times, after neck shaping has been worked, bind off from shoulder edge (beg of WS rows) 4 sts 8 times.

Panel 16

Work as for panel 4 for 9 rows. Reverse neck and shoulder shaping in panel 15.

SLEEVES

(Note: Work inc for sleeves as foll: 1 st each side every 6th row 15 times, every 8th row 5 times—93 sts.)
Cast on 53 sts.

Next row (RS) K2, work 12-st rep of chart for panel 2 for 4 times, k3. Cont in pats through row 18 working inc sts into St st. Mark center st of sleeve. Mark center st of square chart. Beg with row 47 and omit m1 incs, work through row 74 (28 rows) working inc sts into rev St st—67 sts.

Next row (RS) P1, work chart E over 8 sts (omit first st of chart) 8 times, end p2. Cont in chart through row 16. Work rows 47-51 of square chart (5 rows). K 1 row on WS. Work 12-st rep of panel 2 for 18 rows. Work rows 47-74 of square chart, adding 1 diamond to each side—89 sts.

Next row (RS) P4, work chart E over 8 sts (omit first st of chart) 10 times, end p5. Work rows 47-51. K 1 row on WS—total of 136 rows and piece measures approx 19"/48cm from beg.

Cap shaping

Next row (RS) Ssk, work 12-st rep of chart for panel 2 for 7 times, k5, k2tog. Work in pat through row 18, then cont in rev St st, AT SAME TIME, dec 1 st each side every row 19 times more. Bind off rem 53 sts.

FINISHING

Block pieces. (Note: Block squares 11-14 into square shape.) Sew pieces tog foll schematic. Sew shoulder seams. Sew top of sleeve to straight edge of armholes, then sew dec armhole sts of front and back to dec sts of sleeve. Sew side and sleeve seams.

Neckband

With RS facing and crochet hook, beg at right shoulder seam, work as foll:
Rnd 1 (3 dc, 1 sc) in same space evenly around, join with sl st to first dc.
Rnd 2 Do not turn; skip 3 dc, *(1 sc, 3 dc) in sp between 3rd dc and sc of rnd 1; rep from * around. Fasten off.

Sleeve and lower edges

Work edging as for neckband. ●

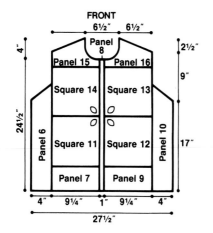

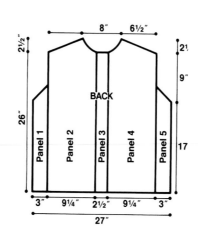

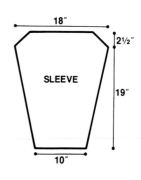

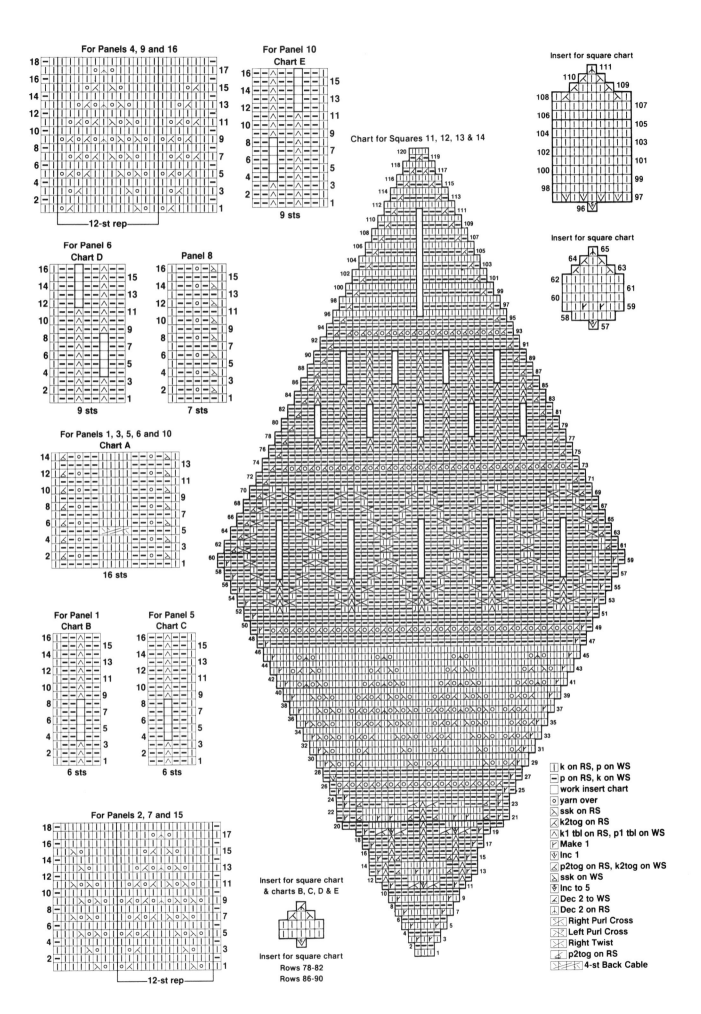

For Panels 4, 9 and 16

For Panel 10
Chart E
9 sts

Chart for Squares 11, 12, 13 & 14

Insert for square chart

For Panel 6
Chart D
9 sts

Panel 8
7 sts

Insert for square chart

For Panels 1, 3, 5, 6 and 10
Chart A
16 sts

For Panel 1
Chart B
6 sts

For Panel 5
Chart C
6 sts

For Panels 2, 7 and 15
12-st rep

Insert for square chart
& charts B, C, D & E

Insert for square chart
Rows 78-82
Rows 86-90

k on RS, p on WS
p on RS, k on WS
work insert chart
yarn over
ssk on RS
k2tog on RS
k1 tbl on RS, p1 tbl on WS
Make 1
Inc 1
p2tog on RS, k2tog on WS
ssk on WS
Inc to 5
Dec 2 to WS
Dec 2 on RS
Right Purl Cross
Left Purl Cross
Right Twist
p2tog on RS
4-st Back Cable

A gently flared tunic with the casual attitude and relaxed style that is trademark DKNY. Very oversized, it rounds up decreasing cables with a circular yoke and turtleneck. The Flared Cable Tunic first appeared in the Fall '91 issue of *Vogue Knitting*.

Flared Cable Tunic

FOR INTERMEDIATE KNITTERS

SIZES
One size. To fit 34-40"/86-101cm bust.

KNITTED MEASUREMENTS
- Bust at underarm 58½"/148.5cm.
- Length 31"/78.5cm.
- Sleeve width at upper arm 17½"/44.5cm.

MATERIALS
Original Yarn
- 14 3½oz/100g balls (each approx 160yd/147m) of Hayfield/Cascade *Brig Aran* (wool 5) in #19001 ecru

Substitute Yarn
- 12 3½oz/100g balls (each approx 190yd/175m) of Brown Sheep *Lamb's Pride Worsted* (wool/mohair 4) in #M10 creme
- One pair each sizes 7 and 8 (4.5 and 5mm) needles OR SIZE TO OBTAIN GAUGE
- Two size 8 (4.5mm) circular needles 36"/90cm long
- One size 8 (4.5mm) circular needle 24"/60cm long
- One set each size 7 and 8 (4.5 and 5mm) double-pointed needles (dpn)
- Cable needle (cn) and stitch markers
- Stitch holders

Note
The original yarn used for this sweater is no longer available. A comparable substitute has been made, which is available at the time of printing. Check gauge of substitute yarns very carefully before beginning.

GAUGE
58 sts to 8"/20.5cm and 26 rows to 4"/10cm over cable pat (slightly stretched) using size 8 (5mm) needles. FOR PERFECT FIT, TAKE TIME TO CHECK GAUGE.

Note
Due to large st numbers, yoke can be worked on two 36"/90cm circular needles, working from one to the other, as sts dec change to shorter length needle or dpn as needed.

STITCH GLOSSARY
12-st Cable Sl 6 sts to cn and hold to *front*, k6, k6 from cn.
Cable Pat (multiple of 14 sts + 2 extra) (Note: Cable pat is a rep of 16 rows, though each rep in yoke will have fewer sts.)
Row 1 (RS) *P2, 12-st cable; rep from *, end p2.
Row 2 and all WS rows K the knit sts and p the purl sts.
Rows 3, 5, 7, 9, 11, 13 and 15 *P2, k12; rep from * to end. Rep rows 1-16 for cable pat.

BACK
With smaller needles, cast on 212 sts. Work in k2, p2 rib for 1"/2.5cm, end with a WS row. Change to larger needles. Work cable pat until row 6 of 8th rep has been worked.
Dec row (RS) *P2, k4, [k2tog] twice, k4; rep from *; end p2—182 sts. Cont in cable pat until piece measures 20"/51cm from beg, end with a row 12. Sl sts to holder for yoke.

FRONT
Work as for back.

SLEEVES
With smaller needles, cast on 50 sts. Work in k2, p2 rib for 1"/2.5cm, inc 22 sts evenly across last WS row—72 sts. Change to larg-er needles. Work in cable pat, AT SAME TIME, inc 1 st each side (working inc sts into cable pat) every other row 6 times, then every 4th row 22 times—128 sts. When row 6 of 7th rep has been worked, work dec row as for back—110 sts. Cont until piece measures 17½"/44.5cm from beg, end with a row 12. Sl sts to holder for yoke.

YOKE
Joining rnd With long circular needles, working sts from back holder, p2tog, work across 178 sts, p2tog, working sts from sleeve holder, p2tog, work across 106 sts, p2tog, working sts from front holder, p2tog, work 178 sts, p2tog, working across sts from sleeve holder, p2tog, work 106 sts, place marker for beg of rnd, p2tog—576 sts. Join. Cont in cable pat in rnds through rnd 16.
Next rnd *P2, sl 5 sts to cn and hold to *front*, k1, [k2tog] twice, k5 from cn, p2, sl 5 sts to cn and hold to *front*, k3, k2tog, (k2tog, k3) from cn; rep from * around—480 sts. Cont in pat until rnd 6 has been worked.
Next rnd *P2, k2 [k2tog] twice, k2, p2, k8; rep from * around—432 sts. Cont in pat until rnd 10 has been worked.
Next rnd *P2, k6, p2, k2 [k2tog] twice, k2; rep from * around—384 sts. Cont in pat until rnd 16 has been worked.
Next rnd *P2, sl 3 sts to cn and hold to *front*, k3, k3 from cn; rep from * around. Work 1 rnd.
Next rnd *P2tog, k6; rep from * around—336 sts. Cont until rnd 8 has been worked.
Next rnd *P1, k2, k2tog, k2; rep from * around—288 sts. Cont in pat until rnd 16 has been worked.
Next rnd *P1, sl 3 sts to cn and hold to *front*, k2, k3 from cn; rep from * around. Work 1 rnd.
Next rnd *P1, k2, k2tog, k1; rep from *

around—240 sts. Work until rnd 16 has been worked.

Next rnd *P1, sl 2 sts to cn and hold to *front*, k2, k2 from cn; rep from * around. Work 1 rnd.

Next rnd *P1, k1, k2tog, k1, p1, k4; rep from * around—216 sts. Work until rnd 14 has been worked.

Next rnd *P1, k3, p1, k1, k2tog, k1; rep from * around—192 sts. Work 1 rnd.

Next rnd *P1, sl 2 sts to cn and hold to *front*, k1, k2 from cn; rep from * around.

Next rnd *K2tog, k2; rep from * around—144 sts.

Next rnd K4, *k2tog, k5; rep from * around—124 sts.

Next rnd K4, *k2tog, k4; rep from * around—104 sts. Change to smaller dpn and work in k2, p2 rib for 8"/20.5cm. Bind off in rib.

FINISHING
Block piece. Sew side and sleeve seams. ●

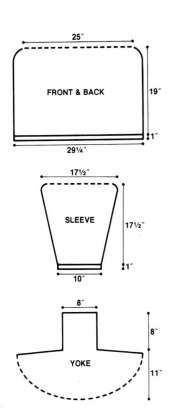

Missoni

MISSONI KNITWEAR IS CELEBRATED around the world for its comfort, grace and brilliantly inventive style. Colors—tossed together in incredibly vivid blends—are the hallmark of Missoni design and are what give the sweaters their unique and unmistakeable energy. Rainbow stripes, geometric motifs, flames and brushstrokes in intense, harmonious hues turn even the simplest of silhouettes into beautiful garments decked out in a kaleidoscope of saturated color.

Since the beginning, Missoni knitwear has been a family affair. The firm was founded by the husband-and-wife team of Ottavio and Rosita Missoni. Ottavio developed the trademark stitch patterns, while Rosita provided the setting, selecting colors and silhouettes to fit the fashion mood of each season. Together, they created knits that are relaxed yet refined, casual yet luxurious.

The Missonis began by making sweaters for a popular Milan boutique, then soon expanded to developing small collections for a large Italian department store. Their big break came in 1968, when Diana Vreeland, then Editor-in-Chief of *Vogue* magazine, came to Italy and suggested that they show their merchandise in the United States. Their first New York show was

Photo courtesy of Missoni, Inc.

The Missoni fashion formula is at once timeless and completely modern.

an instant triumph and the fashion world subsequently went Missoni-mad. To attest to their popularity, in the late 1970s the Missonis were honored as the subject of a retrospective at New York's Whitney Museum. Their success as designers for both women's and men's knitwear continued to grow throughout the succeeding decades, with the Missonis garnering numerous retailing awards along the way.

In 1996, the Missoni's daughter, Angela, began designing and overseeing licensing for the Missoni collection. She has brought a new enthusiasm to the line, updating the collection with streamlined silhouettes while maintaining the distinctive coloring and patterning that has become synonymous with the name Missoni.

The Missoni fashion formula is at once timeless and completely modern. Their use of color has influenced the entire fashion industry, bringing new life to traditional styles. The Missonis produce their own line of knitting yarns and offer a group of sweaters each season specifically designed for hand knitting. The family has expressed enormous pride and satisfaction that now the whole world can make their own Missonis.

Man's Cardigan

That famous Missoni mystique captured in a man's or woman's oversized, twisted rib cardigan with set-in sleeves, doubled shawl collar, front pockets and fold-back double ribbed lower edge and cuffs. Shown in size 40-42. The Man's Cardigan first appeared in the Winter '89 issue of *Vogue Knitting*.

FOR INTERMEDIATE KNITTERS

SIZES
To fit 36-38 (40-42, 44-46)"/91-96 (101-106, 112-116)cm bust/chest. Directions are for smallest size with larger sizes in parentheses. If there is only one figure it applies to all sizes.

KNITTED MEASUREMENTS
● Bust/chest at underarm (buttoned) 47 (48¼, 50)"/117 (121, 125)cm.
● Length 29½ (30½, 31)"/74 (76.5, 78)cm.
● Sleeve width at upper arm 21¾"/54.5cm.

MATERIALS
Original Yarn
● 17 (17, 18) 1¾oz/50g balls (each approx 57yd/52m) of Filatura di Crosa/Stacy Charles *Malta* (mohair/wool/nylon 4) in #701 blue/grey tweed (A)
● 9 (9, 10) 1¾oz/50g balls (each approx 126yd/115m) of Filatura di Crosa/Stacy Charles *Ponza* (wool/cotton/polyamide 4) in #806 purple (B) and #803 olive (C)
Substitute Yarn
● 20 (20, 24) 1¾oz/50g balls (each approx 43yd/40m) of Missoni/Stacy Charles *Saigon* (mohair/wool/viscose/polymide/elastic 4) in #102 purple tweed (A)
● 8 (8, 9) 1¾oz/50g balls (each approx 147yd/136m) of Filatura di Crosa/Stacy Charles *Sympathie*

Tweed (wool/acrylic/mohair/viscose 4) in #169 blue-grey tweed (B)
● 8 (8, 9) 1¾oz/50g balls (each approx 147yd/136m) of Filatura di Crosa/Stacy Charles *Sympathie* (wool/mohair/acrylic 4) in #1012 olive (C)
● One pair each sizes 7 and 9 (4.5 and 5.5mm) needles OR SIZE TO OBTAIN GAUGE
● Five ⅞"/23mm buttons
● Stitch holders
Note
The original yarn used for this sweater is no longer available. A comparable substitute has been made, which is available at the time of printing. Check gauge of substitute yarns very carefully before beginning.

GAUGE
21 sts and 22 rows to 4"/10cm over twisted rib in stripe pat using size 9 (5.5mm) needles. FOR PERFECT FIT, TAKE TIME TO CHECK GAUGE.

STITCH GLOSSARY
Twisted Rib (over an even # of sts)
Row 1 (RS) *K1 through back loop (tbl), p1 tbl; rep from * to end. Rep row 1 for twisted rib.
Stripe Pat
*1 row A, 1 row B, 1 row C; rep from * (3 rows) for stripe pat.

BACK
With smaller needles and B, cast on 106 (110, 114) sts. Work in k2, p2 rib

(do not twist sts) and stripe pat for 7"/18cm, inc 16 sts evenly across last row—122 (126, 130) sts. Change to larger needles. Work in twisted rib and cont stripe pat until piece measures 20 (21, 21½)"/50.5 (53, 54.5)cm from beg.

Armhole shaping
Bind off 3 sts at beg of next 2 rows, 2 sts at beg of next 2 rows, dec 1 st each side every other row twice—108 (112, 116) sts. Work even until armhole measures 12"/30cm.

Shoulder shaping
Bind off 13 sts at beg of next 2 rows, 12 (13, 14) sts at beg of next 4 rows. Bind off rem 34 sts for back neck.

Pocket linings (make 2)
With larger needles and B, cast on 26 sts. Work in St st and stripe pat for 5"/12cm. Place sts on a holder.

LEFT FRONT
With smaller needles and B, cast on 44 (46, 48) sts. Work in k2, p2 rib and stripe pat for 7"/18cm, inc 12 sts evenly across last row—56 (58, 60) sts. Change to larger needles. Work in twisted rib and cont stripe pat until piece measures 12"/30cm from beg, end with a WS row.

Pocket joining
Next row (RS) Work 10 (12, 14) sts, place next 26 sts on holder, with RS of pocket lining facing, cont pat over sts of 1 pocket lining, work to end. When

same length as back to armhole, work armhole shaping at side edge only (beg of RS rows) as for back—49 (51, 53) sts. Work even until armhole measures 4½"/11cm, end with a WS row.

Neck and shoulder shaping
Next row (RS) Work to last 3 sts, k2tog, p1 tbl. Dec 1 st at neck edge every 4th row 11 times, AT SAME TIME, when same length as back to shoulder, work shoulder shaping at side edge only as for back.

RIGHT FRONT
Work to correspond to left front, reversing all shaping and placement of pocket.

SLEEVES
With smaller needles and B, cast on 46 sts. Work in k2, p2 rib and stripe pat for 5½"/14cm, inc 16 sts evenly across last row—62 sts. Change to larger needles. Work in twisted rib and cont stripe pat, inc 1 st each side (working inc sts into pat) every other row 2 (1, 0) times, every 4th row 24 (25, 26) times—114 sts. Work even until piece measures 24½ (25, 25½)"/61.5 (62.5, 64)cm from beg, end with a WS row.

Cap shaping
Bind off 6 sts at beg of next 16 rows. Bind off rem 18 sts.

FINISHING
Block pieces. Sew shoulder seams. Set in sleeves. Sew side and sleeve seams. Fold lower edge and sleeve rib bands in half to WS and sew in place.

Buttonband
With smaller needles and B, cast on 20 sts. Work in k2, p2 rib and stripe pat as foll: Work 1 row even on WS. Cast on 4 sts at beg of next (RS) row (working inc sts into k2, p2 rib) and cont to cast on at same edge 4 sts 9 times more, then cast on 82 (84, 86) sts once—142 (144, 146) sts. Work even

until last cast-on edge of band measures 2¼"/5.5cm, place markers for center of band. Work next half to correspond as foll: Work 2¼"/5.5cm more, end with a WS row. Bind off 82 (84, 86) sts at beg of next (RS) row and cont to bind off from same edge 4 sts 10 times. Bind off rem 20 sts. With RS of band facing RS of piece, sew cast-on edge of band to right front (for men) or sew bound-off edge to left front (for women) with shorter side at lower edge and longer side at center back neck. Place markers on band for 5 buttons with the first 1¼"/3cm from lower edge, the next one 2½"/6.5cm up from first marker, last at beg of neck shaping and 2 others evenly between.

Buttonhole band
Work as for buttonband, reversing shaping (casting on and binding off at beg of WS rows), and working 5 buttonholes opposite markers 1"/2.5cm above last cast-on edge by binding off 3 sts for each buttonhole. On foll row, cast on 3 sts over bound-off sts. Then work a 2nd set of buttonholes on 2nd half of band to correspond to 1st set of buttonholes the same distance from the center marker. Sew band to opposite edge. Sew bands tog at center back neck. Fold band to WS and sew in place. Using buttonhole st, sew buttonholes tog through both thicknesses. Sew ends of bands at lower edge. Sew on buttons.

Pocket edge
With smaller needles and B, working sts from holder, inc 1 st in first st, work in k2, p2 rib to last st, inc 1 st in last st. Cont in stripe pat and rib, k first and last st, until rib measures 3"/7.5cm. Bind off. Fold rib in half to WS and sew in place. Sew side edges of pocket ribs. Sew pocket lining to fronts. ●

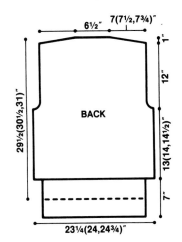

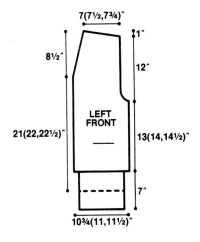

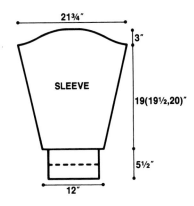

Hooded Cardigan

Bright solids, muted tweeds and bold patterning—the winning ingredients for this oversized, hooded cardigan. It features a dramatic diagonal color-blocked-pattern, striped bands and modified set-in sleeves. The Hooded Cardigan first appeared in the Fall '91 issue of *Vogue Knitting*.

Hooded Cardigan

FOR EXPERIENCED KNITTERS

SIZES
One size. To fit 34-42"/86-106cm.

KNITTED MEASUREMENTS
● Bust at underarm (buttoned) 58½"/148.5cm.
● Length 31¼"/79.5cm.
● Sleeve width at upper arm 16¼"/41cm.

MATERIALS
Original Yarn
● 9 1¾oz/50g balls (each approx 93yd/84m) of Filatura di Crosa/Stacy Charles *Giglio* (wool 4) in #613 black (A)
● 5 balls in #617 grey (B)
● 3 balls each #618 purple (C), #628 orange (D) and #626 green (E)
● 3 1¾oz/50g balls (each approx 117yd/105m) of Filatura di Crosa/Stacy Charles *Andros* (mohair/cotton/polyester/nylon 4) in #202 yellow/green variegated (F)
● 2 balls each in #203 pink/orange variegated (G) and #204 purple/pink variegated (H)
Substitute Yarn
● 9 1¾oz/50g balls (each approx 93yd/84m) of Missoni/Stacy Charles *Giglio* (wool 4) in #613 black (A)
● 3 balls each in #642 orange (D) and #665 teal green (E)
● 6 1¾oz/50g balls (each approx 80yd/74m) of Filatura di Crosa/Stacy Charles *Primo* (wool 4) in #234 grey (B)
● 4 balls in #119 purple (C)
● 2 1¾oz/50g balls (each approx 117yd/105m) of Missoni/Stacy Charles

Andros Oxford (wool/kidmohair/polymide 4) in #308 light olive variegated (F), #301 pink/blue variegated (G), and #313 purple/pink variegated (H)
● One pair each sizes 5 and 7 (3.75 and 4.5mm) needles OR SIZE TO OBTAIN GAUGE
● Size 7 (4.5mm) circular needle 36"/90cm long
● Bobbins and stitch holders
● Seven 1"/25mm buttons

Note
Some of the original yarns used for this sweater are no longer available. A comparable substitute has been made, which is available at the time of printing. Check gauge of substitute yarns very carefully before beginning.

GAUGE
36 sts to 7"/18cm and 40 rows to 6½"/16.5cm in St st over chart #2 using size 7 (4.5mm) needles. FOR PERFECT FIT, TAKE TIME TO CHECK GAUGE.

Note
Use bobbins for large blocks of color. When changing colors, twist yarns on WS to prevent holes.

BACK
With smaller needles and A, cast on 144 sts. Work in St st for 16 rows (hem facing). Work rows 1-4 of chart #1 for 4 times. Change to larger needles. Beg chart #2 as foll: Work 36-st rep of chart 4 times. Cont in pat as established through row 60. Rep rows 1-50 once more—piece measures approx 18"/45.5cm from first row of chart #2.

Armhole shaping
Cont in pat, bind off 2 sts at beg of next 4 rows. Dec 1 st each side every other row twice—132 sts. Cont in chart pat until armhole measures 8¾"/22cm.

Shoulder and neck shaping
Bind off 7 sts at beg of next 10 rows, 8 sts at beg of next 2 rows, AT SAME TIME, after 4 rows of shoulder shaping have been worked, bind off center 30 sts for neck, and working both sides at once, bind off from each neck edge 6 sts once, 2 sts once.

Pocket linings (make 2)
With larger needles and A, cast on 34 sts. Work in St st for 40 rows. Place sts on a holder.

LEFT FRONT
With smaller needles and A, cast on 72 sts. Work hem facing and chart #1 as for back. Change to larger needles. Beg chart #2 as foll: Work 36-st rep of chart twice. Cont in pat until 40 rows of chart have been worked.

Pocket joining
Next row (RS) Work 20 sts, place next 34 sts on a holder, with RS of lining facing WS of piece, work in pat across sts of one pocket lining, work to end. Cont in pat until same length as back to armhole. Work armhole shaping at side edge only (beg of RS rows) as for back—66 sts. Work even in pat until armhole measures 8"/20.5cm, end with a RS row.

Neck and shoulder shaping

Next row (WS) Bind off 10 sts (neck edge), work to end. Cont to bind off 3 sts 3 times, then dec 1 st at neck edge every other row 4 times, AT SAME TIME, when same length as back to shoulder, work shoulder shaping at beg of RS rows as for back.

RIGHT FRONT

Work as for left front, reversing all shaping and pocket placement.

SLEEVES

With smaller needles and A, cast on 48 sts. Work hem facing and chart #1 as for back. Change to larger needles.

Next row (RS) Beg with row 41 of chart #2 as indicated, work 36-st rep once, end as indicated. Cont in pat inc 1 st each side (working inc sts into pat) every other row 4 times, every 4th row 14 times—84 sts. Work even in pat until piece measures 11½"/29cm from beg of chart #2, ending with row 50.

Cap shaping

Cont in chart pat, bind off 6 sts at beg of next 10 rows. Bind off rem 24 sts.

HOOD
Left half

With larger needles and E, cast on 10 sts. Work chart pat and inc simultaneously as foll: Beg with row 43 of chart #2, inc 3 sts at end of next row and every WS row (back edge of hood) 5 times more. Cast on 20 sts at end of next WS row—48 sts. Work even in chart pat as established until piece measures approx 8"/20.5cm from last inc row, end with row 48 of chart. Dec 1 st at beg of next RS row (back edge of hood), then at same edge 5 times more, 3 sts once, 5 sts once, 6 sts once. Bind off rem 28 sts.

Right half

Work as for left half reversing all shaping.

FINISHING

Block pieces. Sew shoulder seams. Sew back edge of hood, then sew hood along neck edge, easing to fit.

Left front band

With circular needle and A, cast on 228 sts. Work 16 rows in St st (facing). Work rows 1-4 of chart #1 for 4 times. Bind off. Sew bound-off edge of band along left front edge to center of hood. Place markers for 7 buttons, the first 1"/2.5cm lower edge and last at neck edge with 5 others evenly between.

Right front band

Work as for left front band, working buttonholes opposite markers on row 7 of facing and row 11 of stripe pat by binding off 2 sts and then casting on 2 sts on next row. Sew right band as for left, seaming band tog at center of hood. Fold band to WS and sew in place. Sew through both thicknesses around buttonholes. Sew on buttons. Set in sleeves. Sew side and sleeve seams. Fold hem facings to WS and sew in place. ●

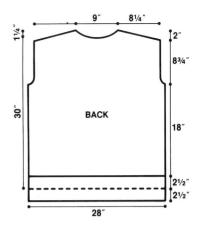

BACK

9" 8¼" 2" 1¼" 8¾" 30" 18" 2½" 2½" 28"

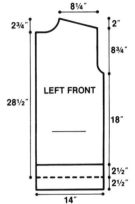

LEFT FRONT

8¼" 2¾" 2" 8¾" 28½" 18" 2½" 2½" 14"

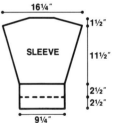

SLEEVE

16¼" 1½" 11½" 2½" 2½" 9¼"

LEFT ½ HOOD

3" 8" 2" 9¼"

Chart #2

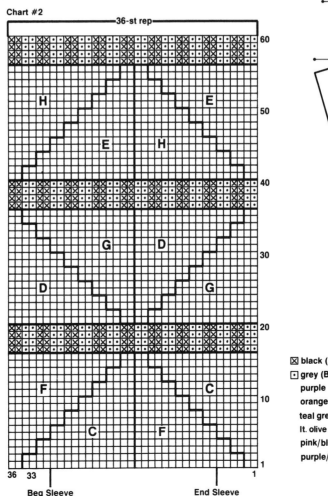

36-st rep

60
50
40
30
20
10
1

36 33   1

Beg Sleeve   End Sleeve

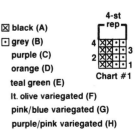

⊠ black (A)
⊡ grey (B)
   purple (C)
   orange (D)
   teal green (E)
   lt. olive variegated (F)
   pink/blue variegated (G)
   purple/pink variegated (H)

4-st rep
4   3
2   1
Chart #1

That Missoni way with color, pattern and texture adds up to a cardigan of undeniable appeal. Knit in reverse stockinette on a striped sawtooth colorwork pattern, this standard-fitting cardigan features angled armholes and high, stand-up collar. Shown in size Medium. The Sawtooth Cardigan first appeared in the Fall '90 issue of *Vogue Knitting*.

Sawtooth Cardigan

FOR EXPERIENCED KNITTERS

SIZES
To fit Small (Medium, Large). Directions are for smallest size with larger sizes in parentheses. If there is only one figure it applies to all sizes.

KNITTED MEASUREMENTS
● Bust at underarm (buttoned) 40¾ (44, 48)"/101.5 (111.5,120)cm.
● Length 30 (31, 31½)"/75 (78, 79.5)cm.
● Sleeve width at upper arm 20 (21, 22)"/50 (52, 55)cm.

MATERIALS
Original Yarn
● 5 (6, 6) 1¾oz/50g balls (each approx 93yd/84m) of Filatura di Crosa/Stacy Charles *Pianosa* (wool/mohair/acrylic/nylon/polyester 4) in #107 fuchsia variegated (A)
● 4 (4,5) balls in #106 blue variegated (B)
● 2 (3,3) balls in #103 green variegated (C)
● 3 (4, 4) 1¾oz/50g balls (each approx 93yd/84m) of Filatura di Crosa/Stacy Charles *Giglio* (wool 4) in #614 red (D), #604 fuchsia (E), and #610 olive (F)
Substitute Yarn
● 5 (6, 8) 1¾oz/50g balls (each approx 93yd/84m) of Filatura di Crosa/Stacy Charles *Flora* (wool/polymide 4) in #9 fuchsia variegated (A)
● 4 (4, 5) balls in #12 purple-blue variegated (B)
● 2 (3, 3) balls in #6 green variegated (C)
● 3 (3, 4) 1¾oz/50g balls (each approx 93yd/84m) of Missoni/Stacy Charles *Giglio* (wool 4) in #659 brick (D), #664

fuchsia (E), and #668 dark olive (F)
● One pair each sizes 6 and 8 (4 and 5mm) needles OR SIZE TO OBTAIN GAUGE
● Seven ⅞"/23mm buttons
Note
The original yarn used for this sweater is no longer available. A comparable substitute has been made, which is available at the time of printing. Check gauge of substitute yarns very carefully before beginning.

GAUGE
17 sts and 21 rows to 4"/10cm over chart pat in Rev St st using size 8 (5mm) needles. FOR PERFECT FIT, TAKE TIME TO CHECK GAUGE.

Note
When a stitch is worked in a new color, k it on RS rows or p it on WS rows.
Note for chart key
All stitches are worked in Rev St st, p on RS, K on WS. See note on working new colors.

BACK
With smaller needles and E, cast on 86 (94, 102) sts. Work in k1, p1 rib in foll stripes: *1 row E, 1 row C, 1 row F, 1 row A, 1 row D, 1 row B; rep from * (6 rows) once more. Change to larger needles.
Beg chart pat: Row 1 (RS) Beg with st 1, work 13-st rep 6 (7, 7) times, work next 8 (3, 11) sts outside rep, ending with st 21 (16, 24). Cont in pat as established through row 86 (90, 90)—piece measures approx 18½ (19, 19)"/46 (48, 48)cm from beg.

Armhole shaping
Bind off 2 (3, 4) sts at beg of next 2 rows. Dec 1 st each side every other row 5 (6, 7) times—72 (76, 80) sts. Work even through chart row 108, then work first 30 (36, 40) rows once more—armhole measures approx 10 (10½, 11)"/25 (26,27.5)cm.

Shoulder shaping
Bind off 5 sts at beg of next 6 (2, 0) rows, 6 sts at beg of next 2 (6, 8) rows. Bind off rem 30 (30, 32) sts for back neck.

LEFT FRONT
With smaller needles and E, cast on 40 (44, 48) sts. Work rib as for back. Change to larger needles.
Beg chart pat: Row 1 (RS) Beg with st 8 (3, 11), work to end of rep, work 13-st rep 2 (2, 3) times, work next 8 (7, 6) sts outside rep, ending with st 21 (20, 19). Cont in pat as established until same length as back to armhole. Work armhole shaping at side edge only (beg of RS rows) as for back—33 (35, 37) sts. Work even in pat until armhole measures 7½ (8, 8½)"/19 (20, 21.5)cm, end with a RS row.

Neck and shoulder shaping
Next row (WS) Bind off 5 (5, 6) sts (neck edge), work to end. Cont to dec 1 st at neck edge every other row 5 times, every 4th row twice, AT SAME TIME, when same length as back to shoulder, work shoulder shaping at beg of RS rows as for back.

RIGHT FRONT

Work as for left front, reversing chart pat as foll:

Beg chart pat: Row 1 (RS) Beg with st 1 (10, 6), work to end of rep, work 13-st rep 2 (3, 3) times, work 1 st outside rep, ending with st 14. Complete to correspond to left front, reversing all shaping.

SLEEVES

With smaller needles and E, cast on 34 (36, 36) sts. Work rib as for back for 6 rows, inc 10 sts evenly across last row—44 (46, 46) sts. Change to larger needles.

Beg chart pat: Row 1 (RS) Beg with st 1, work 13-st rep 3 times, work next 5 (7, 7) sts outside rep, ending with st 18 (20, 20). Cont in pat as established, inc 1 st each side (working inc sts into pat) every other row 1 (1, 5) times, every 4th row 20 (21, 19) times—86 (90, 94) sts. Work even in pat through row 86 (90, 90)—piece measures approx 17½ (18, 18)"/43.5 (45.5, 45.5)cm from beg.

Cap shaping

Bind off 2 (3, 4) sts at beg of next 2 rows. Dec 1 st each side every other row 5 (6, 7) times. Bind off rem 72 sts.

FINISHING

Block pieces. Sew shoulder seams.

Neckband

With RS facing, smaller needles and B, pick up and k77 (77, 81) sts. Work in k1, p1 rib in foll stripes: *1 row D, 1 row A, 1 row F, 1 row C, 1 row E, 1 row B; rep from * (6 rows) for 5"/12.5cm. Bind off in rib. Fold band in half to WS and sew in place.

Left front band

With RS facing, smaller needles and A, beg at top of neckband, (working through both thicknesses) pick up and k103 (107, 109) sts along left front edge. Work in k1, p1 rib in

stripes (beg with color F) as for neckband for 9 rows. With E, bind off with tapestry needle. Place markers on band for 7 buttons, the first ¾"/2cm from lower edge, last ¾"/2cm from top edge, and 5 others evenly between.

Right front band

Work as for left front band, working buttonholes opposite markers on 5th row by binding off 3 sts for each buttonhole. On next row, cast on 3 sts over bound-off sts. Sew top of sleeve to straight edge of armhole, then sew dec armhole sts of front and back to dec sts of sleeve. Sew side and sleeve seams. Sew on buttons. ●

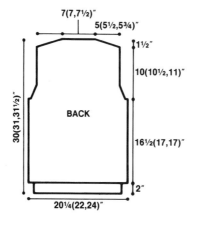

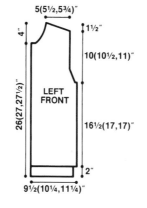

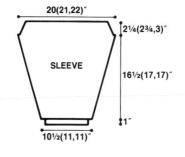

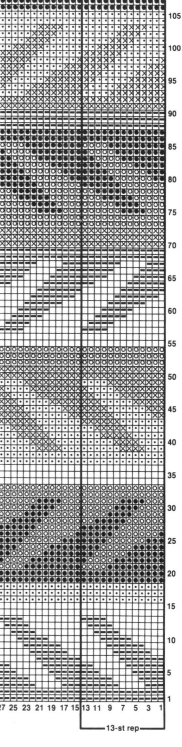

- ◎ fuchsia variegated (A)
- ☐ blue variegated (B)
- ⊠ green variegated (C)
- ⊟ red (D)
- ⊡ fuchsia (E)
- ◉ olive (F)

One-Piece T-Shirt Pullover

This oversized T-shirt pullover is a beautiful example of Missoni color in action. Knit in one piece using color-blended yarns, it sports alternating triangular stripes and foldover sleeve and neck borders. The One-Piece T-Shirt Pullover first appeared in the Spring/Summer '92 issue of *Vogue Knitting*.

One-Piece T-Shirt Pullover

FOR EXPERIENCED KNITTERS

SIZES
One size. To fit 34-42"/86-106cm.

KNITTED MEASUREMENTS
● Bust at underarm 46½"/118cm.
● Length 22"/56cm.
● Sleeve width at upper arm 19"/48cm.

MATERIALS
Original Yarn
● 4 1¾oz/50g balls (each approx 121yd/109m) of Filatura di Crosa/Stacy Charles *Pharos* (cotton/acrylic/nylon 3) in #303 red (MC)
● 3 balls each in #304 turquoise (B), #306 orange (C), and #307 blue (E)
● 2 balls each in #305 green (A) and #302 yellow (D)
Substitute Yarn
● 5 1¾oz/50g balls (each approx 115yd/106m) of Missoni/Stacy Charles *Kos* (viscose/polymide 3) in #264 red variegated (MC)
● 3 balls each in #300 turquoise/pink variegated (B) and #264 orange variegated (C)
● 2 balls each in #16 green variegated (A)
● 3 1¾oz/50g balls (each approx 121yd/110m) of Missoni/Stacy Charles *Caprera* (cotton 3) in #149 teal blue (E) and #169 yellow (D)
● One pair each sizes 4 and 5 (3.5 and 3.75mm) needles OR SIZE TO OBTAIN GAUGE
● Size 4 (3.5mm) circular needle 16"/40cm long

Note
The original yarn used for this sweater is no longer available. A comparable substitute has been made, which is available at the time of printing. Check gauge of substitute yarns very carefully before beginning.

GAUGE
22 sts and 32 rows to 4"/10cm over St st and chart pat using size 5 (3.75mm) needles. FOR PERFECT FIT, TAKE TIME TO CHECK GAUGE.

Notes
1 Use bobbins for large blocks of color. When changing colors, twist yarns on WS to prevent holes.
2 Garment is worked in one piece beg at lower front edge and ending at lower back edge.

BODY
With smaller needles and MC, cast on 128 sts. Work in St st (k on RS, p on WS) for 20 rows (hem facing). Change to larger needles.
Beg chart pat: Row 1 (RS) Work 32-st rep of chart 4 times. Cont in St st and chart pat as established until row 100 has been worked and piece measures approx 12½"/31.5cm above hem facing.

Sleeve shaping
Cont in pat, inc 1 st each side every other row (working inc sts into chart pat) 4 times, 2 sts 6 times, 5 sts 3 times—190 sts. Cont to work even through row 176, AT SAME TIME, when row 152 of chart has been worked and piece measures approx 19"/48cm above hem facing, work neck shaping as foll:

Neck shaping
Next row (RS) Cont in pat, work 87 sts, join 2nd ball of yarn, bind off 16 sts, work to end. Working both sides at once, bind off from each neck edge 3 sts twice, 2 sts twice, then 1 st every other row 6 times—71 sts each side. Mark shoulder at row 176. At row 179 work back neck shaping as foll: inc 1 st at each neck edge once, then 5 sts twice.
Next row (RS) Work 82 sts, cast on 26 sts, work to end—190 sts. Cont to work through row 192, then beg with row 160, work chart in reverse to row 1, AT SAME TIME, beg at row 124, work sleeve shaping as foll: bind off 5 sts each side 3 times, 2 sts 6 times, dec 1 st each side every other row 4 times—128 sts. Cont to work chart through row 1. Change to smaller needles and MC. Work 20 rows in St st (hem facing). Bind off.

FINISHING
Block piece.

Neck border
With RS facing, circular needle and MC, pick up and k92 sts around neck edge. Join and work in St st for 10 rows. Bind off. Fold border in half to WS and sew in place.

Sleeve border

With RS facing, smaller needles and MC, pick up and k72 sts along straight edge of sleeve. Work in St st for 10 rows. Bind off. Sew side and underarm seams. Fold border in half to WS. Sew in place. Fold hem facing to WS, matching edge to row 16 of chart. Sew in place. (Note: Approx 2 rows of hem facing will be visible on front after finishing.) ●

Second Half of Chart

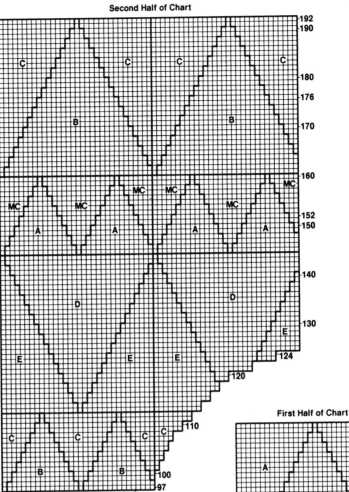

First Half of Chart

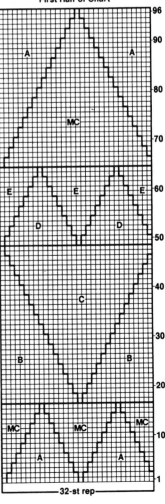

red variegated (MC)

green variegated (A)

turquoise/pink variegated (B)

orange variegated (C)

yellow (D)

teal blue (E)

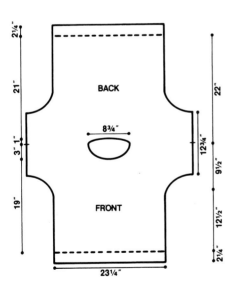

Classic tweeded yarns in soft tones, reminiscent of Persian tapestry, lend this flame-stitched cardigan subtle warmth. The cardigan is oversized with modified set-in sleeves and V-neck. Shown in size Small/Medium. The Flame Stitch Cardigan first appeared in the Fall '92 issue of *Vogue Knitting*.

Flame Stitch Cardigan

FOR EXPERIENCED KNITTERS

SIZES
To fit Small-Medium (Large, X-Large). Directions are for smaller size with larger size in parentheses. If there is only one figure it applies to both sizes.

KNITTED MEASUREMENTS
● Bust at underarm (buttoned) 47 (55½)"/119.5 (141)cm.
● Length 32"/81.5cm.
● Sleeve width at upper arm 14¾ (17)"/37.5 (43)cm.

MATERIALS
● 7 (8) 1¾oz/50g balls (each approx 93yd/84m) of Missoni/Stacy Charles *Brazza* (wool/viscose/nylon 4) in #530 violet (A), #520 brown/black (B), and #527 rust (D)
● 6 balls in #425 grey (C)
● One pair size 7 (4.5mm) needles OR SIZE TO OBTAIN GAUGE
● Size 4 (3.5mm) circular needle 24"/60cm long
● Bobbins and stitch holders
● Seven 1¼"/3cm buttons

Note
The original color used for this sweater is no longer available. A comparable color substitute has been made, which is available at the time of printing.

GAUGE
18 sts and 25 rows to 4"/10cm in St st over chart pat using size 7 (4.5mm) needles. FOR PERFECT FIT, TAKE TIME TO CHECK GAUGE.

Notes
1 Use bobbins for separate blocks of color. When changing colors, twist yarns on WS to prevent holes.
2 Work rib back and forth on circular needle to avoid breaking yarn at end of each row. When changing colors, return to beg of row where color is attached and work in rib pat as established.

BACK
With circular needle and B, cast on 102 (122) sts. Work in k1, p1 rib in foll stripes: * 1 row D, 1 row A, 1 row C, 1 row B; rep from * once more, end with 1 row D. Change to larger needles and St st.
Beg chart pat: Row 1 (RS) Work st(s) 20 (10-20) once, work 20-st rep 5 times, then work st(s) 1 (1-11). Cont in pat as established, work 48 rows of chart twice then rows 1-28 once—piece measures approx 21"/53.5cm from beg.

Armhole shaping
Cont in pat, bind off 4 sts at beg of next 2 rows, 2 sts at beg of next 6 rows. Dec 1 st each side every other row 5 times—72 (92) sts. Cont in chart pat until armhole measures 10"/25.5cm, end with a WS row.

Shoulder and neck shaping
Bind off 7 (10) sts at beg of next 6

rows, AT SAME TIME, after 2 rows of shoulder shaping have been worked, bind off center 20 sts for neck. Working both sides at once, bind off from each neck edge 5 sts once.

Pocket linings (make 2)
With larger needles and B, cast on 26 sts. Work in St st for 36 rows. Sl sts to holder.

LEFT FRONT
With circular needle and B, cast on 52 (62) sts and work stripe rib as for back. Change to larger needles and St st.
Beg chart pat: Row 1 (RS) Work st(s) 20 (20-10) once, work 20-st rep twice, then sts 1-11. Cont in pat until row 2 of 2nd rep of 48 rows of chart has been worked.

Pocket joining
Next row (RS) Work 9 (18) sts, place next 26 sts on holder. With RS of lining facing WS of piece, work in pat across sts of one pocket lining, work to end. Cont in pat until same length as back to armhole.

Armhole and V-neck shaping
Work armhole shaping at side edge only (beg of RS rows) as for back, AT SAME TIME dec 1 st every 4th row 16 (17) times at neck edge (end of RS rows). When same length as back to shoulder, shape shoulder at beg of RS rows as for back.

RIGHT FRONT
Work stripe rib as for left front. Change

to larger needles and St st.
Beg chart pat: Row 1 (RS) Beg with st 11, work to end of rep, work 20-st rep twice, then work st(s) 20 (20-10). Cont in pat until same length as left front to pocket joining.

Pocket joining
Next row (RS) Work chart pat across 17 (18) sts, place next 26 sts on holder, cont in pat across 26 sts of pocket lining, work to end. Cont as for left front, reversing armhole, neck and shoulder shaping.

SLEEVES
With circular needle and B, cast on 44 sts and work in stripe rib as for back. Change to large needles and St st.
Beg chart pat: Next row (RS) Beg with row 27 and st 19, work to end of rep, work 20-st rep twice, end with st 2 of chart. Cont in chart pat for 7 (0) rows more, then inc 1 st each side (working inc sts into pat) every 8th (6th) row 11 (16) times—66 (76) sts. Cont in pat until 98 rows have been worked (row 28 of chart)—piece measures approx 17"/43cm from beg.

Cap shaping
Cont in chart pat, bind off 3 (6) sts at beg of next 2 rows, [dec 1 st each side every other row 6 times, then 1 st each side every 4th row] once, [dec 1 st each side every other row 5 times, then 1 st each side every 4th row once] 3 times. Bind off rem 10 (14) sts.

FINISHING
Block pieces. Sew shoulder seams.

Pocket bands
With circular needle and B, work in k1, p1 rib across 26 sts on stitch holder. Cont in stripe rib as for body ribs.

Front bands
With RS facing, B and circular needle, pick up 198 sts along left front edge and half of back neck. Working rib as

for back, work 1 row D, 1 row A, 1 row C, 1 row B, 1 row D, 1 row A and 1 row C. Bind off with B. Mark for 7 buttons with first ½"/1.5cm from lower edge and last at beg of neck shaping and 5 more evenly spaced between. Work right band as for left band, working buttonholes on rows C and B opposite markers as foll: Bind off 4 sts. On next row, cast on 4 sts above bound-off sts. Sew back neck seam. Set in sleeves. Sew side and sleeve seams. Sew pocket linings in place. Sew on buttons. ●

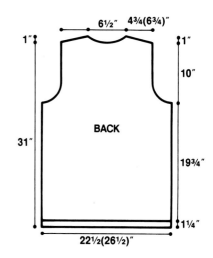

BACK

6½" 4¾(6¾)"
1"
1"
10"
31"
19¾"
1¼"
22½(26½)"

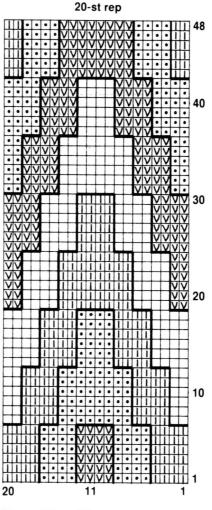

20-st rep

48
40
30
20
10
1
20 11 1

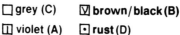

□ grey (C)   ☑ brown/black (B)
⊞ violet (A)   ⊡ rust (D)

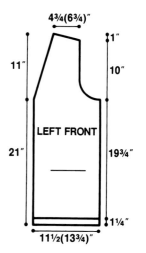

LEFT FRONT

4¾(6¾)"
11"
1"
10"
21"
19¾"
1¼"
11½(13¾)"

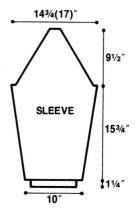

SLEEVE

14¾(17)"
9½"
15¾"
1¼"
10"

Summer Cardigan

Pattern plays a leading role in this over-sized striped cardigan jacket. It features combined colorwork and tuck-stitching in a flat and comfortable cotton, with corded ridges, drop shoulders, V-neck shaping and foldover bands. Shown in size Medium. The Summer Cardigan first appeared in the Spring/Summer '93 issue of *Vogue Knitting*.

Summer Cardigan

FOR EXPERIENCED KNITTERS

SIZES
To fit Small (Medium, Large). Directions are for smallest size with larger sizes in parentheses. If there is only one figure it applies to all sizes.

KNITTED MEASUREMENTS
● Bust at underarm (overlapped) 43¼ (46½, 49¼)"/110 (118, 125)cm.
● Length 27½ (28½, 29½)"/70 (72.5, 75)cm.
● Sleeve width at upperarm 16¼ (17¼, 18¼)"/41.5 (43.5, 46.5)cm.

MATERIALS
Original Yarn
● 2 (3, 3) 1¾oz/50g balls (each approx 98yd/88m) of Filatura di Crosa/Stacy Charles *Oki* (viscose/cotton/polyester 3) in #206 blue variegated (A), #205 red/yellow variegated (B), and #202 turquoise/green variegated (C)
● 6 (7, 7) 1¾oz/50g balls (each approx 121yd/110m) of Filatura di Crosa/Stacy Charles *Caprera* (cotton 3) in #129 navy (H)
● 2 balls each in #141 red (D), #134 olive green (E), #133 yellow (F), #136 royal blue (G), #130 off-white (J), #138 teal (K), and #143 fuchsia (L)
Substitute Yarn
● 2 (3, 3) 1¾oz/50g balls (each approx 115yd/106) of Missoni/Stacy Charles *Kos* (viscose/polymide 3) in #301 blue variegated (A), #319 red/yellow/green variegated (B), and #300 turquoise/green/pink variegated (C)
● 6 (7, 7) 1¾oz/50g balls (each approx 121yd/110m) of Filatura di Crosa/Stacy Charles *Caprera* (cotton 3) in #154 dark navy (H)
● 2 balls each in #168 red (D), #146 olive green (E), #169 yellow (F), #166 royal blue (G), #108 off-white (J), #149 teal (K), and #173 deep lavender (L)
● One pair size 4 (3.5mm) needles OR SIZE TO OBTAIN GAUGE
● Size 3 and 4 (3.25 and 3.5mm) circular needles 29"/80cm long

Note
The original yarn used for this sweater is no longer available. A comparable substitute has been made, which is available at the time of printing. Check gauge of substitute yarns very carefully before beginning.

GAUGE
27 sts to 4"/10cm and 42 rows to 4½"/11.5cm over chart pat and St st using size 4 (3.5mm) needles.
FOR PERFECT FIT, TAKE TIME TO CHECK GAUGE.

Notes
1 When changing colors, twist yarns on WS to prevent holes.
2 When working with more than one color, carry yarn not in use loosely across back of work.
3 Block swatch and finished pieces by pressing lightly with damp cloth and warm iron. Do not put iron directly on knitted pieces.

STITCH GLOSSARY
Chart Pat #1
Work stripe and colorwork pat in St st foll chart #1 for rows 1-90. Corded st row is worked on first k row immediately foll 6 rows of bi-color stripe pats as foll:
Corded St (worked on chart rows 1C, 19C, 31C, 49C, 61C, 79C) (RS) K1, *wyib, insert RH needle to purl side of work and pick up carried strand 6 rows below; place on LH needle and k it tog with next st; k1; rep from * to end.

BACK
With D cast on 145 (153, 161) sts.
Border Pat P 1 row. K 1 row. P 1 row.
Next row (RS) *K2 E, k2 D; rep from *, end k1 E.
Next row (WS) P1 E, *p2 D, p2 E; rep from * to end. Rep these 2 rows 3 times more—11 rows in border pat.
Beg chart pat #1: Next row (RS) Work 8-st rep of chart #1 for 18 (19, 20) times, then end with st 1. Cont to rep rows 1-90 of chart #1 until piece measures approx 26 (27, 28)"/66 (68.5, 71)cm from beg.

Shoulder and neck shaping
Bind off 7 sts at beg of next 14 (8, 2) rows, 8 sts at beg of next 0 (6, 12) rows, AT SAME TIME, bind off center 17 (19, 21) sts for neck and working both sides at once bind off from each neck edge 5 sts once, 4 sts once, 3 sts once, 2 sts once, dec 1 st once.

LEFT FRONT

With D cast on 72 (76, 80) sts.
Border Pat P 1 row. K 1 row.
P 1 row.
Next row (RS) *K2 E, k2 D;
rep from * to end.
Next row (WS) *P2 D, p2 E; rep
from * to end. Rep these 2 rows 3
times more—11 rows in border pat.
Beg chart pat #1: Next row
(RS) Work 8-st rep 9 (9, 10) times,
then end with st 0 (4, 0). Cont to
rep rows 1-90 of chart #1 until piece
measures approx 15½ (16, 16½)"/
39.5 (40.5, 42)cm from beg, end with
a WS row.

V-neck shaping

Next row (RS) K, dec 1 st at end
(neck edge). Cont to dec 1 st at neck
edge alternately [every 4th row once,
every 6th row once] for a total of
22 (23, 24) dec, AT SAME TIME, when
piece measures same length as
back to shoulder, bind off 7 sts from
shoulder edge 7 (4, 1) times, 8 sts
0 (3, 6) times.

RIGHT FRONT

Work as for left front reversing shaping
and working chart #1 as foll: Beg with
st 0 (5, 0), work to end of rep, work 8-
st rep 9 (9, 10) times.

SLEEVES

With D cast on 66 (68, 70) sts. Work
border pat as for back.
Beg chart #1: Next row (RS) Beg
with st 8 (7, 6), work to end of rep, then
work 8-st rep 8 times, end with st 1 (2,
3). Cont to work in chart #1, AT SAME
TIME, inc 1 st each side (working inc
sts into chart #1) every 8th row 16 (10,
4) times, then every 6th row 6 (14, 22)
times—110 (116, 122) sts. Work even
until piece measures approx 17¾"/45cm
from beg, end with a WS row.

Cap shaping

Cont in chart pat, bind off 9 sts at beg of
next 10 rows. Bind off rem 20 (26, 32) sts.

FINISHING

Block pieces. Sew shoulder seams.

Left border band

With circular needle, using colors
F and G and beg at back neck,
working row 1 of chart #2, pick up
and k192 (200, 208) sts evenly to
lower left front edge, working 8-st
rep of chart #2 for 24 (25, 26) times.
Work band through row 20 of chart.
Bind off loosely.

Right border band

Beg at lower right front edge, pick up
and work as for left border band. Sew
bands tog at center back neck. Turn
band in half to WS and sew in place.
Place markers 8¼ (8¾, 9¼)"/21 (22,
23.5)cm down from shoulders on
front and back for armholes. Sew
sleeves between markers. Sew side
and sleeve seams. ●

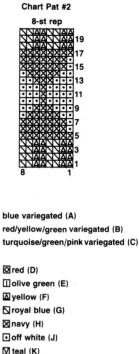

Chart Pat #1

Chart Pat #2

8-st rep

blue variegated (A)
red/yellow/green variegated (B)
turquoise/green/pink variegated (C)

red (D)
olive green (E)
yellow (F)
royal blue (G)
navy (H)
off white (J)
teal (K)
deep lavender (L)

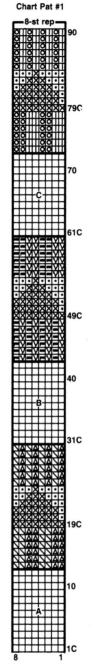

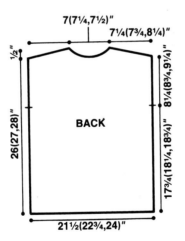

BACK

26(27,28)"

7(7¼,7½)"

7¼(7¾,8¼)"

8¼(8¾,9¼)"

17¾(18¼,18¾)"

21½(22¾,24)"

½"

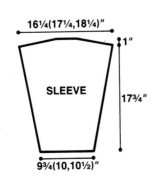

SLEEVE

16¼(17¼,18¼)"

17¾"

1"

9¾(10,10½)"

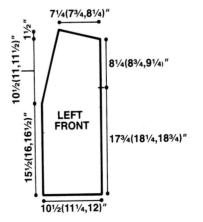

LEFT
FRONT

7¼(7¾,8¼)"

1½"

½"

8¼(8¾,9¼)"

10½(11,11½)"

15½(16,16½)"

17¾(18¼,18¾)"

10½(11¼,12)"

A harmonious blend of intense colors in a trendy T-shirt shape. With a rolled bottom edge and raglan sleeves, this close-fitting mock turtleneck has casual appeal. Shown in size Medium. The Funnel-Neck Short Pullover first appeared in the Winter '96 issue of *Vogue Knitting*.

Funnel-Neck Short Pullover

FOR INTERMEDIATE KNITTERS

SIZES
To fit sizes X-Small (Small, Medium and Large). Directions are for smallest size with larger sizes in parentheses. If there is only one figure it applies to all sizes.

KNITTED MEASUREMENTS
● Bust at underarm 32 (34, 36, 38)"/81 (86.5, 91.5, 96.5)cm.
● Length 20 (20½, 20½, 21)"/51 (52, 52, 53.5)cm.
● Sleeve width at upper arm 13 (13½, 13¾, 14)"/33 (34, 35, 35.5)cm.

MATERIALS
● 3 (3, 4, 4) 1¾oz/50g balls (each approx 158yd/145m) of Missoni/Stacy Charles *Rebun* (wool/polyamid/acrylic 4) in #423 orange tweed (A) and #422 white tweed (B)
● 1 ball each in #429 blue tweed (C), #430 dark blue (D), #441 light olive tweed (E), #440 light olive (F), #424 orange (G), and #444 red (H)
● Size 5 (3.75mm) circular needles 16"/40cm and 24"/60cm long OR SIZE TO OBTAIN GAUGE
● Stitch holders
● Stitch markers

Note
The original color used for this sweater is no longer available. A comparable color substitute has been made, which is available at the time of printing.

GAUGE
22 sts and 52 rnds/rows to 4"/10cm over slip st color pat using size 5 (3.75mm) circular needle. FOR PERFECT FIT, TAKE TIME TO CHECK GAUGE.

STITCH GLOSSARY
Slip St Pat (even # of sts)
Rnds 1 and 2 Purl.
Rnds 3 and 4 *P1, sl 1 with yarn in front (wyif); rep from *. Rep rnds 1-4 for slip st pat.
To work Slip St Pat in rows:
Row 1 (RS) Purl.
Row 2 Knit.
Row 3 *P1, sl 1 wyif; rep from *.
Row 4 *Sl 1 with yarn in back k1; rep from *. Rep rows 1-4 for slip st pat.

Stripe Pat
Work 2 rnds/rows in each color as foll: *B, G, A, C, B, H, A, F, B, G, A, D, B, H, A, E; rep from * (32 rnds) for stripe pat.
Note
Lower edges will roll naturally. Measure pieces with edges rolled.

BODY
With 24"/60cm circular needle and A, cast on 156 (168, 180, 188) sts. Being careful not to twist sts, place marker (pm), join and k 9 rnds as foll: 1 rnd B, 1 rnd A, 7 rnds B. Place 2nd marker for side seam after 78 (84, 90, 94) sts. Beg with rnd 1, work in slip st pat and stripe pat, AT SAME TIME, inc 1 st before and after each marker (working inc sts into slip st pat) every 10th rnd 5 times—176 (188, 200, 208) sts. Work even until piece measures 13"/33cm

from beg, end with pat rnd 4, color D and 6 sts before joining marker.
Next rnd With B, bind off 6 sts before and after each marker—76 (82, 88, 92) sts across both front and back. Place all sts on holder.

SLEEVES
(Note: Work back and forth in rows on 16"/40cm circular needle.)
With A, cast on 44 (44, 46, 46) sts. Beg with a p row, work 7 rows in St st as foll: 1 row A, 2 rows B, 2 rows A, 2 rows B. Work slip st pat and stripe pat as for body, AT THE SAME TIME, inc 1 st each side (working inc sts into pat) every 18th (14th, 14th, 14th) row 5 (3, 3, 11) times every 16th row 9 (12, 12, 5) times—72 (74, 76, 78) sts. Work even until piece measures 20"/51cm from beg, end with pat row 2 and color A.
Next row (RS) With D, bind off 6 sts, work pat row 3 to end.
Next row With D, bind off 6 sts, work pat row 4 to end—60 (62, 64, 66) sts. Place sts on holder.

Join sleeves to body
With RS facing 24"/60cm circular needle and B, p across 60 (62, 64, 66) sts of left sleeve, pm, p76 (82, 88, 92) sts of front, pm, p60 (62, 64, 66) sts of right sleeve, pm, p76 (82, 88, 92) back sts. Place marker for beg of rnd, join and work 1"/2.5cm even in pat, end at rnd marker.

Shape raglan armholes
Cont pat, dec 1 st before and after each marker every 4th rnd 15 times,

every other rnd 5 (6, 7, 8) times, then
dec 1 st each side of front and back
only, every other rnd 3 (5, 5, 6) times—
30 (30, 34, 34) sts across both front
and back, 20 sts across each sleeve.
Piece measures 27 (27½, 27½,
28)"/68.5 (70, 70, 71)cm from beg.

Funnel neck
Work 1½"/3.8cm even. K 8 rnds for neck
facing as foll: 5 rnds A, 1 rnd B, 1 rnd
A, 1 rnd B. Bind off loosely with B. Fold
neck facing to WS and sew in place.

FINISHING
Sew sleeve seams. Sew bound-off sts
of sleeves to body. ●

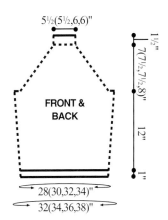

5½(5½,6,6)"

FRONT &
BACK

1½"

7(7½,7½,8)"

12"

1"

28(30,32,34)"
32(34,36,38)"

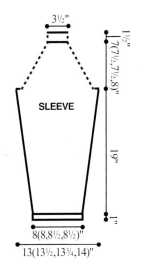

3½"

1½"

7(7½,7½,8)"

SLEEVE

19"

1"

8(8,8½,8½)"
13(13½,13¾,14)"

Calvin Klein

WITH THE BELIEF THAT line and shape determine the function and beauty of any design, Calvin Klein combines a palette of muted colors with fine quality natural fibers to create knitwear that is practical yet luxurious. The supple shaping and soft silhouettes of his sweaters adapt easily to different seasons and various looks, depending on the color and type of yarn chosen and the clothing with which they are paired. Recognizing that sweaters are a very important aspect of dressing, Klein strives to create knit designs that are pure, simple, classic and lasting.

Born and raised in New York, Klein decided to become a clothing designer at a remarkably early age, teaching himself how to draw and sew while still a child. In 1962, he graduated from the Fashion Institute of Technology, and by 1968, he had started his own label in partnership with longtime friend Barry Schwartz. Success came quickly to the young company, laying the foundation for what is today a fashion empire with a wide variety of divisions, including men's and women's apparel, accessories, and fragrance. Klein's achievements were quickly recognized by the fashion industry. He was the youngest designer ever to win a Coty Award, and has since gone on to garner numerous awards for fashion design.

Calvin Klein designs clothes geared for the modern woman, with adaptable styles to suit varied and hectic schedules. His clothing is admired worldwide for its elegantly simple lines and shapes that show off but never overpower the woman wearing them.

Klein feels it is important to have different kinds of fashion available to meet individual needs and desires. "It's wonderful...that women who love designer sweaters can use these patterns, select the same yarns or their own choice of yarns, and bring their own creativity to the sweaters." He encourages knitters to interpret these sweaters their own way, building upon his clean lines, spare shapes, simplicity and elegance to create one-of-a-kind designer fashions.

Photo courtesy of Calvin Klein, Inc.

> Recognizing that sweaters are a very important aspect of dressing, Klein strives to create knit designs that are pure, simple, classic and lasting.

This fitted cable crewneck pullover with deep raglan sleeves is the sort of weekend classic you will reach for again and again. Shown in size 34. The Fitted Cable Sweater first appeared in the Holiday '87 issue of *Vogue Knitting*.

Fitted Cable Sweater

FOR EXPERIENCED KNITTERS

SIZES
To fit 32 (34, 36, 38, 40)"/81 (86, 91, 96, 101)cm bust. Directions are for smallest size with larger sizes in parentheses. If there is only one set of figures it applies to all sizes.

KNITTED MEASUREMENTS
● Bust at underarm 35 (37, 39, 41, 43)"/87 (92, 97, 102, 107)cm.
● Length 23 (24, 24¼, 25, 25¾)"/57 (61, 61.5, 63, 64.5)cm.
● Sleeve width at upper arm 14½ (15, 15½, 16, 16½)"/36.5 (38, 38.5, 40, 41.5)cm.

MATERIALS
Original Yarn
● 13 (14, 15, 16, 17) 1¾oz/50g balls (each approx 110yd/100m) of Bernat *Cassino* (cotton 3) in #4559 ecru
Substitute Yarn
● 12 (13, 14, 15, 16) 1¾oz/50g balls (each approx 123yd/114m) of Reynolds *Saucy Sport* (cotton 3) in #809 creme fraisce
● One pair each sizes 2 and 5 (2.75 and 3.75mm) needles OR SIZE TO OBTAIN GAUGE
● Size 2 (2.75mm) circular needle 16"/40cm long
● Cable needle (cn)
Note
The original yarn used for this sweater is no longer available. A comparable substitute has been made, which is available at the time of printing. Check gauge of substitute yarns very carefully before beginning.

GAUGE
28 sts and 36 rows to 4"/10cm over cable pats using size 5 (3.75mm) needles. FOR PERFECT FIT, TAKE TIME TO CHECK GAUGE.

Note
Work gauge swatch as foll: With larger needles, cast on 36 sts.
Preparation row (RS) [P2, k4, p2, k6] twice, p2, k4, p2.
Next row K the knit sts and p the purl sts. Work rows 1-6 of chart, beg with first st of rep, until 38 rows have been worked from beg. Bind off. Steam lightly. Piece measures approx 5¼ X 4¼"/13 X 10.5cm.

STITCH GLOSSARY (for chart)
4-st Cable Sl 2 sts to cn and hold to *front*, k2, k2 from cn.
6-st Cable Sl 3 sts to cn and hold to *front*, k3, k3 from cn.

BACK
With smaller needles, cast on 105 (111, 119, 125, 133) sts. Work in k1, p1 rib for 1¾"/4.5cm, inc 1 st at end of last row—106 (112, 120, 126, 134) sts. Change to larger needles.
Preparation row (RS) P2 (0, 0, 0, 2), k4 (0, 0, 2, 4), p2 (0, 1, 2, 2), k6 (3, 6, 6, 6), *p2, k4, p2, k6; rep from *, end p2 (2, 1, 2, 2), k4 (4, 0, 2, 4), p2 (2, 0, 0, 2), k0 (3, 0, 0, 0).
Next row K the knit sts and p the purl sts. Beg and end as indicated, work rows 1-6 of chart, inc 1 st each end (working inc sts into pat) every 12th row 8 times—122 (128, 136, 142, 150) sts. Work even, if necessary, until piece measures 12½ (13, 13¼, 13½, 13¾)"/31 (33, 33.5, 34, 34.5)cm from beg, end with a WS row.

Raglan shaping
Dec row 1 (RS) K3, SKP, work cable pats to last 5 sts, k2tog, k3.
Dec row 2 P3, p2tog, work to last 5 sts, p2tog tbl, p3. Rep last 2 rows 3 (0, 2, 2, 4) times more, then work dec row 1 every other row 34 (40, 38, 40, 40) times. Bind off rem 38 (44, 48, 50, 50) sts as foll: [K2tog] twice, *pass first k2tog over 2nd k2tog; k2tog; rep from * to end. Fasten off.

FRONT
Work as for back to raglan shaping.

Raglan and neck shaping
Work dec rows 1 and 2 as for back 4 (1, 3, 3, 5) times, then work dec row 1 every other row 29 (33, 32, 36, 36) times, then work dec rows 1 and 2 for 1 (2, 1, 0, 0) times, AT SAME TIME, when armhole measures 6¾ (7¼, 7¼, 7¾, 8¼)"/17 (18, 18, 19, 21)cm, bind off center 22 (24, 26, 26, 26) sts (working bind-off as for back neck). Working both sides at once, bind off from each neck edge 4 (4, 5, 5, 5) sts twice, 3 (5, 5, 6, 6) sts once.

LEFT SLEEVE

With smaller needles, cast on 50 (52, 52, 56, 60) sts. Work in k1, p1 rib for 1½"/4cm. Change to larger needles.

Preparation row (RS) K0 (1, 1, 3, 5), [p2, k4, p2, k6] 3 times, p2, k4, p2, k0 (1, 1, 3, 5).

Next row K the knit sts and p the purl sts. Beg with 11th (10th, 10th, 8th, 6th) st of chart, work cable pats, inc 1 st each end (working inc sts into pat) every other row once, every 4th row 7 (8, 9, 8, 7) times, every 6th row 18 (18, 18, 19, 20) times—102 (106, 108, 112, 116) sts. Work even until piece measures 17½ (18, 18, 18½ ,19)"/44 (45, 45, 46.5, 48)cm from beg, end with a WS row.

Raglan cap shaping

Work dec row 1 as for back every other row 34 (36, 36, 38, 41) times, end with a WS row—34 (34, 36, 36, 34) sts.

Next row (RS) K3, SKP (back edge), work to end.

Next row Bind off 5 (4, 4, 4, 5) sts (front edge), work to last 5 sts, p2tog tbl; p3. Cont to work dec rows 1 and 2 at back edge, AT SAME TIME, bind off from front edge 5 (4, 4, 4, 5) sts 1 (4, 2, 2, 1) times more, 6 (0, 5, 5, 6) sts twice. Bind off rem 4 sts.

RIGHT SLEEVE

Work to correspond to left sleeve, reversing raglan cap shaping.

FINISHING

Block pieces. Sew back edge of raglan sleeve to back armhole and front edge of sleeve to front armhole. Sew side and sleeve seams.

Neckband

With RS facing and circular needle, pick up and k88 (94, 106, 110, 110) sts evenly around neck edge. Join and work in k1, p1 rib for 1"/2.5cm. Bind off. ●

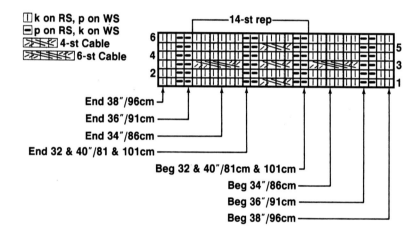

☐ k on RS, p on WS
⊟ p on RS, k on WS
⧄ 4-st Cable
⧄ 6-st Cable

14-st rep

End 38"/96cm
End 36"/91cm
End 34"/86cm
End 32 & 40"/81 & 101cm
Beg 32 & 40"/81cm & 101cm
Beg 34"/86cm
Beg 36"/91cm
Beg 38"/96cm

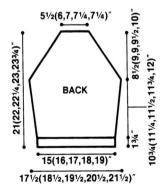

BACK

5½(6,7,7¼,7¼)"
8½(9,9,9½,10)"
21(22,22¼,23,23¾)"
10¾(11¼,11½,11¾,12)"
1¾"
15(16,17,18,19)"
17½(18½,19½,20½,21½)"

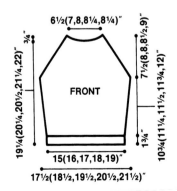

FRONT

6½(7,8,8¼,8¼)"
¾"
7½(8,8,8½,9)"
19¼(20¼,20½,21¼,22)"
10¾(11¼,11½,11¾,12)"
1¾"
15(16,17,18,19)"
17½(18½,19½,20½,21½)"

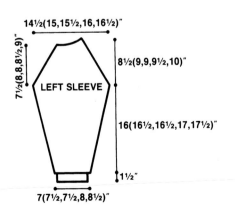

LEFT SLEEVE

14½(15,15½,16,16½)"
8½(9,9,9½,10)"
7½(8,8,8½,9)"
16(16½,16½,17,17½)"
1½"
7(7½,7½,8,8½)"

Stitchwork Cardigan

A clean-cut version of a perennial classic—this crewneck cardigan is a study in fine traditional stitchwork and couture detailing. Done in a guernsey stitch pattern, the cardigan is over-sized, with foldover front and neck rib bands, set-in sleeves and a neat slip-stitch edge. Shown in size 34-36. The Stitchwork Cardigan first appeared in the Spring/Summer '87 issue of *Vogue Knitting*.

Stitchwork Cardigan

FOR EXPERIENCED KNITTERS

SIZES
To fit 30-32 (34-36, 38-40)"/76-81 (86-91, 96-101)cm bust. Directions are for smallest size with larger sizes in parentheses. If there is only one set of figures it applies to all sizes.

KNITTED MEASUREMENTS
● Bust at underarm (buttoned) 35¾ (42, 46¾)"/89 (106, 117)cm.
● Length 25 (26, 27)"/63.5 (66, 68.5)cm.
● Sleeve width at upper arm 16½ (17, 17½)"/41 (42.5, 44)cm.

MATERIALS
Original Yarn
● 16 (17, 18) 1¾oz/50g balls (each approx 147yd/134m) of DMC *Coton Perle 3* (cotton 1) in #920 rust
Substitute Yarn
● 21 (22, 23) 1¾oz/50g balls (each approx 114yd/105m) of Dale of Norway *Kolibri* (cotton 1) in #3907 rust
● One pair each sizes 0, 1 and 3 (2, 2.25 and 3.25mm) needles OR SIZE TO OBTAIN GAUGE
● Size B (2mm) crochet hook
● Five ½"/15mm buttons
Note
The original yarn used for this sweater is no longer available. A comparable substitute has been made, which is available at the time of printing. Check gauge of substitute yarns very carefully before beginning.

GAUGE
26 sts and 36 rows to 4"/10cm over chart pat using size 3 (3.25mm) needles. FOR PERFECT FIT, TAKE TIME TO CHECK GAUGE.

BACK
With size 1 (2.25mm) needles, cast on 117 (135, 153) sts. Work in k1, p1 rib for 2"/5cm. Change to size 3 (3.25mm) needles.
Beg chart pat: Row 1 (RS) Work 18 sts of chart 6 (7, 8) times, then work first 9 sts once more. Cont in chart pat until piece measures 15½ (16, 16½)"/39.5 (40.5, 42)cm from beg.

Armhole shaping
Cont in pat, bind off 3 (4, 4) sts at beg of next 2 rows, dec 1 st each end every other row 4 (5, 6) times—103 (117, 133) sts. Work even until armhole measures 8½ (9, 9½)"/21.5 (23, 24)cm.

Neck and shoulder shaping
Work 42 (48, 54) sts, join 2nd ball of yarn and bind off 19 (21, 25) sts, work to end. Working both sides at once, bind off from each neck edge 3 sts once, 2 sts twice, AT SAME TIME, bind off from each armhole edge 8 (11, 14) sts once, 9 (10, 11) sts 3 times.

LEFT FRONT
With size 1 (2.25mm) needles, cast on 55 (67, 73) sts. Work in k1, p1 rib as for back. Change to size 3 (3.25mm) needles.
Beg chart pat: Row 1 (RS) Work last 0 (12, 0) sts of chart, then rep 18 sts of chart 3 (3, 4) times, k1 (selvage st). (Note: Work 1 st at front edge in St st for selvage st.) Cont in pat, until same length as back to armhole. Work armhole shaping at underarm edge—48 (58, 63) sts. Work even until armhole measures 6½ (7, 7½)"/16.5 (18, 19)cm, end with a RS row.

Neck shaping
Next row (WS) Bind off 5 (7, 6) sts (neck edge), work to end. Cont to bind off from neck edge 2 sts 1 (2, 2) times, then dec 1 st every other row 6 times, AT SAME TIME, when same length as back to shoulder, work shoulder shaping as for back.

RIGHT FRONT
Work as for left front, reversing all shaping and placement of chart pat. Work pat as foll:
Row 1 (RS) K1 (selvage st), work last 9 sts of chart, then rep 18 sts of chart to end.

SLEEVES
With size 1 (2.25mm) needles, cast on 33 (35, 37) sts. Work in k1, p1 rib for 2"/5cm, inc 12 (19, 17) sts evenly across last row—45 (54, 54) sts. Change to size 3 (3.25mm) needles.
Beg chart pat: Row 1 (RS) Work 18 sts of chart 2 (3, 3) times, then work first 9 sts 1 (0, 0) time more. Cont in pat, inc 1 st each end (working inc sts into pat) every 4th row 28 (16, 20) times, every 6th row 3 (12, 10) times—107 (110, 114) sts. Work even until piece measures 17 (17½, 18)"/42.5 (44, 45)cm from beg.

Cap shaping

Bind off 3 (4, 4) sts at beg of next 2 rows. Dec 1 st each end every row 26 (30, 34) times. Bind off 6 (4, 3) sts at beg of next 4 rows. Bind off rem 25 (26, 26) sts.

FINISHING

Block pieces. Sew shoulder seams. Set in sleeves. Sew side and sleeve seams.

Left front band

With RS facing and crochet hook, beg at first neck dec, work a row of sl st along left front edge, spacing sts to keep edge flat. Fasten off. With RS facing and size 0 (2mm) needles, pick up and k220 (230, 240) sts behind sl st edge (sl st should show on RS). Work in k1, p1 rib for 1½"/4cm. Do not bind off. Fold band in half to WS and sew in place by slipping off st onto yarn needle and sewing in place without binding off. Mark band for 4 buttons with the first ¾"/2cm from lower edge, the last 5"/12.5cm from top of band, and 2 evenly between.

Right front band

Work right front band as for left, working 4 one-row buttonholes opposite markers after ¼"/.5cm as foll: *Rib to buttonhole, with yarn in front, sl first st from LH needle to RH needle, place yarn in back of work, [sl next st from LH to RH needle and pass the first st over it] 5 times, sl last bound-off st back to LH needle and turn work; place yarn to back of work, cast on 6 sts and before slipping the last lp on LH needle, bring yarn to front, turn work; sl the first st from LH needle to RH needle, then pass the extra cast-on st over it to close buttonhole; rep from * until all buttonholes are worked. Rib until band measures 1"/2.5cm from buttonhole row. Work buttonholes as before. Complete as for left front band. Sew buttonholes tog with overcast st if desired.

Neckband

With RS facing and crochet hook, work a row of sl st around entire neck edge. Fasten off. With size 0 (2mm) needles, pick up and k150 (156, 162) sts around neck edge behind sl st edge. Work in k1, p1 rib for ¼"/.5cm. Work a buttonhole as before ½"/1.5cm in from right front edge. Rib until band measures 1"/2.5cm from buttonhole. Make another buttonhole in same place. Rib until band measures 1½"/4cm. Complete as for left front band. Sew on buttons. ●

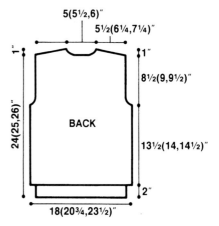

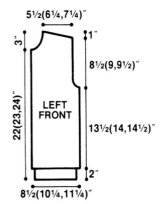

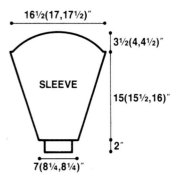

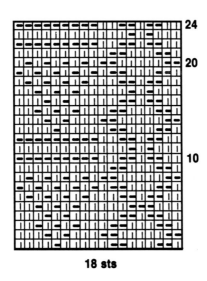

18 sts

☐ **k on RS, p on WS**
⊟ **p on RS, k on WS**

Decisively clean lines, forceful cables and rich colors—the sum total of this classic design. This sporty pullover has a small V-shaped collar, set-in sleeves, precise V-shaped cabling and eyelets. The Cable V-Neck originally appeared in the Fall/Winter '84 issue of *Vogue Knitting*.

Cable V-Neck

FOR EXPERIENCED KNITTERS

SIZES
To fit 32-34 (36, 38)"/81-86 (91, 96)cm bust. Directions are for smallest size with larger sizes in parentheses. If there is only one set of figures it applies to all sizes.

KNITTED MEASUREMENTS
● Bust at underarm 37 (39, 41)"/93 (97,103)cm.
● Length 23 (23½, 24¼)"/58.5 (59.5, 61.5)cm.
● Sleeve width at upper arm 14¼ (14½, 15)"/35.5 (36.5, 37.5)cm.

MATERIALS
Original Yarn
● 14 (14, 15, 15) 1¾oz/50g balls (each approx 90yd/85m) of Berger du Nord *Prodiges* (wool 5) in #7202 red
Substitute Yarn
● 15 (15, 16, 16) 1¾oz/50g balls (each approx 88yd/80m) of Brown Sheep *Prairie Silk* (wool/mohair/silk 5) in #400 ruble red
● One pair each sizes 5 and 7 (3.75 and 4.5mm) needles OR SIZE TO OBTAIN GAUGE
● Stitch markers
● Cable needle (cn)
Note
The original yarn used for this sweater is no longer available. A comparable substitute has been made, which is available at the time of printing. Check gauge of substitute yarns very carefully before beginning.

GAUGE
20 sts and 26 rows to 4"/10cm over St st using size 7 (4.5mm) needles. 1 cable panel (34 sts) to approx 5"/12.5cm. FOR PERFECT FIT, TAKE TIME TO CHECK GAUGES.

STITCH GLOSSARY
Cable Pat (8 sts)
Row 1 (RS) P1, k6, p1.
Row 2 and all WS rows K1, p6, k1.
Row 3 P1, sl next 3 sts to cn and hold at *back* of work, k3, k3 from cn, p1.
Rows 5 and 7 Rep row 1.
Row 8 Rep row 2. Rep rows 1-8 for cable pat.

Openwork Pat (5 sts)
Row 1 (RS) Knit.
Row 2 and all WS rows Purl.
Row 3 K2, yo, k2tog, k1.
Rows 5 and 7 Knit.
Row 8 Purl. Rep rows 1-8 for openwork pat.

BACK
With smaller needles, cast on 91 (95, 101) sts.
Beg rib and cable pats: Row 1 (RS) K0 (0, 1), [p1, k1] 4 (5, 6) times, *work row 1 of cable pat over next 8 sts, [k1, p1] twice, k1*; rep between *'s once more, work row 1 of cable pat over next 8 sts, [k1, P1] 3 times, k1; rep between *'s twice, work row 1 of cable pat over next 8 sts, [k1, p1] 4 (5, 6) times, k0 (0, 1).
Row 2 P0 (0, 1), [k1, p1] 4 (5, 6) times, *work row 2 of cable pat over next 8 sts, p1, [k1, p1] twice*; rep between *'s once more, work row 2 of cable pat over next 8 sts, [p1, k1] 3 times, p1; rep between *'s twice, work row 2 of cable pat over next 8 sts, [p1, k1] 4 (5, 6) times, p0 (0, 1). Cont in pats as established, work k1, p1 rib between cables until 32 rows have been worked from beg (4 cable pat reps) and back measures approx 3½"/9cm from beg. Change to larger needles.
Beg cable and openwork pats:
Row 1 (RS) K8 (10, 13), *work row 1 of cable pat over next 8 sts, row 1 of openwork pat over next 5 sts*; rep between *'s once more, work row 1 of cable pat over next 8 sts, place marker, inc 1 st in next st, k5, inc 1 st in next st, place marker; rep between *'s twice, work row 1 of cable pat over next 8 sts, k8 (10, 13)—93 (97, 103) sts.
Row 2 P8 (10, 13), *work row 2 of cable pat over next 8 sts, row 2 of openwork pat over next 5 sts*; rep between *'s once more, work row 2 of cable pat over next 8 sts, sl marker, p9, sl marker; rep between *'s twice, work row 2 of cable pat over next 8 sts, p8 (10, 13). Cont in pats as established, working first and last sts in St st, sl markers every row and inc 1 st after first marker and 1 st before 2nd marker every pat row 1 (every 8th row), working inc sts in St st until back measures approx 15"/38cm from beg, end with pat row 4 of 10th cable and openwork pat rep. There are 111 (115, 121) sts.

Armhole shaping
Being sure to cont incs at markers

every pat row 1 for 6 (6, 7) times more (a total of 16 (16, 17) inc rows), bind off 4 (5, 6) sts at beg of next 2 rows, 2 sts at beg of next 2 (2, 4) rows. Dec 1 st each end every other row 2 (3, 3) times. Cont incs, work in pats until armhole measures 8 (8½, 9¼)"/20.5 (21.5, 23.5)cm. Bind off all 107 (107, 109) sts.

FRONT
Work as for back until armhole measures 3½ (4, 4¾)"/9 (10, 12)cm, end with a WS row.

V-neck shaping
(Note: When working V-neck shaping, be sure to cont incs at markers every pat row 1 as before.)
Next row (RS) Work pat to center st, join 2nd ball of yarn and bind off center st, work pat to end. Working both sides at once, dec 1 st at each neck edge every row 13 times, then every other row 6 times. When there are same number of rows and incs as

back to shoulder, bind off rem 34 (34, 35) sts each side for shoulders.

SLEEVES
With smaller needles, cast on 44 (46, 48) sts. Work in k1, p1 rib for 3¼"/8.5cm, inc 36 sts evenly spaced across last WS row—80 (82, 84) sts. Change to larger needles.

Beg cable and openwork pats:
Row 1 (RS) K23 (24, 25), *work row 1 of cable pat over next 8 sts, row 1 of openwork pat over next 5 sts*; rep between *'s once, work row 1 of cable pat over next 8 sts, k23 (24, 25).
Row 2 P23 (24, 25), *work row 2 of cable pat over next 8 sts, row 2 of openwork pat over next 5 sts*; rep between *'s once, work row 2 of cable pat over next 8 sts, p23 (24, 25). Cont in pats as established (working first and last sts in St st) until sleeve measures 17½ (18, 18)"/44.5 (45.5, 45.5)cm from beg or desired length to underarm, end with a WS row.

Cap shaping
Bind off 4 (5, 6) sts at beg of next 2 rows, 2 sts at beg of next 2 rows. Dec 1 st each end every other row 10 (12, 14) times. Bind off 4 (2, 2) sts at beg of next 2 (2, 6) rows, 3 sts at beg of next 8 (8, 4) rows. Bind off rem 16 sts.

Collar
With smaller needles, cast on 46 sts. Work in k1, p1 rib for 1 row.
Next row Cast on 4 sts at beg of row, rib across all sts—50 sts. Rep this row 19 times more—126 sts. Bind off 4 sts at beg of next 20 rows—46 sts. Work even for 1 row. Bind off.

FINISHING
Block pieces to measurements. Sew shoulder, side and sleeve seams. Set in sleeves. Fold collar in half lengthwise and sew to neck edge through both thicknesses. ●

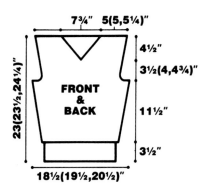

7¾" 5(5,5¼)"
4½"
3½(4,4¾)"
23(23½,24¼)"
FRONT & BACK
11½"
3½"
18½(19½,20½)"

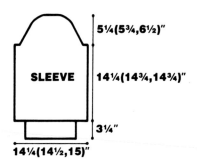

5¼(5¾,6½)"
SLEEVE
14¼(14¾,14¾)"
3¼"
14¼(14½,15)"

Cable Cardigan

This oversized, below-hip length V-neck cardigan in distinctive cable counterpoint, features angled armholes, front pockets and vertical ribbed bands. Shown in size 34-36. The Cable Cardigan first appeared in the Fall '89 issue of *Vogue Knitting*.

Cable Cardigan

FOR INTERMEDIATE KNITTERS

SIZES
To fit 30-32 (34-36, 38-40)"/76-81 (86-91, 96-101)cm bust. Directions are for smallest size with larger sizes in parentheses. If there is only one figure it applies to all sizes.

KNITTED MEASUREMENTS
● Bust at underarm (buttoned) 38 (44, 48)"/95 (109.5, 121)cm.
● Length 28½ (30, 31½)"/71.5 (75.5, 78.5)cm.
● Sleeve width at upper arm 19 (20, 21)"/48 (50, 52)cm.

MATERIALS
● 12 (13, 15) 3½oz/100g balls (each approx 215yd/196m) of Baruffa/Lane Borgosesia *Knitaly®* (wool 4) in #90094 mushroom
● One pair each sizes 5 and 7 (3.75 and 4.5mm) needles OR SIZE TO OBTAIN GAUGE
● Five ¾"/20mm buttons
● Cable needle (cn) and stitch holders

GAUGE
33 sts and 30 rows to 4"/10cm over cable chart using size 7 (4.5mm) needles. FOR PERFECT FIT, TAKE TIME TO CHECK GAUGE.

STITCH GLOSSARY
6-st Right Cable Sl 3 sts to cn and hold to *back*, k3, k3 from cn.
6-st Left Cable Sl 3 sts to cn and hold to *front*, k3, k3 from cn.

BACK
With smaller needles, cast on 150 (170, 186) sts.
Rib row 1 K2, *p2, k2; rep from * to end.
Rib row 2 P2, *k2, p2; rep from * to end. Rep last 2 rows for 2¾"/7cm, inc 7 (11, 13) sts evenly across last row—157 (181, 199) sts. Change to larger needles.
Beg cable chart: Row 1 (RS) K0 (0, 1), beg with 21st (9th, 1st) st of chart, work to end of chart, then work 28-st rep 5 (5, 6) times, work first 9 (21, 1) sts of chart once more, k0 (0, 1). Cont in pat until piece measures 19 (20, 21)"/47.5 (50.5, 52.5)cm from beg, end with a WS row.

Armhole shaping
Dec 1 st each side every row 16 (18, 21) times—125 (145, 157) sts. Work even until armhole measures 9½ (10, 10½)"/24 (25, 26)cm. Bind off.

Pocket linings (make 2)
With larger needles, cast on 36 (43, 43) sts. Work in St st for 4"/10cm. Place sts on holder.

LEFT FRONT
With smaller needles, cast on 70 (78, 90) sts. Rib as for back for 2¾"/7cm, inc 4 (8, 6) sts evenly across last row—74 (86, 96) sts. Change to larger needles.
Beg cable chart: Row 1 (RS) K0 (0, 1), beg with 21st (9th, 1st) st of chart, work to end of chart, then work 28-st rep twice, work first 10 sts of chart once more, k0 (0, 1). Cont in pat until 30 rows of chart have been worked and piece measures 6¾"/17cm, end with a WS row.

Pocket joining
Next row (RS) Work across 9 (14, 23) sts, join 2nd ball of yarn and bind off 34 (41, 41) sts, work to end.
Next row (WS) Work to 1 st before bound-off sts, with RS of pocket lining facing WS of work, p next st on needle tog with first st on holder, p next 34 (41, 41) sts, p last st on holder tog with next st on needle, work in pat to end. Work even in pat until piece measures 16½ (18, 19½)"/41.5 (45.5, 48.5)cm from beg, end with a WS row.

Neck and armhole shaping
Next row (RS) Work to last 3 sts, k2tog, k1. Cont to dec 1 st at neck edge every other row 0 (0, 10) times, then every 4th row 20 (20, 15) times, AT SAME TIME, when same length as back to armhole, work armhole shaping at side edge only (beg of RS rows) as for back. When same length as back, bind off rem 37 (47, 49) sts.

RIGHT FRONT

Work to correspond to left front, reversing all shaping.

SLEEVES

With smaller needles, cast on 54 (58, 58) sts. Work in k2, p2 rib for 2½"/6.5cm, inc 38 (38, 40) sts evenly across last WS row—92 (96, 98) sts.
Beg cable chart: Row 1 (RS) Beg with 11th (9th, 8th) st of chart, work to end of chart, then work 28-st rep twice, work first 18 (20, 21) sts once more. Cont in pat, inc 1 st each side (working inc sts into cable chart) every other row 12 (14, 17) times, every 4th row 20 times—156 (164, 172) sts. Work even until piece measures 17 (17½, 18)"/43 (44, 45)cm, end with a WS row.

Cap shaping

Dec 1 st each side every row 16 (18, 21) times. Bind off rem 124 (128, 130) sts.

FINISHING

Block pieces. Sew shoulder seams.

V-neck band

With smaller needles, cast on 11 sts.

Row 1 (RS) [K1, p1] 5 times, sl 1 wyib.
Row 2 K1, *k1, p1; rep from * to end. Rep last 2 rows until piece fits along right front to center back neck. Place sts on holder and sew in place. Mark placement for 5 buttons with the first ½"/1.5cm from lower edge and the last at the first neck dec and others evenly between. Rib to just below first marker.
Next row Rib 5, join a 2nd ball of yarn, rib to end. Work both sides at once, rib 2 rows more.
Next row Work across all sts, cut 2nd ball. Cont in rib working rem buttonholes opposite markers. Sew 2nd half of band in place.

Pocket edging

Cast on and rib as for V-neck band, until rib fits horizontally along top of pocket. Sew k1 row along pocket edge (sl st row to the outside). Sew side edges. Sew linings to fronts. Sew top of sleeve to straight edge of armhole, then sew dec armhole sts on front and back to dec sts of sleeve. Sew side and sleeve seams. Sew on buttons. ●

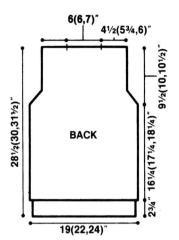

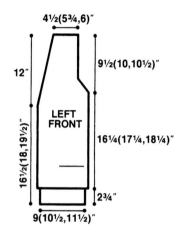

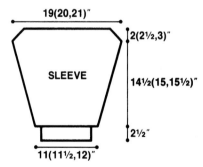

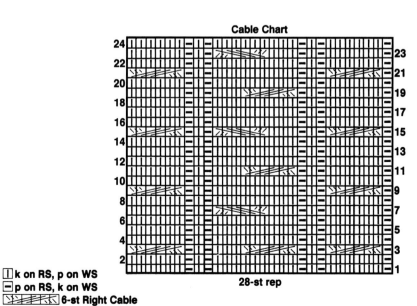

Cable Chart

28-st rep

☐ k on RS, p on WS
☐ p on RS, k on WS
6-st Right Cable
6-st Left Cable

Well-defined rope cables carve out this flawless, loose-fitting pullover. A classic Calvin Klein look, with angled armholes and ribbed turtleneck. Shown in size 36. The Cable Turtleneck first appeared in the Fall '89 issue of *Vogue Knitting*.

Cable Turtleneck

FOR INTERMEDIATE KNITTERS

SIZES
To fit 32 (34, 36, 38)"/81(86, 91, 96)cm bust. Directions are for smallest size with larger sizes in parentheses. If there is only one figure it applies to all sizes.

KNITTED MEASUREMENTS
● Bust at underarm 38 (40, 42, 44)"/96 (101, 105, 111)cm.
● Length 22½ (23½, 24, 25)"/57 (59.5, 61, 63)cm.
● Sleeve width at upper arm 18 (19, 19, 20)"/45 (48, 48, 50)cm.

MATERIALS
Original Yarn
● 10 (11, 12, 13) 1¾oz/50g balls (each approx 254yd/232m) of Filatura di Crosa/Stacy Charles *Camelhair* (camel hair/wool 2) in #1 beige
Substitute Yarn
● 13 (14, 16, 17) 1¾oz/50g balls (each approx 199yd/182m) of Filatura di Crosa/Stacy Charles *Alpaca Peru* (alpaca 2) in #55 beige
● One pair each sizes 1 and 3 (2.25 and 3.25mm) needles OR SIZE TO OBTAIN GAUGE
● Size 1 (2.25mm) circular needle 16"/40cm long
● Cable needle (cn)
Note
The original yarn used for this sweater is no longer available. A comparable substitute has been made, which is available at the time of printing. Check gauge of substitute yarns very carefully before beginning.

GAUGE
44 sts and 44 rows to 4"/10cm over cable chart (slightly stretched) using size 3 (3.25mm) needles. FOR PERFECT FIT, TAKE TIME TO CHECK GAUGE.

STITCH GLOSSARY
6-st Right Cable Sl 3 sts to cn and hold to *back*, k3, k3 from cn.

BACK
With smaller needles, cast on 230 (242, 250, 266) sts.
Rib row 1 K2, *p2, k2; rep from* to end.
Rib row 2 P2,*k2, p2; rep from * to end. Rep last 2 rows for 2"/5cm, dec 20 (20, 20, 22) sts evenly across last row—210 (222, 230, 244) sts. Change to larger needles.
Beg cable chart: Row 1 (RS) P0 (2, 2, 1), work first 2 sts of chart once then work 8-st rep 26 (27, 28, 30) times, p0 (2, 2, 1). Cont in pats, working sts outside chart in rev St st (p on RS, k on WS) until piece measures 13½ (14, 14½, 15)"/34.5 (35.5, 37, 38)cm from beg, end with a WS row.

Armhole shaping
Dec 1 st each side every row 16 (18, 18, 18) times—178 (186, 194, 208) sts. Work even until armhole measures 8 (8½, 8½, 9)"/20 (21.5, 21.5, 22.5)cm.

Neck shaping
Next row (RS) Work 60 (62, 66, 70) sts, join 2nd ball of yarn and bind off 58 (62, 62, 68) sts, work to end. Working both sides at once, dec 1 st at neck edge every row 10 times. Bind

off rem 50 (52, 56, 60) sts each side for shoulders.

FRONT
Work as for back until armhole measures 6½ (7, 7, 7½)"/16 (17.5, 17.5, 18.5)cm, end with a WS row.

Neck shaping
Next row (RS) Work 72 (74, 78, 82) sts, join 2nd ball of yarn and bind off 34 (38, 38, 44) sts, work to end. Working both sides at once, bind off from each neck edge 3 sts twice, 2 sts twice, then dec 1 st every other row 4 times, every row 8 times. Work even until same length as back. Bind off rem 50 (52, 56, 60) sts each side for shoulders.

SLEEVES
With smaller needles, cast on 78 (78, 82, 82) sts. Work in k2, p2 rib for 2"/5cm, inc 20 (20, 24, 24) sts evenly across last row—98 (98, 106, 106) sts. Change to larger needles.
Beg cable chart: Row 1 (RS) Work first 2 sts of chart, then work 8-st rep 12 (12, 13, 13) times. Cont in pat, inc 1 st each side (working inc sts into cable chart) every other row 11 (19, 11, 20) times, every 4th row 39 (36, 40, 37) times—198 (208, 208, 220) sts. Work even until piece measures 19 (19½, 19½, 20)"/47.5 (48.5, 48.5, 50)cm from beg, end with a WS row.

Cap shaping
Dec 1 st each side every row 16 (18, 18, 18) times. Bind off rem 166 (172, 172, 184) sts.

FINISHING
Block pieces. Sew shoulder seams.

Turtleneck
With RS facing and circular needle, beg at right shoulder, pick up and k164 (172, 172, 184) sts evenly around neck edge. Join and work in k2, p2 rib for 8"/20.5cm. Bind off in rib. Sew top of sleeve to straight edge of armholes, then sew dec armhole sts on front and back to dec sts of sleeve. Sew side and sleeve seams. ●

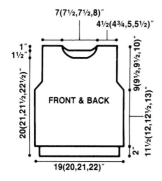

7(7½,7½,8)"
4½(4¾,5,5½)"
1"
1½"
9(9½,9½,10)"
FRONT & BACK
20(21,21½,22½)"
11½(12,12½,13)"
2"
19(20,21,22)"

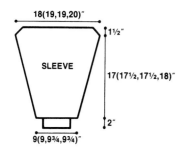

18(19,19,20)"
1½"
SLEEVE
17(17½,17½,18)"
2"
9(9,9¾,9¾)"

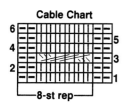

Cable Chart
6
4
2
5
3
1
8-st rep

☐ k on RS, p on WS
⊟ p on RS, k on WS
6-st Right Cable

Perry Ellis

PERRY ELLIS, PERHAPS MORE THAN ANY other American designer, sparked the resurgence in the popularity of handknits. His use of cables in simple shapes, worked in visually alluring, tweeded yarns, became a trademark of his terrific style. Part of what brought Ellis' knit designs almost instant success was his ability to mix the functional with the fanciful. His adventurous and witty approach captures a perfect blend of classic styling with innovative design.

Perry Ellis began his career in department store retailing. Before long, his own talent for design became evident and he was recruited by a well-known clothing manufacturer as its Design Director. His reputation grew as his clothes became increasingly admired and sought after for their fresh and innovative style. In 1978, Ellis' success enabled him to develop his own sportswear collection. Along with his team of talented designers, he created stylish and sophisticated fashions that redefined the American "classics."

Ellis' company grew rapidly as he began to apply his talent to a long list of fashionable products. He was honored with many Fashion and Design awards, among them the prestigious Coty Fashion Critic's Award and the Council of Fashion Designers of America (CFDA) Award. In fact, Ellis served as the first president of the the CFDA, and his remarkable efforts are honored every year with the presentation of the Perry Ellis Award for the most promising new talent in fashion design.

The fashion world lost a true star with Ellis' death in 1986. Since then, the design team at Perry Ellis International has committed itself to carrying on the Perry Ellis tradition in creating sophisticated and trend-setting fashions. Many talented and well-known designers, such as Marc Jacobs, who designed collections for Perry Ellis from 1988 to 1993, are responsible for keeping the legacy of the late designer alive.

Always opposed to fashion mandates, Perry Ellis believed clothes should be a personal matter, and strove to provide options to pique each individual's unique fashion sense. The following pages showcase a selection of just a few of his rave-winning designs so you can add a dash of Perry Ellis fashion originality to your wardrobe.

> His adventurous and witty approach captures a perfect blend of classic styling with innovative design.

Carrying on the spirited legacy of the late designer, former design director Marc Jacobs lent his innovative wit to knits with this "bubble" sweater. Very oversized in thigh-length, this popular pullover features angled pockets and a deeply ribbed yoke rising to a funnel neck. The Bubble Sweater first appeared in the Fall '89 issue of *Vogue Knitting*.

Bubble Sweater

FOR EXPERT KNITTERS

SIZES
One size fits all.

KNITTED MEASUREMENTS
● Length 30"/76.5cm.
● Width of lower edge rib 36"/44.5cm.
● Width from sleeve cuff to sleeve cuff 73"/185.5cm.

MATERIALS
● 13 1½oz/40g balls (each approx 90yd/82m) of Classic Elite *La Gran* (mohair/wool/nylon 5) in #6564 purple basil (A) and #6548 slate (B)
● Sizes 10 and 11 (6 and 8mm) circular needles 29"/80cm long OR SIZE TO OBTAIN GAUGE
● Size 10 (6mm) circular needle 16"/40cm long
● Size 11 (8mm) double pointed needles (dpn)
● Stitch markers and stitch holders
Note
The original color used for this sweater is no longer available. A comparable color substitute has been made, which is available at the time of printing.

GAUGE
12 sts and 16 rows to 4"/10cm over St st and 1 strand each A and B held tog, using size 11 (8mm) needle.
13 sts to 4"/10cm over twisted rib and 1 strand each A and B held tog, using size 11 (8mm) needle. FOR PERFECT FIT, TAKE TIME TO CHECK GAUGES.

Notes
1 As gauge may differ between working back and forth and working in rounds, check work after a few inches and adjust needle size if necessary.
2 Body of sweater is knit in one circular piece to underarm. Sleeves are knit separately to underarm, then joined to body at yoke.
3 Work with 1 strand each A and B held tog throughout.
4 To enlarge rib at lower edge, cast on 128 sts and omit incs on rnd 1.

BODY
With larger 29"/80cm needle and 1 strand each A and B, cast on 116 sts. Join, taking care not to twist sts on needle. Place marker for end of rnd, and sl marker every rnd.
Twisted rib: Rnd 1 (RS) *K1 tbl, p1; rep from * around. Rep rnd 1 for twisted rib for 2½"/6.5cm. Work in St st as foll:
Rnd 1 *K10, inc 1 st as foll: k in 1 strand of st, then k in 2nd strand of same st, [k8, inc 1] twice; rep from * 3 times more—128 sts. K 4 rnds. (Note: Use a different color marker for inc rnds to distinguish them from end of rnd marker.)
Rnd 6 *K7, inc 1 (placing marker

between 2 new sts), k16, inc 1 (placing marker), k14, inc 1 (placing marker), k16, inc 1 (placing marker), k7; rep from * once more—136 sts.
Rnd 7 *K to 3 sts before next marker, inc 1; rep from * around—144 sts. K 5 rnds, sl markers every rnd.
Rnd 13 *K to next marker, remove marker, inc 1 (placing marker between 2 new sts); rep from * around—152 sts. Rep rnds 7-13 for 5 times more, then work rnd 7 once more, AT SAME TIME, after 18 rnds have been worked above rib and there are 160 sts on needle, work as foll:

Pocket linings (make 2)
With larger needle and 1 strand each A and B, cast on 18 sts. Work in St st for 4¾"/12cm. Sl sts to a holder.

Pocket joining
Rnd 19 K12, sl next 18 sts to a holder for left pocket, removing marker, k across sts on one lining, placing marker on lining in correct position, k20, sl next 18 sts to a holder for right pocket, k across sts of 2nd lining, k to end of rnd. After all incs have been worked, work even on rem 240 sts until piece measures 17"/43cm from beg.

Divide for front and back
Bind off 6 sts (underarm) or sl sts to a holder to graft tog, work until there are 108 sts from bind-off, sl sts to a holder for front, bind off next 12 sts (underarm), work until there are 108 sts from bind-off, sl sts to a holder for back, bind off rem 6 sts.

SLEEVES

With 16"/40cm needle and 1 strand each A and B, cast on 52 sts. Join, taking care not to twist sts. Work in twisted rib for 1¼"/3cm. Change to size 11 (8mm) dpn and k 5 rnds. (Note: Change to circular needle once there are enough sts to fit around needle.)
Rnd 6 [Inc 1 st, k12] 4 times—56 sts. K 5 rnds.
Rnd 12 [Inc 1 st, k13] 4 times—60 sts. K 5 rnds. Cont in this way to inc 4 sts (adding 1 more st between incs each inc rnd) every 6th rnd 6 times more—84 sts. K 7 rnds.
Next rnd [Inc 1 st, k13] 6 times—90 sts. Work even until piece measures 16½"/42cm from beg. Bind off 6 sts, work until there are 78 sts from bind-off, sl sts to a holder, bind off rem 6 sts.

YOKE
Next (joining) row With larger 29"/80cm needle, k sts from holders as foll: 108 sts of front, 78 sts of right sleeve, 108 sts of back, 78 sts of left sleeve—372 sts. Join and work in rnds as foll: K 4 rnds.
Rnd 5 *K6, k2tog, [k6, k2tog, k7, k2tog] 5 times; rep from * 3 times more—328 sts. K 4 rnds.
Rnd 10 *K2, [k2tog, k6, k2tog, k5] 5 times, k2tog, k3; rep from * 3 times more—284 sts. K 4 rnds.
Rnd 15 *K4, k2tog, [k4, k2tog, k5, k2tog] 5 times; rep from * 3 times more—240 sts. K 4 rnds.
Rnd 20 *K1, [k2tog, k4, k2tog, k3] 5 times, k2tog, k2; rep from * 3 times more—196 sts. K 4 rnds.
Rnd 25 *K2, k2tog, [k3, k2tog, k2, k2tog] 5 times; rep from * 3 times more—152 sts. K 4 rnds. Work in k2, p2 rib for 2½"/6.5cm. Change to smaller circular needle.
Next rnd *K2, p2tog; rep from * around—114 sts. Work in k2, p1 rib for 2½"/6.5cm.
Next rnd *K2tog, p1; rep from * around—76 sts. Work in twisted rib as for body for 5"/12.5cm. Bind off in rib.

FINISHING
Sew bound-off armhole sts tog at underarm or graft tog.

Right pocket edging
With RS facing and larger needle, work sts from holder as foll:
Next row K6, turn, p to end.
Next row K12, turn, purl to end.
Next row K18. Change to smaller needle and work in twisted rib for 1"/2.5cm. Bind off. With WS of pocket facing, work left pocket edging to correspond to right pocket. Sew pocket linings to WS of front. Sew sides of pockets to front. ●

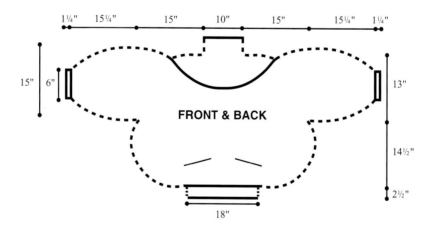

FRONT & BACK

Stitchwork Turtleneck

A softened elegance defines this loose-fitting turtleneck. A modern classic with a fluid drape and set-in sleeves, it has lots of surface interest in the multistitch design, all taking shape in ultra chic camel-colored yarn. Shown in size 34. The Stitchwork Turtleneck first appeared in the Fall '86 issue of *Vogue Knitting*.

Stitchwork Turtleneck

FOR EXPERIENCED KNITTERS

SIZES
To fit 32 (34, 36, 38)"/81 (86, 91, 96)cm bust. Directions are for smallest size with larger sizes in parentheses. If there is only one set of figures it applies to all sizes.

KNITTED MEASUREMENTS
● Bust at underarm 38 (40, 42, 44)"/96 (100, 106, 110)cm.
● Length 19½ (20, 21, 22)"/49.5 (51, 53, 55)cm.
● Sleeve width at upper arm 16 (17, 18, 19)"/40 (43, 45, 48)cm.

MATERIALS
Original Yarn
● 10 (11, 11, 12) 1½oz/40g balls (each approx 220yd/201m) of Wm. Unger *Precious* (camel hair/lambswool 2) in #2 camel
Substitute Yarn
● 30 (33, 33, 36) ⅞oz/25g balls (each approx 73yd/67m) of Rowan *Lightweight Double Knitting* (wool 2) in #11 camel
● One pair each sizes 1 and 3 (2.5 and 3.25mm) needles OR SIZE TO OBTAIN GAUGE
● Size 1 (2.5mm) circular needle 24"/60cm long
Note
The original yarn used for this sweater is no longer available. A comparable substitute has been made, which is available at the time of printing. Check gauge of substitute yarns very carefully before beginning.

GAUGE
26 sts and 32 rows to 4"/10cm over St st using size 3 (3.25mm) needles. FOR PERFECT FIT, TAKE TIME TO CHECK GAUGE.

BACK
With smaller needles cast on 114 (120, 126, 134) sts.
Rib row 1 K2 (1, 2, 0), *p2, k2; rep from *, end p2, k2 (1, 2, 0).
Rib row 2 K the knit sts and p the purl sts. Rep last 2 rows for 2½"/6.5cm, end with a RS row. Change to larger needles. Work inc and pats as foll: Inc 1 st each end every 12th (12th, 12th, 18th) row 5 (5, 5, 4) times, and AT SAME TIME, work pats as foll:
Beg pat st #1: Next row (WS) P2 (5, 2, 0), *k2, p10; rep from *, end k2, p2 (5, 2, 0).
Next row Knit. Work in pat #1 until piece measures 5"/13cm from beg—116 (122, 128, 136) sts.
Beg pat st #2: Next row (WS) K0 (3, 0, 0), p8 (8, 8, 6), *k4, p8; rep from * end, k4, p8 (8, 8, 6), k0 (3, 0, 0).
Next row Knit. Cont in pat #2 until piece measures 11 (11, 11½, 12)"/28 (28, 29.5, 30)cm from beg and there are 124 (130, 136, 142) sts.

Armhole shaping
Cont in pat #2, bind off 3 sts at beg of next 2 rows, 2 sts at beg of next 2 (2, 2, 0) rows. Dec 1 st each end every other row 2 (2, 2, 3) times—110 (116, 122, 130) sts.
Beg pat st #3 (RS) Work even foll chart through row 27.

Beg pat st #4: Next row (WS) P1 (1, 1, 2), *k3, p3; rep from *, end p1 (1, 1, 2).
Next row Knit. Work even in pat #4 until piece measures 19½ (20, 21, 22)"/49.5 (51, 53, 55)cm from beg. Bind off 36 (39, 40, 44) sts at beg of next 2 rows for shoulders. Bind off 38 (38, 42, 42) sts.

FRONT
Work as for back until armhole measures 5½ (6, 6½, 7)"/14 (15.5, 16, 17.5)cm.

Neck shaping
Next row (RS) Cont in pat st #4, work 48 (51, 53, 57) sts, join 2nd ball of yarn and bind off center 14 (14, 16, 16) sts for neck, work to end. Working both sides at once, and cont in pat, bind off from each neck edge 2 sts 2 (2, 1, 1) times, 3 sts 0 (0, 1, 1) time, 1 st 8 times. Bind off rem 36 (39, 40, 44) sts each side.

SLEEVES
With smaller needles cast on 52 (52, 58, 58) sts.
Rib row 1 P1 (1, 0, 0), *k2, p2; rep from *, end k2, p1 (1, 0, 0). Cont in rib as for back for 2½"/6.5cm. Change to larger needles.
Beg pat #1: Next row (WS) P1 (1, 4, 4), *k2, p10; rep from *, end k2, p1 (1, 4, 4). Cont in pat #1, inc 1 st each end every 4th row 16 (23, 24, 31) times, every 6th row 10 (6, 6, 2) times, and AT SAME TIME, when piece measures 6¼"/16cm from beg and there are 66 (66, 72, 72) sts, work as foll:

Beg pat #2: Next row (WS) P1 (1, 4, 4), *k4, p8; rep from *, end k4, p1 (1, 4, 4). Cont in pat #2 until piece measures 12½ (13, 13½, 14)"/32.5 (34, 35, 36.5)cm from beg and there are 88 (94, 102, 104) sts, end with a WS row.

Beg pat #3 Work chart through row 27—98 (104, 112, 116) sts.

Beg pat #4: **Next row** (WS) P3 (2, 1, 3), k3, *p3, k3; rep from *, end p2 (3, 0, 2).

Next row Knit. Work even in pat #4 until all inc have been worked and there are 104 (110, 118, 124) sts— piece measures 18½ (19, 19½, 20)"/46.5 (48, 49.5, 50)cm from beg.

Cap shaping

Cont in pat #4, bind off 12 (12, 12, 14) sts at beg of next 2 rows, 6 sts at beg of next 10 (8, 10, 10) rows, 5 (7, 6, 9) sts at beg of next 4 (2, 4, 4) rows, 0 (4, 5, 0) sts at beg of next 0 (6, 2, 0) rows.

FINISHING

Block pieces. Brush lightly, if desired, to add fullness to original yarn only. Sew shoulder seams.

Neckband

With RS facing and circular needle, pick up and k38 (38, 42, 42) sts along back neck edge and 70 (70, 74, 74) sts along front neck edge— 108 (108, 116, 116) sts. Join and work in rnds of k2, p2 rib for 7"/18cm. Bind off in rib. Set in sleeves. Sew side and sleeve seams. ●

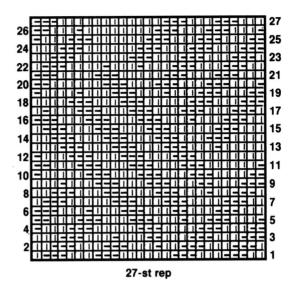

27-st rep

☐ St st (k on RS, p on WS)
⊟ rev St st (p on RS, k on WS)

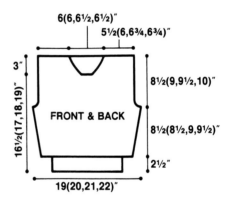

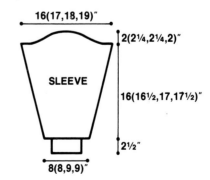

This winning little cardigan is shirt collared in reverse stockinette for a stylish twist. It's close-fitting with angled armholes and front cable dart detailing that creates vest-like shaping. Shown in size 34. The Cable Dart Cardigan first appeared in the Winter '89 issue of *Vogue Knitting*.

Cable Dart Cardigan

FOR INTERMEDIATE KNITTERS

SIZES
To fit 32 (34, 36, 38, 40)"/81 (86, 91, 96, 101)cm bust. Directions are for smallest size with larger sizes in parentheses. If there is only one figure it applies to all sizes.

KNITTED MEASUREMENTS
● Bust at underarm (buttoned) 34 (36, 38, 40, 42)"/85.5 (90.5, 94.5, 99.5, 106.5)cm.
● Length 20 (20, 20½, 21, 22)"/ 50.5 (50.5, 52, 53, 55.5)cm.
● Sleeve width at upper arm 18 (18, 19, 19, 20)"/45 (45, 48, 48, 50)cm.

MATERIALS
Original Yarn
● 8 (8, 9, 10, 11) 1¾oz/50g balls (each approx 126yd/115m) of Filatura di Crosa/Stacy Charles *Ponza* (wool/cotton/polyamide 4) in #805 rust tweed
Substitute Yarn
● 7 (7, 8, 9, 10) 1¾oz/50g balls (each approx 147yd/136m) of Filatura di Crosa/Stacy Charles *Sympathie Tweed* (acrylic/mohair/wool/viscose 4) in #167 red tweed
● One pair each sizes 5 and 7 (3.75 and 4.5mm) needles OR SIZE TO OBTAIN GAUGE
● Seven ¾"/20mm buttons
● Cable needle (cn) and stitch holders

Note
The original yarn used for this sweater is no longer available. A comparable substitute has been made, which is available at the time of printing. Check gauge of substitute yarns very carefully before beginning.

GAUGE
22 sts and 30 rows to 4"/10cm over rev St st using size 7 (4.5mm) needles. FOR PERFECT FIT, TAKE TIME TO CHECK GAUGE.

STITCH GLOSSARY
8-st Left Cable Sl 4 sts to cn and hold to *front*, k4, k4 from cn.
8-st Right Cable Sl 4 sts to cn and hold to *back*, k4, k4 from cn.

BACK
With smaller needles, cast on 74 (77, 82, 86, 88) sts. Work in k1, p1 rib for 1"/2.5cm. Change to larger needles. Work in rev St st (p on RS, k on WS), inc 1 st each side every 10th row 3 (3, 3, 3, 0) times, every 8th row 1 (0, 0, 0, 3) times, every 4th row 6 (8, 8, 9, 11) times—94 (99, 104, 110, 116) sts. Work even until piece measures 9½ (9½, 9½, 10, 10½)"/24 (24, 24, 25, 26.5)cm from beg.

Armhole shaping
Dec 1 st each side on next row, then every other row 3 (4, 0, 0, 0) times, every row 0 (0, 6, 6, 7) times—86 (89, 90, 96, 100) sts. Work even until arm-hole measures 9 (9, 9½, 9½, 10)"/22.5 (22.5, 24, 24, 25)cm.

Shoulder shaping
Bind off 4 sts at beg of next 12 (10, 10, 6, 2) rows, 5 sts at beg of next 0 (2, 2, 6, 10) rows. Bind off rem 38 (39, 40, 42, 42) sts.

LEFT FRONT
With larger needles, cast on 4 sts. P 1 row on WS (center 4 sts of cable chart).
Next row (RS) Cast on 4 (4, 4, 4, 5) sts, p2 (2, 2, 2, 3), k6.
Next row (WS) Cast on 4 (4, 4, 4, 5) sts, k2 (2, 2, 2, 3), p8 (row 4 of chart #1), k2 (2, 2, 2, 3). Cont to cast on 4 sts at beg of next 6 (4, 2, 0, 0) rows, 5 sts at beg of next 0 (2, 4, 6, 6) rows, AT SAME TIME, cont cable pat on center 8 sts foll chart (and rem sts in rev St st) as foll: beg with row 5 of chart #1, work through row 8, then rep rows 1-8 for 6 times, rep rows 1-4 once more, then dec 2 sts across cable on next (RS) row and discontin-ue cable, AT SAME TIME, after all sts have been cast on and there are 36 (38, 40, 42, 44) sts, cont in pat, work-ing incs at side edge only (beg of RS rows) as for back—44 (47, 49, 52, 56) sts. Work even until side edge mea-sures same as back to armhole (not including 1"/2.5cm rib). Work armhole shaping at side edge only as for back—40 (42, 42, 45, 48) sts. Work even until armhole measures 8½ (8½, 9, 9, 9½)"/21 (21, 22.5, 22.5, 23.5)cm, end with a RS row.

Neck shaping

Next row (WS) Bind off 6 (7, 7, 8, 9) sts (neck edge), work to end. Cont to bind off from neck edge 3 sts once, 2 sts twice. Dec 1 st every other row 3 times, AT SAME TIME, when same length as back to shoulder, shape shoulder at armhole edge as for back.

RIGHT FRONT

Work as for left front (working cable chart #2 instead of cable chart #1), until there are 36 (38, 40, 42, 44) sts. Work to correspond to left front, reversing all shaping.

SLEEVES

With smaller needles, cast on 45 (45, 47, 47, 48) sts. Work in k1, p1 rib for 2½"/6.5cm. Change to larger needles. Work in rev St st, inc 1 st each side [every 4th row once, every 6th row once] 10 (12, 8, 10, 7) times, every 4th row 7 (3, 13, 9, 17) times—99 (99, 105, 105, 110) sts. Work even until piece measures 20 (20½, 20½, 21, 21½)"/51 (52, 52, 53.5, 54.5)cm from beg, end with a WS row.

Cap shaping

Dec 1 st each side on next row, then every other row 3 (4, 0, 0, 0) times, every row 0 (0, 6, 6, 7) times. Bind off rem 91 (89, 91, 91, 94) sts.

FINISHING

Block pieces. Sew shoulder seams.

Left front band

With smaller needles, cast on 61 (63, 65, 69, 71) sts. Work in k1, p1 rib for 1"/2.5cm, end with a WS row.
Next row (RS) Bind off 53 (55, 57, 61, 63) sts in rib, rib to end. Cont rib on rem 8 sts until band fits along left front edge to beg of neck shaping.

Place sts on a holder. Sew band along lower and front edge. Place markers on band for 6 buttons, with the first 1¼"/3cm from lower edge and the last 3"/7.5cm below first neck dec, and 4 others evenly between.

Right front band

Work to correspond to left front band, reversing shaping, and working buttonholes opposite markers as foll:
Buttonhole row (RS) Rib 3 sts, bind off 2 sts, rib to end. On next row, cast on 3 sts over bound-off sts.

Collar

With RS facing and smaller needles, rib across 8 sts of right front band, pick up and k101 (101, 103, 109, 109) sts around neck edge, rib across sts of left front band—117 (117, 119, 125, 125) sts. Work in k1, p1 rib for 1"/2.5cm, working buttonhole on right front band after ¼"/.5cm. Bind off 9 sts at beg of next 2 rows—99 (99, 101, 107, 107) sts. Rib until collar measures 2½"/6.5cm. Cont in rib and work short rows as foll: (Note: Before turning work, wrap the next st.)
Next row (RS) Rib 33 (33, 34, 36, 36), turn. Rib to end. Rib 1 row on all sts.
Next row (WS) Rib 33 (33, 34, 36, 36), turn. Rib to end. Rib 1 row on all sts.
Next row (RS) Rib 21 (21, 22, 24, 24), turn. Rib to end. Rib 1 row on all sts.
Next row (WS) Rib 21 (21, 22, 24, 24), turn. Rib to end. Rib 1 row on all sts.
Next row (RS) Rib 9 (9, 10, 12, 12), turn. Rib to end. Rib 1 row on all sts.
Next row (WS) Rib 9 (9, 10, 12, 12), turn. Rib to end. Rib 1 row on all sts. Bind off in rib. Sew top of sleeve to straight edge of armholes, then sew dec armhole sts of front and back to dec sts of sleeve. Sew side and sleeve seams. Sew on buttons. ●

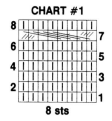

CHART #1

8 sts

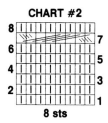

CHART #2

8 sts

☐ k on RS, p on WS

8-st Right Cable

8-st Left Cable

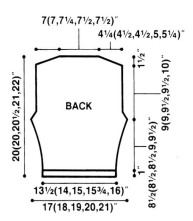

7(7,7¼,7½,7½)"
4¼(4½,4½,5,5¼)"
1½"
20(20,20½,21,22)"
BACK
9(9,9½,9½,10)"
8½(8½,8½,9,9½)"
1"
13½(14,15,15¾,16)"
17(18,19,20,21)"

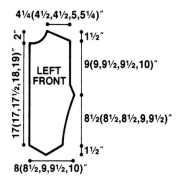

4¼(4½,4½,5,5¼)"
1½"
2"
17(17,17½,18,19)"
LEFT FRONT
9(9,9½,9½,10)"
8½(8½,8½,9,9½)"
1½"
8(8½,9,9½,10)"

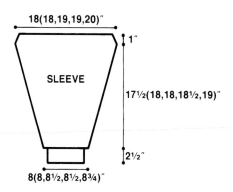

18(18,19,19,20)"
1"
SLEEVE
17½(18,18,18½,19)"
2½"
8(8,8½,8½,8¾)"

Zebra Print Pullover

Perry Ellis' spectacular crewneck pullover in wildly exciting zebra striping. Untamed lines give this sweater a wonderfully natural, sportive elegance. Shown in size Medium. The Zebra Print Pullover first appeared in the Fall/Winter '83 issue of *Vogue Knitting*.

Zebra Print Pullover

FOR EXPERT KNITTERS

SIZES
To fit 32-34 (36-38)"/81-86 (91-96)cm bust. Directions are for medium size with larger size in parentheses. If there is only one set of figures it applies to both sizes.

KNITTED MEASUREMENTS
● Bust at underarm 38 (42)"/95 (105)cm.
● Length 24½"/61.5cm.
● Sleeve width at upper arm 18"/45cm.

MATERIALS
Original Yarn
● 6 (7) 1¾oz/50g balls (each approx 140yd/125m) of Pingouin *Type Shetland* (wool 4) in #15 black (A) and #18 cream (B)
Substitute Yarn
● 5 (6) 4oz/114g skeins (each approx 172yd/159m) of Reynolds/JCA Paternayan® *Persian Yarn* (wool 4) in #220 black and #261 cream
● One pair each sizes 5 and 6 (3.75 and 4.5mm) needles OR SIZE TO OBTAIN GAUGE
● Stitch holders
Note
The original yarn used for this sweater is no longer available. A comparable substitute has been made, which is available at the time of printing. Check gauge of substitute yarns very carefully before beginning.

GAUGE
21 sts and 21 rows to 4"/10cm over colorwork pat using size 6 (4.5mm) needles. FOR PERFECT FIT, TAKE TIME TO CHECK GAUGE.

Note
When working with more than one color, carry yarn not in use loosely across back of work. To avoid excessively long loose strands or long "floats" at back of work, weave or twist yarns not in use around working yarn every 3 or 4 sts.

BACK
With smaller needles and A, cast on 89 (99) sts. Work in k1, p1 rib for 2"/5cm, end with a RS row. Change to larger needles and p next row inc 11 sts evenly across row—100 (110) sts. Beg colorwork pat as foll:
Pat row 1 (RS) Foll row 1 of chart from right to left and beg as indicated for chosen size, k across row, ending as indicated for chosen size.
Pat row 2 (WS) Foll row 2 of chart from left to right, p across row. Cont even in St st foll chart from right to left on RS rows and from left to right on WS rows until chart row 72 is completed.

Armhole shaping
Bind off 5 (8) sts at beg of next 2 rows as indicated on chart—90 (94) sts. Cont in pat foll chart through chart row 120.
Next row (RS) Bind off first 30 (32) sts, sl center 30 sts onto a holder for back of neck, rejoin yarn and bind off rem 30 (32) sts.

FRONT
Work as for back through row 104 of chart.

Neck shaping
Next row—Pat row 105 K in pat across first 38 (40) sts, sl next 52 (54) sts onto a holder. Working left side of neck first, cont foll chart and bind off 2 sts at neck edge on next row, then on every other row once, dec 1 st at neck edge on next row, then on every other row 3 times—30 (32) sts. Work even through chart row 120. Bind off for shoulder. With RS facing, sl first 14 sts onto a holder for center front neck, k in pat across rem 38 (40) sts. Work next row in pat. Complete right side of neck as for left side reversing shaping.

SLEEVES
With smaller needles and A, cast on 39 sts. Work in k1, p1 rib for 2½"/ 6.5cm, end with a RS row. Change to larger needles and p next row inc 13 sts evenly across row—52 sts.
Pat row 1 (RS) Follow row 1 of chart from right to left and beg as indicated for sleeve, k across row, ending as indicated for sleeve.
Pat row 2 (WS) Foll row 2 of chart from left to right, p across. Cont in St st foll chart and AT SAME TIME inc 1 st at each end of every 3rd row 10 times, then at each end of every 4th row 11 times—94 sts. Work even in pat through chart row 90. Bind off.

FINISHING
Press pieces lightly on WS with damp cloth and warm iron. Sew shoulder

seams. Sew top of sleeve to straight edge of armhole. Sew bound-off sts at underarm to side of sleeve. Sew side and sleeve seams.

Neckband
With RS facing, circular needle and A, k30 sts from back neck holder, pick up and k17 sts evenly along left front neck to holder, k14 sts from center front neck holder, pick up and k17 sts evenly along right front neck—78 sts. Work in k1, p1 rib for ¾"/2cm. Bind off loosely in rib. ●

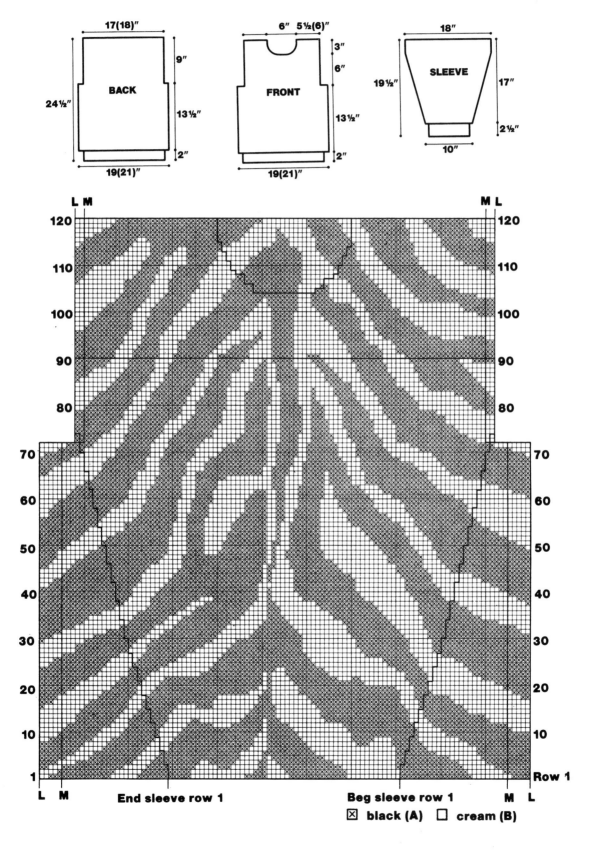

End sleeve row 1   Beg sleeve row 1

☒ black (A)   ☐ cream (B)

Perry Ellis colors up the casual man's pullover with vertical stripes of blue, purple and grey. This oversized, multi-pattern pullover, suitable for a man or woman, is knit in one piece with dolman-sleeves and crew neck. Shown in size 40. The Man's Aran first appeared in the Holiday '87 issue of *Vogue Knitting*.

Man's Aran

FOR EXPERT KNITTERS

SIZES
To fit 36-38 (40, 42-44)"/91-96 (101, 106-112)cm bust/chest. Directions are for smallest size with larger sizes in parentheses. If there is only one set of figures it applies to all sizes.

KNITTED MEASUREMENTS
● Bust/chest at underarm 41 (43, 46)"/102 (108, 115)cm.
● Length 28 (29, 29)"/71 (73.5, 73.5)cm.
● Width from sleeve edge to sleeve edge (including cuffs) 61½ (63½, 66)"/153 (159, 164.5)cm.

MATERIALS
Original Yarn
● 6 (6, 7) 1½oz/50g balls (each approx 137yd/125m) of Aarlan *Royal* (wool/acrylic/mohair 3) in #4237 teal (A)
● 6 balls in #4248 purple (B)
● 5 balls in #4331 royal (C)
● 4 balls in #4305 heather blue (D)
● 3 balls in #4236 turquoise (E)
Substitute Yarn
● 6 (6, 7) 1¾oz/50g balls (each approx 68yd/62m) of Tahki *Cottage Chunky* (wool 5) in #572 teal (A)
● 6 balls in #571 purple (B)
● 5 balls in #588 navy (C)
● 4 balls in #586 heather grey (D)
● 3 balls in #587 heather blue (E)
● One pair each sizes 8 and 9 (5 and 5.5mm) needles OR SIZE TO

OBTAIN GAUGE
● Size 8 (5mm) circular needle 16"/40cm long
● Size 9 (5.5mm) circular needle 36"/90cm long
● Cable needle and stitch markers
Note
The original yarn used for this sweater is no longer available. A comparable substitute has been made, which is available at the time of printing. Check gauge of substitute yarns very carefully before beginning.

GAUGE
16 sts and 24 rows to 4"/10cm over chart #6 using size 9 (5.5mm) needles. FOR PERFECT FIT, TAKE TIME TO CHECK GAUGE.

Notes
1 When changing colors, twist yarns on WS to prevent holes.
2 Pullover is made in one piece.

STITCH GLOSSARY (for charts)
Right Twist (over 2 sts) Sl next st to cn and hold to *back*, k1, k1 from cn.
Right Purl Twist (over 2 sts) Sl next st to cn and hold to *back*, k1, p1 from cn.
Left Purl Twist (over 2 sts) Sl next st to cn and hold to *front*, p1, k1 from cn.
Right Purl Twist (over 3 sts) Sl next st to cn and hold to *back*, k2, p1 from cn.
Left Purl Twist (over 3 sts) Sl next 2 sts to cn and hold to *front*, p1, k2 from cn.

Right Purl Twist (over 5 sts) Sl next 2 sts to cn and hold to *back*, k3, p2 from cn.
Left Purl Twist (over 5 sts) Sl next 3 sts to cn and hold to *front*, p2, k3 from cn.
4-st Right Cable Sl next 2 sts to cn and hold to *back*, k2, k2 from cn.
4-st Left Cable Sl next 2 sts to cn and hold to *front*, k2, k2 from cn.
6-st Right Cable Sl next 3 sts to cn and hold to *back*, k3, k3 from cn.
6-st Left Cable Sl next 3 sts to cn and hold to *front*, k3, k3 from cn.

FRONT
With smaller needles and A, cast on 95 (101, 108) sts. Work in k1, p1 rib for 2"/5cm. Change to larger needles.
Preparation row (WS) With C, [k2, p4] 3 (4, 4) times, k2; with B, p1, k1, p2, k1, p3, k1, p2, k1, p1, k1; with A, [p6, k1] 2 (2, 3) times, p6; with D, k1, p2, k3, p2, k4, p2, k3, p2, k1; with B, [p6, k1] 3 times.
Beg chart pats: Row 1 (RS) Work as foll, matching colors: 7-st rep of chart #1 for 3 times, 20 sts of chart #2, 7-st rep of chart #3 for 2 (2, 3) times, work first 6 sts once more, 14 sts of chart #4, 20 (26, 26) sts of chart #5. Cont in pats until piece measures 16"/40.5cm from beg.

Sleeve shaping
Note
Work inc sts into chart pats as foll:
For left sleeve With E, 10 (12, 12) sts chart #6; with D, 17 sts chart #7; with A, 8 sts chart #8; with C, 32 sts

chart #9; with B, 14 sts chart #3, p1; with E, 8 sts chart #6.

For right sleeve With A, 14 sts chart #3; with D, 11 sts chart #6; with E, p1, 7 sts chart #3, k1, p1, 7 sts chart #3; with A, 10 (12, 12) sts chart #10; with B, 11 sts chart #11; with C, 17 sts chart #7. Change to larger circular needle. Work inc sts as foll:

For left sleeve Cast on at beg of RS rows, 6 (7, 7) sts 2 (1, 1) times, 4 sts 18 (16, 16) times, 6 (3, 3) sts 1 (7, 7) times for a total of 90 (92, 92) sts cast-on;

For right sleeve Cast on at beg of WS rows, 2 sts 2 (7, 7) times, 4 sts 19 (17, 17) times for a total of 80 (82, 82) sts. After all sts have been cast on,

there are 265 (275, 282) sts on needle. Work even until piece measures 1½"/3.5cm from last cast-on row.

Neck shaping

Next row (RS) Work 130 (133, 137) sts, join 2nd ball of yarn and bind off center 15 (17, 18) sts, work to end. Working both sides at once, bind off from each neck edge 3 sts once, 2 sts once, dec 1 st every other row 5 times. Work even until piece measures 5"/12.5cm from last cast-on row. Mark each end of last row for shoulder seam. On next row, cast on 35 (37, 38) sts at center of row for back neck. Work back, cont in pats as for front, omitting neck shap-

ing, and reversing sleeve shaping by binding off instead of casting on.

FINISHING
Block piece.

Neckband
With RS facing, smaller circular needle and A, pick up and k94 (98, 100) sts around neck edge. Work in k1, p1 rib for 1"/2.5cm. Bind off.

Sleeve cuff
With smaller needles and A, pick up and k36 sts along lower edge of sleeve. Work in k1, p1 rib for 1½ (1½, 2)"/4 (4, 5)cm. Bind off loosely in rib. Sew side and sleeve seams. ●

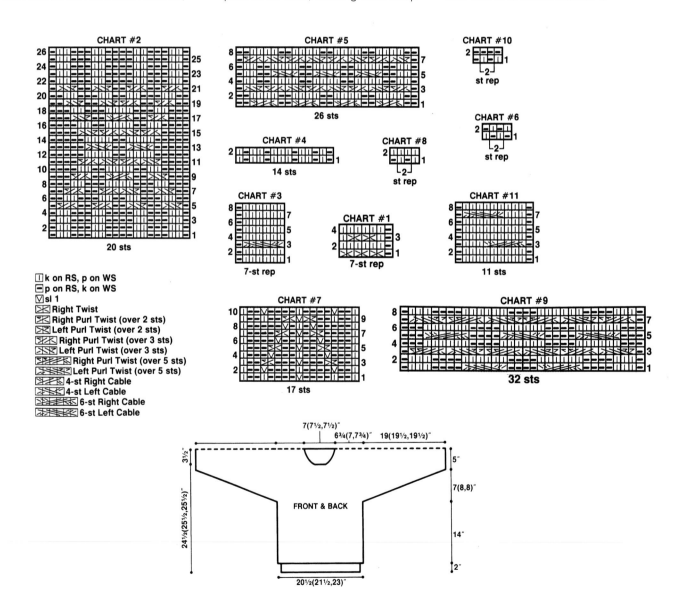

Fair Isle Crew Neck

Marc Jacobs for Perry Ellis gets right to the point in a very oversized, circular-knit Fair Isle crew neck with ⅞ length sleeves and wide cuffs. A quirky stitch change in the ribbing pulls together a shape reminiscent of the designer's "bubble" sweater. Shown in size Medium. The Fair Isle Crew Neck first appeared in the Fall '90 issue of *Vogue Knitting*.

Fair Isle Crew Neck

FOR EXPERIENCED KNITTERS

SIZES
To fit Small (Medium, Large). Directions are for smallest size with larger sizes in parentheses. If there is only one figure it applies to all sizes.

KNITTED MEASUREMENTS
● Bust at underarm 45½ (49, 52½)"/114 (122.5, 131)cm.
● Length 29½ (30½, 31)"/74.5 (77, 78.5)cm.
● Sleeve width at upperarm 20 (21, 22)"/50 (52.5, 55)cm.

MATERIALS
● 10 (11, 12) 3½oz/100g (each 110yd/100m) of Reynolds *Andean Alpaca Regal* (alpaca/wool 5) in #6 ecru (MC)
● 2 balls each in #5 brown (A) and #13 navy (B)
● Sizes 9 and 10 (5.5 and 6mm) circular needles 36"/90cm long OR SIZE TO OBTAIN GAUGE
● Sizes 9 and 10 (5.5 and 6mm) circular needles 16"/40cm long
● Stitch holders and stitch markers

GAUGE
16 sts and 20 rows to 4"/10cm over St st using size 10 (6mm) needles. FOR PERFECT FIT, TAKE TIME TO CHECK GAUGE.

Notes
1 To simulate a circular piece, work a flat swatch on RS rows only by breaking yarn at end of every row and reattaching at beg of row.
2 Body and sleeves of sweater are knit circularly to underarm, then joined at yoke.
3 All chart rnds are worked from right to left.

BODY
With smaller size 36"/90cm needle and MC, cast on 172 (184, 200) sts. Join, taking care not to twist sts on needle. Place marker for end of rnd and sl marker every rnd. Work in k2, p2 rib for 2"/5cm. K next rnd, inc 2 (2, 4) sts evenly around—174 (186, 204) sts. Work in k3, p3 rib for 3"/7.5cm more. K next rnd, inc 8 (10, 6) sts evenly around—182 (196, 210) sts. Change to larger 36"/90cm needle. Work in St st (k every rnd) as foll: Work rnds 1-17 of chart #1. Cont with MC only until piece measures 16 (17, 17½)"/40.5 (43, 44.5)cm from beg. Place sts on a holder.

SLEEVES
With smaller size 16"/40cm needle and MC, cast on 72 (76, 84) sts. Join. Work in k2, p2 rib for 1"/2.5cm. K next rnd, inc 0 (2, 0) sts—72 (78, 84) sts. Work in k3, p3 rib for 2"/5cm more. K next rnd, inc 12 (6, 0) sts evenly around—84 sts. Change to larger 36"/90cm needle. Work rnds 1-17 of chart #1. K next rnd in MC, dec 4 (0, inc 4) sts evenly around—80 (84, 88) sts. Cont in St st with MC until piece measures 13 (13½, 14)"/33 (34, 35.5)cm from beg. Place sts on holder.

YOKE
Next (joining) rnd With larger 36"/90cm needle and MC, k across sts from holders as foll: first 91 (98, 105) sts of body (back), 80 (84, 88) sts of one sleeve, last 91 (98, 105) sts of body (front), 80 (84, 88) sts of 2nd sleeve—342 (364, 386) sts. Join and place marker for beg of rnd. (Note: When too few sts for longer needle, change to 16"/40cm needle.) Work in St st with MC for 4 rnds. K next rnd, dec 6 (12, 2) sts evenly around—336 (352, 384) sts. K 1 rnd. Work rnds 1-15 of chart #2—294 (308, 336) sts. K 1 rnd with MC, inc 3 (0, dec 6) sts evenly around—297 (308, 330) sts. Work rnds 1-13 of chart #3—243 (252, 270) sts.
Next rnd With MC, [k7, k2tog] 27 (28, 30) times—216 (224, 240) sts. Work rnds 1-6 of chart #4.
Next rnd With MC, [k2, k2tog] 52 (56, 60) times, k8 (0, 0)—164 (168, 180) sts. Work rnds 1-6 of chart #5—123 (126, 135) sts. Cont with MC only as foll: K 1 rnd.
Small size only: Next rnd
[K4, k2tog] 18 times, [k3, k2tog]

3 times—102 sts.

Medium size only: Next rnd [K5, k2tog] 18 times—108 sts.

Large size only: Next rnd [K7, k2tog] 15 times—120 sts. K 4 rnds for all sizes.

Next rnd [K1, k2tog] 34 (36, 40) times—68 (72, 80) sts. K next rnd, dec 2 (4, 10) sts evenly around—66 (68, 70) sts. Change to smaller 16"/40cm needle. Work in k1, p1 rib for 1½"/4cm. Bind off.

FINISHING

Block sweater. ●

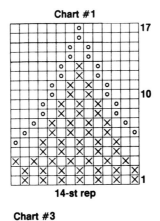

Chart #1
14-st rep

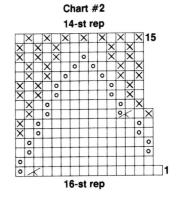

Chart #2
14-st rep
16-st rep

Chart #3
10-st rep 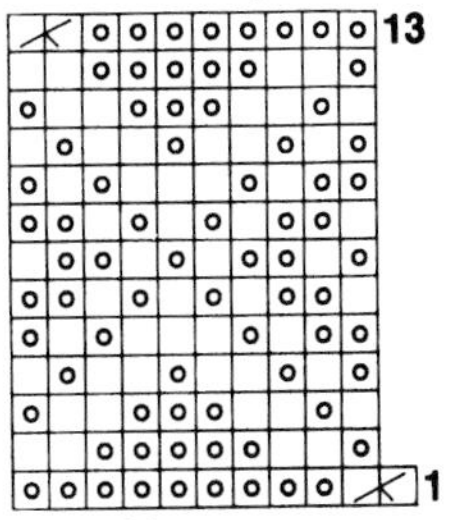
11-st rep

Chart #4 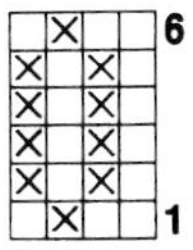
4-st rep

Chart #5 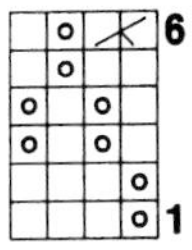
4-st rep

☐ ecru (MC)
☒ brown (A)
⊙ navy (B)
╱ k2tog
⊙╱ With B, k2tog tbl

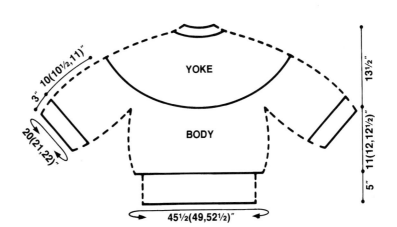

YOKE

BODY

3" 10(10½,11)"

20(21,22)"

13½"

5" 11(12,12½)"

45½(49,52½)"

A summer standout—this pink, sweater-girl pullover is knit in two pieces, with staggered cables, short dolman sleeves, and an applied round and back scooped neck. Designed by Patricia Pastor for Perry Ellis, the top is cropped and very close-fitting for a smart, true-to-form look. Shown in size 34. The Short Top first appeared in the Spring/Summer '88 issue of *Vogue Knitting*.

Short Top

VERY EASY VERY VOGUE

SIZES
To fit 30-32 (34, 36, 38, 40)"/76-81 (86, 91, 96, 101)cm bust. Directions are for smallest size with larger sizes in parentheses. If there is only one set of figures it applies to all sizes.

KNITTED MEASUREMENTS
● Bust at underarm 30 (32½, 35½, 38, 41)"/74 (81, 88, 95, 102)cm.
● Length 16½ (17, 17½, 18½, 19)"/42.5 (44, 45, 48, 49)cm.
● Finished waist 26 (28½, 31½, 34, 37)"/64 (71, 78, 85, 92)cm.
● Width from sleeve edge to sleeve edge (including cuffs) 26¾ (28, 29½, 31, 32¼)"/67 (70.5, 74, 77.5, 81)cm.

MATERIALS
Original Yarn
● 9 (9, 9, 10,11) 1¾oz/50g balls (each approx 66yd/60m) of Crystal Palace *Luxor* (cotton 4) in #1018 hot pink
Substitute Yarn
● 9 (9, 9, 10,11) 1¾oz/50g balls (each approx 70yd/65m) of Crystal Palace *Monterey* (cotton 4) in #018 hot pink
● One pair each sizes 6 and 8 (4 and 5mm) needles OR SIZE TO OBTAIN GAUGE
● Cable needle (cn) and stitch markers
Note
The original yarn used for this sweater is no longer available. A comparable substitute has been made, which is available at the time of printing. Check gauge of substitute yarns carefully before beginning.

GAUGE
20 sts and 26 rows to 4"/10cm over cable pat using size 8 (5mm) needles. FOR PERFECT FIT, TAKE TIME TO CHECK GAUGE.

Notes
1 Pullover is made in two pieces with *front* worked first.
2 Knit first and last st of every row for selvage sts.

STITCH GLOSSARY
Left Cable Sl 3 sts to cn and hold to *front* of work, k3, k3 from cn.

FRONT
With smaller needles, cast on 66 (73, 80, 87, 94) sts. Work in k1, p1 rib for 2½"/6.5cm. Change to larger needles.
Beg cable pat: Row 1 (RS) K1 (selvage st), work 14-st rep of chart 4 (5, 5, 6, 6) times, work first 8 sts of chart 1 (0, 1, 0, 1) time more, p0 (1, 0, 1, 0), k1 (selvage st). Cont in pat until piece measures 7 (7, 7½, 8, 8½)"/18 (18, 19, 20.5, 21.5)cm from beg. Inc 1 st each end (working inc sts into pat) every other row 3 times, every 4th row twice—76 (83, 90, 97, 104) sts and piece measures 9¾ (9¾, 9¾, 10¼, 10¾)"/24 (24, 25, 26.5, 27.5)cm from beg.

Sleeve shaping
Cast on 4 sts at beg of next 12 rows, 3 sts at beg of next 2 rows—130 (137, 144, 151, 158) sts. Place marker each end of last row. Work even until piece measures 3½ (4, 4, 4½, 4½)"/8.5 (10, 10, 11.5, 11.5)cm above markers, end with a WS row.

Neck shaping
Next row (RS) Work 57 (60, 63, 66, 69) sts, join 2nd ball of yarn and bind off 16 (17, 18, 19, 20) sts, work to end. Work both sides at once as foll: Work 1 row even.
Next row (RS) Work to 5 sts before center bound-off sts, k3tog, k2; with 2nd ball of yarn, k2, sl 1-k2tog-psso, work to end.
Next row Work to 5 sts before center, p3tog tbl, p2; with 2nd ball of yarn, p2, p3tog, work to end. Rep last 2 rows until there are 43 (46, 49, 52, 55) sts each side. Work even until piece measures 5 (5½, 5½, 6, 6)"/12.5 (14, 14, 15.5, 15.5)cm above markers. Bind off rem sts.

BACK
Work as for front until piece measures 2 (2½, 2½, 3, 3)"/5 (6.5, 6.5, 8, 8)cm above markers, end with a WS row.

Neck shaping
Next row (RS) Work 58 (61, 64, 67, 70) sts, join 2nd ball of yarn and bind off 14 (15, 16, 17, 18) sts, work to end. Work both sides at once as foll: Work 1 row even.
Next row (RS) Work to 4 sts before center, k2tog, k2; with 2nd ball of yarn, k2, sl 1-k1-psso, work to end.
Next row Work to 4 sts before center, p2tog tbl, p2; with 2nd ball of yarn, p2, p2tog, work to end. Rep last 2 rows until there are 43 (46, 49, 52, 55) sts each side. Work even until same length as front. Bind off rem sts.

FINISHING

Block pieces. Sew shoulder and upper sleeve seams.

Neckband

With smaller needles, cast on 11 sts.
Row 1 (RS) K1 (selvage st), [k1, p1] 4 times, k1, sl 1.
Row 2 P2, [k1, p1] 4 times, k1. Rep last 2 rows until piece fits around entire neck edge. Bind off. Sew side with selvage sts to neck edge. Sew ends of band tog.

Sleeve cuff

With smaller needles, pick up and k48 (52, 52, 56, 56) sts along lower edge of sleeve. Work in k1, p1 rib for ½"/1.5cm. Bind off loosely in rib. Sew side and sleeve seams, including rib cuffs. ●

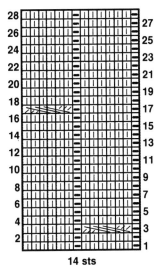

14 sts

☐ k on RS, p on WS
⊟ p on RS, k on WS
▨ Left Cable

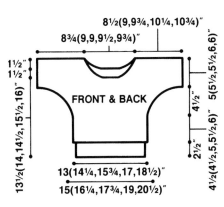

8½(9,9¾,10¼,10¾)"

8¾(9,9,9½,9¾)"

1½"
1½"

FRONT & BACK

5(5½,5½,6,6)"

4½"

13½(14,14,14½,15½,16)"

2½"

4½(4½,5,5½,6)"

13(14¼,15¾,17,18½)"

15(16¼,17¾,19,20½)"

Joan Vass

INNOVATIVE CHOICES OF YARN combined with a contemporary attitude are what make Joan Vass' knits look so modern, so right for now. Vass draws upon her background in the arts to create sweaters that are a triumph of form and function. She is drawn to yarns with both visual and tactile appeal—cashmere and silks; pure cottons; natural fibers blended with superior synthetics. Shunning the trend towards nostalgia, Vass designs sweater styles that look appropriate for the moment. "I like clothes that feel comfortable, look individual and express a social attitude for the proper time and place."

Joan Vass entered the fashion world mid-life, switching from a career in the fine arts and publishing to design by way of a non-profit organization. In the early 1970s, she volunteered her marketing services to a group of struggling artisans, helping them increase sales and distribution by developing modern designs using the finest materials possible. Within this context, Vass discovered her own talent for creating fashions with wide-ranging appeal. Her career as a clothing designer has been flourishing ever since. Joan Vass, Inc., formed in 1977, has grown to include multiple clothing and accessory lines. As a testament to her success, Vass was honored in 1978 by the Smithsonian Institution as an Extraordinary Woman of Fashion. In 1979, she received both the Prix de Cachet and a Coty Award.

Handknits were what brought Joan Vass to the fore of the fashion world. She approaches sweater design with the integrity of an artist, considering self-truth as integral as form and function. Knowing yourself, defining and expressing a self-image and staying true to that image is, in her mind, the only meaningful way to put fashion in your life. By selecting yarns and designing sweaters that please herself, Joan Vass has found a way to please many others.

> She approaches sweater design with the integrity of an artist, considering self-truth as integral as form and function.

Joan Vass takes a simple shape and adds dramatic texture. This easy-to-knit, close-fitting cropped turtleneck is all garter stitch—the "eyelash" texture is created by using two interesting yarns held together. Shown in size Small. The Eyelash Turtleneck first appeared in the Winter '96/97 issue of *Vogue Knitting*.

Eyelash Turtleneck

VERY EASY VERY VOGUE

SIZES
To fit Small (Medium, Large). Directions are for smallest size with larger sizes in parentheses. If there is only one figure it applies to all sizes.

KNITTED MEASUREMENTS
● Bust at underarm 35 (38, 41)"/89 (96.5, 104)cm.
● Length 16 (16½, 17)"/40.5 (42, 43)cm.
● Sleeve width at upperarm 14 (14¾, 15½)"/35.5 (37, 39.5)cm.

MATERIALS
Original Yarn
● 12 (15, 17) .7oz/20g balls (each approx 74yd/67m) of Trendsetter *Shadow* (polyester) in #470 tumbleweed (A)
● 10 (12, 14) 1½oz/50g balls (each approx 88yd/80m) of Ornaghi Filati/Trendsetter *Zeus* (wool/acrylic 4) in primary colors #91 (B)
Substitute Yarn
● 12 (15, 17) .7oz/20g balls (each approx 74yd/67m) of Trendsetter *Shadow* (polyester) in #470 tumbleweed (A)
● 9 (11,12) 1¾oz/50g balls (each approx 105yd/97m) of Ornaghi Filati/Trendsetter *Mirage* (acrylic/polyamide 4) in carnival #5 (B)
● One pair each sizes 9 and 11 (5.5 and 8mm) needles OR SIZE TO OBTAIN GAUGE
● Size 9 (5.5mm) circular needle 16"/40cm long
● Stitch holders

Note
Some of the original yarns used for this sweater are no longer available. A comparable substitute has been made, which is available at the time of printing. Check gauge of substitute yarns very carefully before beginning.

GAUGE
13 sts and 24 rows to 4"/10 cm over garter stitch using larger needles and 1 strand each A and B held tog. FOR PERFECT FIT, TAKE TIME TO CHECK GAUGE.

STITCH GLOSSARY
Garter Stitch Knit each row.

BACK
With smaller needles and 1 strand each A and B held tog, cast on 58 (62, 66) sts. Work in k2, p2 rib for 6"/15cm. Change to larger needles. Work even in garter stitch until piece measures 16 (16½, 17)"/40.5 (42, 43)cm from beg, end with a WS row.
Next row (RS) Bind off 16 (18, 19) sts, work 26 (26, 28) sts and place on a holder, bind off rem 16 (18, 19) sts.

FRONT
Work as for back.

SLEEVES
With smaller needles and 1 strand each A and B held tog, cast on 42 (44, 46) sts. Work in k2, p2 rib for 6"/15cm. Change to larger needles. Work in garter stitch, inc 1 st each side every other row twice—46 (48, 50) sts. Work even until

piece measures 19 (19½, 20)"/48 (49.5, 51)cm from beg. Bind off all sts.

FINISHING
Block pieces to measurements. Sew shoulder seams.

Turtleneck
With RS facing, circular needle and 1 strand each A and B held tog, beg at a shoulder and pick up and k 2 sts, then 26 (26, 28) sts from first stitch holder, 4 sts at other shoulder, then 26 (26, 28) sts from second holder, and 2 sts at beg shoulder—60 (60, 64) sts. Join and work in rnds of k2, p2 rib for 6"/15cm. Bind off in rib. Place markers 7 (7½, 7½)"/18 (19,19.5)cm down from shoulder seams on front and back for armholes. Sew top of sleeves between markers. Sew side and sleeve seams. ●

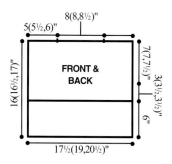

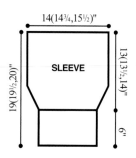

Joan Vass makes an easy-going fashion statement with this cropped, very over-sized pullover with dropped shoulders and casual hood. A perfect, wear-with-everything piece knit with variegated yarn to enhance textural interest. Shown in size Medium/Large. The Cropped Hooded Sweater first appeared in the Winter '94/95 issue of *Vogue Knitting*.

Cropped Hooded Sweater

VERY EASY VERY VOGUE

SIZES
To fit Small (Medium/Large). Directions are for smaller size with larger size in parentheses. If there is only one figure it applies to both sizes.

KNITTED MEASUREMENTS
● Bust at underarm 64 (80)"/162.5 (203)cm.
● Length 18"/46cm.
● Sleeve width at upper arm 13"/33cm.

MATERIALS
Original Yarn
● 5 (7) 1¾oz/50g balls (each approx 143yd/130m) of Lang/Berroco *Calibra* (wool/nylon/mohair 6) in #7091 black ombre
Substitute Yarn
● 5 (7) 1¾oz/50g balls (each approx 148yd/137m) of Unger/JCA *Shades* (wool/nylon/mohair 6) in #39 variegated
● One pair size 11 (8mm) needles OR SIZE TO OBTAIN GAUGE
● Size J/10 (6mm) crochet hook
● Stitch markers
Note
The original yarn used for this sweater is no longer available. A comparable substitute has been made, which is available at the time of printing. Check gauge of substitute yarns very carefully before beginning.

GAUGE
12 sts and 18 rows to 4"/10cm over St st using size 11 (8mm) needles. FOR PERFECT FIT, TAKE TIME TO CHECK GAUGE.

BACK
Cast on 96 (120) sts. Beg with a purl row, work in St st (k on RS, p on WS) until piece measures 18"/46cm from beg. Bind off all sts.

FRONT
Work as for back until piece measures 14"/35.5cm from beg, end with a WS row.

Front opening
Next row (RS) K48 (60) sts, join 2nd ball of yarn and k48 (60) sts. Working both sides at once, work even until piece measures 17"/43cm from beg, end with a WS row.

Neck shaping
Next row (RS) K45 (60); on 2nd side, bind off 8 sts, work to end.
Next row (WS) P40 (52); on 2nd side bind off 8 sts, work to end.
Next row (RS) K40 (52); on 2nd side, bind off 8 sts, work to end.
Next row (WS) K32 (44); on 2nd side, bind off 8 sts, work to end. Bind off rem 32 (44) sts each side.

SLEEVES
Cast on 30 sts. Beg with a purl row, work in St st, AT SAME TIME, inc 1 st each side every 8th row 5 times—40 sts. Work even until sleeve measures 9½"/24.5cm from beg. Bind off all sts.

FINISHING
Block pieces. Sew shoulder seams.

Hood
With RS facing, beg at right front neck edge, pick up and k16 sts to shoulder, 32 sts along back neck, 16 sts to left front neck edge—64 sts. Beg with a purl row, work even in St st until piece measures 14"/35.5cm from beg, end with a WS row.

Top of hood shaping
Bind off 24 sts at beg of next 2 rows—16 sts. Work even until center of hood measures 8"/20.5cm from bound-off edges. Bind off 16 sts. Sew bound-off sts to each side of center section, easing to fit. Place markers 6½"/16.5cm down from shoulders on front and back. Sew straight edge of sleeves between markers. Sew side and sleeve seams. Make front ties as foll: With RS facing and hook, join yarn 1"/2.5cm above beg of hood at center front edge. Ch 20. Turn and work sl st in each ch to beg. Fasten off. ●

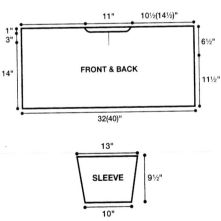

The diagonal, V-front sweater takes on a figure flattering shape and drape by cleverly increasing and decreasing in ribbing at the same time. Variegated yarn gives this close-fitting, long sleeve pullover a modern appeal. Shown in size Small. The Diagonal V-Front Sweater first appeared in the Spring/Summer '96 issue of *Vogue Knitting*.

Diagonal V-Front Sweater

FOR INTERMEDIATE KNITTERS

SIZES
To fit Small (Medium, Large). Directions are for smallest size with larger sizes in parentheses. If there is only one figure it applies to all sizes.

KNITTED MEASUREMENTS
● Bust at underarm 35 (38, 41)"/89 (96.5, 104)cm.
● Length 17½ (18, 18½)"/44.5 (45.5, 47)cm.
● Sleeve width at upper arm 13 (14, 15½)"/33 (35.5, 39.51)cm.

MATERIALS
● 6 (7, 7) 1¾oz/50g balls (each approx 150yd/135m) of Tahki Yarns *Hand Dyed Cotton Ribbon* (cotton/nylon 4) in #38 Egyptian
● One pair size 9 (5.5mm) needles OR SIZE TO OBTAIN GAUGE
● Size 9 (5.5mm) circular needle 16"/40cm long
● Stitch markers and holders

GAUGE
18 sts and 26 rows to 4"/10cm over k2, p2 rib (slightly stretched), using size 9 (5.5mm) needles. FOR PERFECT FIT, TAKE TIME TO CHECK GAUGE.

BACK
With size 9 (5.5mm) needles, cast on 98 (106, 114) sts. Work in k2, p2 rib as foll:
Row 1 (RS) [K2, p2] 12 (13, 14) times, place marker, k2, place marker, [p2, k2] 12 (13, 14) times.
Row 2 and all WS rows K the knit sts and p the purl sts.
Row 3 K2, m1, rib to 2 sts before marker, k2tog, sl marker, k2, sl marker, k2tog, rib to last 2 sts, m1, k2. Rep rows 2 and 3, working inc and dec sts into k2, p2 rib, until piece measures 17½ (18, 18½)"/44.5 (45.5, 47)cm from beg (measure at center of work). Bind off 30 (33, 36) sts at beg of next 2 rows for shoulders. Place rem 38 (40, 42) sts on a holder for back neck.

FRONT
Work as for back.

SLEEVES
With size 9 (5.5mm) needles, cast on 42 (42, 46) sts. Work in k2, p2 rib as foll:
Row 1 (RS) K0 (0, 2), [k2, p2] 5 times, place marker, k2, place marker, [p2, k2] 5 times, k0 (0, 2).
Row 2 and all WS rows K the knit sts and p the purl sts.
Row 3 K2, m1, rib to 2 sts before marker, k2tog, sl marker, k2, sl marker, k2tog, rib to last 2 sts, m1, k2. Rep rows 2 and

3, working inc and dec sts into k2, p2 rib, AT THE SAME TIME, inc 2 sts (instead of 1) each side every 6th row 16 (18, 20) times—74 (78, 86) sts. Work even until piece measures 18 (18½, 19)"/45.5 (47, 48)cm from beg (measure at center of work). Bind off all sts.

FINISHING
Sew shoulder seams.

Neckband
With RS facing and circular needle, beg at one shoulder, pick up 2 sts in shoulder seam, rib across sts of one holder, pick up 2 sts at other shoulder seam, rib across sts on 2nd holder. Join and cont in k2, p2 rib for ¾"/2cm. Bind off in rib. Place markers 6½ (7, 7¾)"/16.5 (18, 19.5)cm down from shoulder seams on front and back for armholes. Sew top of sleeves between markers. Sew side and sleeve seams. ●

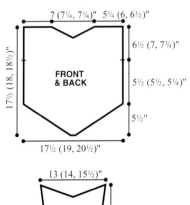

7 (7¼, 7¼)"   5¼ (6, 6½)"
6½ (7, 7¾)"
FRONT & BACK
17½ (18, 18½)"
5½ (5½, 5¼)"
5½"
17½ (19, 20½)"

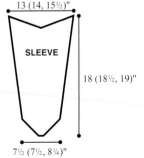

13 (14, 15½)"
SLEEVE
18 (18½, 19)"
7½ (7½, 8¼)"

This ultra-cool cropped tank top is a breeze to knit in variegated yarn. It's close-fitting with knit shoulder straps, back buttoned closure and angled armholes. Shown in size Small. The Tank Top first appeared in the Spring/Summer '96 issue of *Vogue Knitting*.

Tank Top

VERY EASY VERY VOGUE

SIZES
To fit Small (Medium, Large). Directions are for smallest size with larger sizes in parentheses. If there is only one figure it applies to all sizes.

KNITTED MEASUREMENTS
● Bust at underarm 33 (35, 37)"/83.5 (89, 94)cm.
● Length 15 (15¼, 15½)"/38 (39, 39.5)cm.

MATERIALS
Original Yarn
● 3 (4, 4) 1¾oz/50g balls (each approx 148yd/133m) of Trendsetter *Horizon* (cotton/linen/polyamide 4) in #1
Substitute Yarn
● 3 (4, 4) 1¾oz/50g balls (each approx 153yd/140m) of Zitron/Skacel *Feelings Multi* (cotton/polyamide 4) in #01 warm pastel tones
● One pair size 6 (4mm) needles OR SIZE TO OBTAIN GAUGE
● Size J (6mm) crochet hook
● One small button
● Stitch holders
Note
The original yarn used for this sweater is no longer available. A comparable substitute has been made, which is available at the time of printing. Check gauge of substitute yarns very carefully before beginning.

GAUGE
18 sts and 28 rows to 4"/10cm over St st using size 6 (4mm) needles. FOR PERFECT FIT, TAKE TIME TO CHECK GAUGE.

BACK
With size 10 (6mm) needles, cast on 74 (78, 84) sts *loosely*. Work in St st for 6½"/16.5cm, end with a WS row.

Armhole shaping
Dec 1 st each side on next row, then every other row 17 (20, 25) times more, every 4th row 4 (3, 1) times, AT SAME TIME, when armhole measures 4½ (4¾, 5)"/11.5 (12, 1.5)cm, divide work in half for back neck opening and work both sides at once with separate balls of yarn, until all decs are completed, armhole measures 7½ (7¾, 8)"/19 (19.5, 20.5)cm. Place 15 sts each side on holders.

FRONT
Work as for back to armhole.

Armhole and neck shaping
Dec 1 st each side on next row, then every other row 18 (19, 22) times more, every 4th row 1 (1, 0) times, AT SAME TIME, when armhole measures 4½ (4¾, 5)"/11.5 (12, 12.5)cm, shape neck as foll: bind off center 14 (16, 18) sts and working both sides at once with separate balls of yarn, bind off from each neck edge 4 sts once, 3 sts once, 2 sts once. Fasten off last st each side.

FINISHING
Do not block. Sew side seams, leaving 1"/2.5cm open at lower edge for slits.

Neck and shoulder band
With RS facing and size 10 (6mm) needles, beg at right back neck, k across 15 sts of holder, cast on 13 sts, pick up and k46 (48, 50) sts evenly around front neck, cast on 13 sts, k across 15 sts of left back holder. Work in St st for 2"/5cm. Bind off *loosely*. Fold band in half to WS and sew in place. With RS facing and crochet hook, work a rnd of sc around lower edge of top, including side slits and around armhole and shoulder bands. Sc along back neck opening and make a chain 3 buttonloop at top of left back neckband. Sew button on right back neckband opposite loop. ●

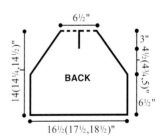

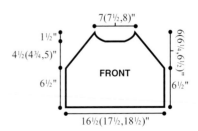

Joan Vass

Joan Vass incorporates great-looking family values into these casual classics with allover cable patterns, drop shoulders and rolled edges. All very wearable and very easy to knit. The Family Cable Pullovers first appeared in the Spring/Summer '95 issue of *Vogue Knitting*. Woman's pullover shown in size Medium. Man's or woman's oversized pullover shown in size Medium. Child's pullover shown in size 6.

Family Cable Pullovers

WOMAN'S PULLOVER

VERY EASY VERY VOGUE

SIZES
To fit Small (Medium, Large). Directions are for smallest size with larger sizes in parentheses. If there is only one figure it applies to all sizes.

KNITTED MEASUREMENTS
● Bust at underarm 44 (46½, 49)"/112 (118, 124.5)cm.
● Length 26 (27, 28)"/66 (68.5, 71)cm.
● Sleeve width at upper arm 18 (18, 19)"/46 (46, 48.5)cm.

MATERIALS
Original Yarn
● 13 (14, 15) 1¾oz/50g balls (each approx 100yd/90m) of Filatura di Crosa/Stacy Charles *Indiana* (cotton 4) in #10 blue/black
Substitute Yarn
● 17 (18, 19) 1¾oz/50g balls (each approx 157yd/145m) of Stahl Wolle/Tahki *Bari* (cotton/acrylic 3) in #602 black
● One pair size 8 (5mm) needles OR SIZE TO OBTAIN GAUGE
● Size 8 (5mm) circular needle 16"/40cm
● Cable needle
● Stitch markers

Note
The original yarn used for this sweater is no longer available. A comparable substitute has been made, which is available at the time of printing. Check gauge of substitute yarns very carefully before beginning.

GAUGE
18 sts and 28 rows to 4"/10cm over St st with 2 strands of yarn using size 8 (5mm) needles.
25 sts and 28 rows to 4"/10cm over cable pat with 2 strands of yarn using size 8 (5mm) needles.
To work gauge swatch Cast on 25 sts. Work 28 rows in cable pat, marking rows 5 and 17. Measure piece across either marked row. FOR PERFECT FIT, TAKE TIME TO CHECK GAUGES.

Note
Use 2 strands of yarn held together throughout.

STITCH GLOSSARY
Cable Pat (multiple of 8 sts plus 1 extra)
Foundation row (WS) K1, *p7, k1; rep from*.
Rows 1 and 3 (RS) P1, *k7, p1; rep from*.
Rows 2 and 4 (WS) K1, *p7, k1; rep from*.
Row 5 P1, *sl 4 sts to cable needle and hold to *back* of work, k3; k4 from cn, p1; rep from *.
Row 6-16 Work the sts as they face you by k the knit sts and p the purl sts.
Row 17 Rep row 5. Rep rows 6-17 for cable pat.

BACK
With 2 strands of yarn, cast on 137 (145, 153) sts. Beg with foundation row, work in cable pat until piece measures 25½ (26½, 27½)"/65 (67, 70)cm from beg, end with a WS row.

Neck shaping
Next row (RS) Work across 40 (43, 47)

sts, join 2nd ball of yarn and bind off 57 (59, 59) sts, work to end. Working both sides at once, work 3 rows even. Bind off.

FRONT
Work as for back.

SLEEVES
With 2 strands of yarn, cast on 65 (73, 73) sts. Beg with foundation row, work in cable pat, AT SAME TIME, inc 1 st each side (working inc sts into cable pat) every 4th row 20 (10, 18) times, every 6th row 4 (10, 5) times—113 (113, 119) sts. Work even until piece measures 17 (17½, 18)"/43.5 (44.5, 46)cm from beg. Bind off all sts.

FINISHING
Block pieces lightly. Sew shoulder seams.

Rolled neck
With RS facing, circular needle and 2 strands of yarn, pick up and k63 (65, 65) sts along back neck, 63 (65, 65) sts along front neck—126 (130, 130) sts. Place marker, join and k every rnd until rolled neck measures 1½"/4cm. Bind off loosely. Place markers 9 (9, 9½)"/23 (23, 24.5)cm down from shoulders on front and back for armholes. Sew top of sleeves between markers. Sew side seams, leaving 4½"/11.5cm open at lower edge for side slits. Sew sleeve seams. ●

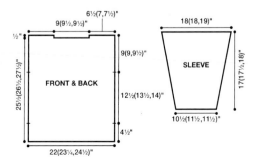

MAN'S PULLOVER

VERY EASY VERY VOGUE

SIZES
To fit Small (Medium, Large, X-Large); Perfect Plus sizes [Plus ½, Plus 3]. Directions are for smallest size with larger sizes in parentheses. If there is only one figure it applies to all sizes.

KNITTED MEASUREMENTS
- Chest at underarm 44 (47, 50, 52)"/112 (119.5, 127, 132)cm; [56, 60"/142, 152cm].
- Length 26 (27, 28, 28½)"/66 (68.5, 71, 72.5)cm; [29, 29½"/73.5, 75cm].
- Sleeve width at upper arm 19 (20, 21, 22)"/48 (51, 53, 56)cm; [21, 22"/53, 56cm].

MATERIALS
Original Yarn
- 18 (19, 20, 21) [21, 22] 1¾oz/50g balls (each approx 92yd/85m) of Pingouin *Corossol* (cotton/acrylic 5) in #02 cream

Substitute Yarn
- 16 (17, 18, 18) [18, 19] 3½oz/100g skeins (each approx 215yd/198m) of Brown Sheep *Cotton Fleece* (cotton/wool 5) in #CW105 putty
- One pair size 9 (5.5mm) needles OR SIZE TO OBTAIN GAUGE
- Size 9 (5.5mm) circular needle 16"/40cm long
- Cable needle
- Stitch markers

Note
The original yarn used for this sweater is no longer available. A comparable substitute has been made, which is available at the time of printing. Check gauge of substitute yarns very carefully before beginning.

GAUGE
16 sts and 22 rows to 4"/10cm over St st with 2 strands of yarn using size 9 (5.5mm) needles.

25 sts to 4½"/11.5cm and 22 rows to 4"/10cm over cable pat with 2 strands of yarn using size 9 (5.5mm) needles.
To work gauge swatch Cast on 25 sts. Work 22 rows in cable pat, marking rows 5 and 15. Measure piece across either marked row. FOR PERFECT FIT, TAKE TIME TO CHECK GAUGES.

Note
Use 2 strands of yarn held together throughout.

STITCH GLOSSARY
See Woman's Cable Pullover pat for cable pat.

Note for Perfect Plus sizes only
Unless otherwise specified, foll all instructions as given for regular sizes. Numbers for Perfect Plus sizes are in brackets. If there is only one number or one set of instructions it applies to both Perfect Plus sizes.

BACK
With 2 strands of yarn, cast on 121 (129, 137, 145) [153, 161] sts.
For regular sizes only Beg with foundation row, work in cable pat until piece measures 25½ (26½, 27½, 28)"/65 (67.5, 70, 71)cm from beg, end with a WS row.
For perfect plus sizes only: Beg pat P[4, 8], place marker (pm), work foundation row of cable pat over 145 sts, pm, p[4, 8]. Working first and last [4, 8] sts in rev St st, cont in pat until piece measures [18½"/47cm] from beg, end with a WS row. Bind off [4, 8] sts at beg of next 2 rows—[145] sts. Work even until armhole is [10½, 11"/27, 28cm] from beg, end with a WS row.

Neck shaping
For all sizes: Next row (RS) Work across 38 (40, 43, 45) [45] sts, join 2nd ball of yarn and bind off 45 (49, 51, 55) [55] sts, work to end. Working both sides at once, work 2 rows even. Bind off all sts.

FRONT
Work as for back.

SLEEVES
With 2 strands of yarn, cast on 65 (65, 73, 73) [73] sts. Beg with foundation row, work in cable pat, AT SAME TIME, inc 1 st each side (working inc sts into cable pat) every 4th row 10 (18, 15, 16) [15, 16] times, every 6th row 10 (5, 7, 8) [7, 8] times—105 (111, 117, 121) [117, 121] sts. Work even until piece measures 19 (19½, 20, 21)"/48 (49.5, 51, 53)cm [19, 20"/48, 51cm] from beg. Bind off all sts.

FINISHING
Block pieces lightly. Sew shoulder seams.

Rolled neck
With RS facing, circular needle and 2 strands of yarn, pick up and k50 (53, 55, 59) [59] sts along back neck, 50 (53, 55, 59) [59] sts along front neck—100 (106, 110, 118) [118] sts. Place marker, join and k every rnd until rolled neck measures 1½"/4cm [1½"/4cm]. Bind off loosely.

For regular sizes Place markers 9½ (10, 10½, 11)"/24.5 (25.5, 26.5, 28)cm down from shoulders on front and back for armholes. Sew top of sleeves between markers.

For plus sizes only Sew top of sleeves to straight edge of armholes. Sew bound-off body sts to side edges of sleeves.

For all sizes Sew side seams, leaving 4½"/11.5cm [5"/12cm] open at lower edge for side slit. Sew sleeve seams. ●

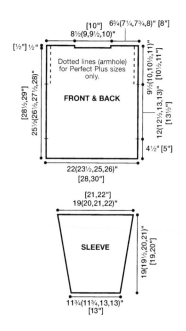

CHILD'S PULLOVER

SIZES
To fit size 4 (6, 8, 10) or 23 (25, 27, 29)"/58 (63, 68, 73)cm chest. Directions are for smallest size with larger sizes in parentheses. If there is only one figure it applies to all sizes.

KNITTED MEASUREMENTS
● Chest at underarm 30 (33, 36, 39)"/76.5 (84, 91.5, 99)cm.
● Length 15½ (16½, 18, 19)"/39.5 (42, 45.5, 48)cm.
● Sleeve width at upper arm 10 (11, 12, 13)"/25.5 (28, 30.5, 33)cm.

MATERIALS
Original Yarn
● 7 (8, 9, 10) 1¾oz/50g balls (each approx 92yd/85m) of Pingouin *Corossol* (cotton/acrylic 5) in #12 black
Substitute Yarn
● 6 (8, 8, 10) 3½oz/100g skeins (each approx 215yd/198m) of Brown Sheep *Cotton Fleece* (cotton/wool 5) in #CW005 cavern
● One pair size 9 (5.5mm) needles OR SIZE TO OBTAIN GAUGE
● Cable needle and stitch markers
Note
The original yarn used for this sweater is no longer available. A comparable substitute has been made, which is available at the time of printing. Check gauge of substitute yarns very carefully before beginning.

GAUGE
16 sts and 22 rows to 4"/10cm over St st with 2 strands of yarn using size 9 (5.5mm) needles.
25 sts to 4½"/11.5cm and 22 rows to 4"/10cm over cable pat with 2 strands of yarn using size 9 (5.5mm) needles.
To work gauge swatch Cast on 25 sts. Work 22 rows in cable pat, marking rows 5 and 15. Measure piece across either marked row. FOR PERFECT FIT, TAKE TIME TO CHECK GAUGES.

Note
Use 2 strands of yarn held together throughout.

STITCH GLOSSARY
Cable Pat (multiple of 8 sts plus 1 extra)
Foundation row (WS) K1,*p7, k1; rep from*.
Rows 1 and 3 (RS) P1, *k7, p1; rep from*.
Rows 2 and 4 K1, *p7, k1; rep from *.
Row 5 P1, *sl 4 sts to cable needle and hold to back of work, k3; k4 from cn, p1; rep from *.
Rows 6-14 Work the sts as they face you by k the knit sts and p the purl sts.
Row 15 Rep row 5. Rep rows 6-15 for cable pat.

BACK
With 2 strands of yarn, cast on 83 (91, 99, 107) sts.
Beg pat: Foundation row (WS) K1, place marker (pm), work foundation row cable pat to last st, pm, k1. Work first and last st in rev St st (p on RS, k on WS) and work rem sts in cable pat until piece measures 15 (16, 17½, 18½)"/38 (41, 44.5, 47)cm from beg, end with a WS row.

Neck shaping
Next row (RS) Work across 22 (25, 29, 31) sts, join 2nd ball of yarn and bind off 39 (41, 41, 45) sts, work to end. Working both sides at once, work 3 rows even. Bind off all sts.

FRONT
Work as for back until piece measures 14 (15, 16½, 17½)"/35.5 (38, 42, 44.5)cm from beg, end with a WS row.

Neck shaping
Next row (RS) Work across 24 (27, 31, 33) sts, join 2nd ball of yarn and bind off 35 (37, 37, 41) sts, work to end. Working both sides at once, work 1 row even. Dec 1 st at each neck edge every other row twice—22 (25, 29, 31) sts. Work even and when piece measures same as back to shoulder, bind off all sts.

SLEEVES
(Note: For size 6 (8) only, work first and last 3 (6) sts in St st until they can be worked into cable pat.)
With 2 strands of yarn, cast on 49 (55, 61, 65) sts.
Beg pat: Foundation row (WS) P0 (3, 6, 0), pm, work foundation row on next 49 (49, 49, 65) sts, pm, end p0 (3, 6, 0). Cont in cable pat, AT SAME TIME, inc 1 st each side (working inc sts into cable pat) every other row 2 (2, 1, 1) times, every 4th row 4 (4, 5, 5) times—55 (61, 67, 71) sts. Work even and when sleeve measures 4 (4, 4½, 5)"/10 (10, 11.5, 13)cm from beg, bind off all sts.

FINISHING
Block pieces lightly. Sew shoulder seams. Place markers 5 (5½, 6½, 7)"/12.5 (14, 16.5, 18)cm down from shoulders on front and back for armholes. Sew top of sleeves between markers. Sew side and sleeve seams. If desired, work 1 row sc evenly around neck edge. ●

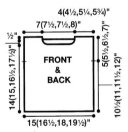

The Innovators

MANY OF TODAY'S most prestigious designers have applied their talents to creating exquisite knit fashions. Thanks to them, *Vogue Knitting* has been able to continuously provide readers with some of the most stylish sweaters of the day. To round out this presentation, we have selected some of our most popular patterns to demonstrate the quality and diversity of today's designer knits. Here are five designers who have made an extraordinary contribution to the knitting craft. Michael Simon, Todd Oldham, Cynthia Rowley, Anna Sui, and Betty Jackson have each lent their distinct sensibility and fashion flair to sweater design.

You'll see here that fashion is not about one idea or mood. Each designer brings his or her unique vision to their sweater creations. Some go for understatement while others have a more dramatic approach. What they all have in common, though, is the ability to combine unique yarns, clever stitchery, appliqués and embroidery, with timeless design and an exceptional attention to detail to create head-turning looks that make designer knits stand out from the rest.

Bright, inventive themes and dimensional flourishes set Michael Simon's sweaters apart. Early in his career, Simon was known for designs with simple, clean lines and bold colors. More recently, he has built a reputation for novel-

ty looks, incorporating embroidery, appliqué and crochet in classic silhouettes. His fanciful, embellished sweaters, often decorated with quirky motifs, appeal to women of all ages, and are great for evening as well as day wear.

Todd Oldham is one of the most visible forces in the fashion world today. Believing that fashion should always charm, Oldham designs sweaters that are sweetly sexy, with a whimsical yet sophisticated attitude. Born in Corpus Christi, Texas, Oldham and his family moved constantly to keep up with the demands of his father's career, including two years spent living in Iran. This experience affected him greatly, removing any fear of trying something new and different. After graduation, Oldham, whose grandmother taught him to sew when he was only 9 years old, took 41 yards of white cotton jersey, dyed it and created a small collection which he then sold to Neiman Marcus. Since then, Oldham and his partner, Tony Longoria, have headed a thriving fashion business whose designs are highly regarded worldwide.

Cynthia Rowley is recognized throughout the world for the wit, originality and sophistication of her sweaters. With artful stitches and an exquisite palette, she has found a way to lend a fresh face to classic styles. In

> You'll see here that fashion is not about one idea or mood. Each designer brings his or her unique vision to their sweater creations.

1995, Rowley was honored by the Council of Fashion Designers of America as the recipient of the New Fashion Talent award. Today, she is considered one of the hottest talents in contemporary fashion design.

An Anna Sui creation is as nostalgic as it is innovative. Shunning the fashion dictates of the day, Sui designs for herself, incorporating some fantasy into her

Cynthia Rowley

Anna Sui

Michael Simon

Award-winning British designer Betty Jackson creates offbeat yet highly wearable sweaters. The bold and graphic patterning of her knitwear makes a thoroughly modern impression, while exquisite yarns lend texture and surface interest. Since establishing her own company in 1981, Jackson has sold clothes worldwide, with multiple design lines ranging from womenswear to menswear and accessories. In 1987, Britain's Royal Society of the Arts awarded Jackson the title of Royal Designer for Industry. In the same year, Jackson received a Member of the British Empire (MBE) from Queen Elizabeth for her contribution to the fashion industry.

Today's top fashion designers continue to find fresh inspiration and exciting possibilities in the knitting craft. From the whimsical embellishments of a Michael Simon creation to the classic subtlety of a Cynthia Rowley, designers continue to bring distinction and artistry to knitwear. The following sweaters were chosen to illustrate the incredible quality and variety of designer fashion knits. Sweaters to adapt to your own personal style, as fun to knit as they are to wear.

Here are five great designers who have made an extraordinary contribution to the knitting craft.

self-perception: she designs clothes she "imagines" she would wear if she were a towering blonde or a small-framed man. After a modest beginning designing sportswear and styling for fashion photographer Steven Meisel, Sui's career took off in 1980 after a small yet highly successful show of her work. Sui has since gained international prominence and fashion stardom, with devotees including many well-known names in the entertainment and fashion industry.

Betty Jackson

Todd Oldham

Playful sophistication with a festive holiday spirit—dancing gingerbread people and cookie cut-outs decorate this boxy, body-skimming cardigan trimmed with twisted, bi-color cording. The cardigan is oversized, with raglan armholes and applied, embroidered, and beaded gingerbread motifs. Shown in size Medium. The Gingerbread Cookie Cardigan first appeared in the Winter '92 issue of *Vogue Knitting*.

Gingerbread Cookie Cardigan

FOR EXPERIENCED KNITTERS

SIZES
To fit Small (Medium, Large). Directions are for smallest size with larger sizes in parentheses. If there is only one figure it applies to all sizes.

KNITTED MEASUREMENTS
- Bust at underarm (buttoned) 42 (46, 50)"/106.5 (117, 127)cm.
- Length 19½ (20½, 21½)"/49.5 (52, 54.5)cm.
- Sleeve width at upper arm 16 (17, 17¾)"/41.5 (43, 45)cm.

MATERIALS
- 10 (11, 13) 1¾oz/50g balls (each approx 110yd/100m) of Reynolds *Paterna Handknitting Yarn* (wool 3) in #50 black (MC)
- 1 ball in #5 white (CC)
- 19 8yd/7.4m skeins of *Paternayan® Persian Yarn* (wool) in #424 brown (A)
- 6 skeins in #261 white (B)
- 12 skeins in #220 black (C)
- 1 skein each in #311 purple (D), #591 turquoise (E), #612 green (F), #726 yellow (G), #942 pink (H), and #969 red (J)
- Four ¾"/20mm buttons
- 16 beads each 14mm, 13 each in 10mm, 37 each in 8mm in assorted colors
- Bugle beads and strung beads, small amount each in red, blue and green
- Matching sewing thread
- One pair each sizes 2, 4, and 7

(2.75, 3.5, and 4.5mm) needles OR SIZE TO OBTAIN GAUGE
- Cable needle (cn) or dpn
- Sizes B/1 and E/4 (2 and 3.5mm) crochet hooks

GAUGE
21 sts and 29 rows to 4"/10cm over St st with MC using size 7 (4.5mm) needles. 32 sts and 44 rows to 4"/10cm over St st with single strand of Persian Yarn using size 2 (2.75mm) needles. FOR PERFECT FIT, TAKE TIME TO CHECK GAUGES.

Note
To aid in seaming, k first and last st of every row for selvage sts. Do not count these sts when measuring pieces.

BACK
With size 7 (4.5mm) needles and MC, cast on 105 (115, 125) sts. Work in St st, inc 1 st each side every 14th row 3 times—111 (121, 131) sts. Work even until piece measures 11 (11½, 12)"/28 (29, 30.5)cm from beg, end with a WS row.

Raglan armhole shaping
Bind off 2 sts at beg of next 2 rows. Work 2 rows even.
Dec row K2, sl next 2 sts to cn and hold at *back*, with cn parallel to LH needle, k next st tog with first st from cn, k next st tog with 2nd st from cn (2-st back dec); k to last 6 sts, sl next 2 sts to cn and hold at *front*, with cn parallel to LH needle, k first st from cn tog with next st on LH needle, k 2nd st from cn

tog with next st on LH needle (2-st front dec), k2. Rep dec row every 4th row 10 times more, then every other row 8 (10, 12) times—31 (33, 35) sts. Bind off.

LEFT FRONT
(Note: Read through instructions before beg.) With size 7 (4.5mm) needles and MC, cast on 55 (60, 65) sts. Work in St st for 6 rows. Inc 1 st at end of next (RS) row (center front edge). Rep inc every 6th row once more, AT SAME TIME, inc 1 st at beg of RS rows (side edge) every 14th row 3 times, AT SAME TIME, when piece measures 3"/7.5cm from beg work buttonholes at center front edge as foll:
Next row (RS) K to last 4 sts, join 2nd ball of yarn, work to end. Cont to work both sides at once for 5 rows for vertical buttonhole. On next row, rejoin piece and work with single strand, rep buttonhole 3 times more every 3½ (3¾, 4¼)"/9 (9.5, 10.5)cm, AT SAME TIME, when piece measures 11 (11½, 12)"/28 (29, 30.5)cm from beg and there are 60 (65, 70) sts, end with a WS row.

Raglan armhole shaping
Bind off 2 sts at beg of next RS row (armhole edge). Work 3 rows even. Work 2-st back dec at beg of next RS row, then every 4th row 8 times more, then every 2nd row 9 (11, 13) times, AT SAME TIME, when center front edge measures 17¼ (18¼, 19¼)"/44 (46.5, 49)cm, end with a RS row.

Neck shaping
Next row (WS) Bind off 7 (8, 9) sts

(neck edge), work to end. Cont to bind off from neck edge 5 sts twice, 3 sts once, and 2 sts once.

RIGHT FRONT

Work right front to correspond to left front, reversing all shaping, working 2-st front dec at end of RS rows for raglan shaping, and omitting buttonholes.

LEFT SLEEVE

With size 7 (4.5mm) needles and MC, cast on 49 (51, 53) sts. Work in St st, inc 1 st each side every 6th row 18 (19, 20) times—85 (89, 93) sts. Work even until piece measures 17 (17½, 18)"/43 (44.5, 45.5)cm from beg.

Raglan cap shaping

Bind off 2 sts at beg of next 2 rows. Work 2-st back dec (beg of RS rows) every 4th row 9 (10, 11) times, then [every 2nd row once, every 4th row once] 8 times, AT SAME TIME, work 2-st front dec (end of RS rows) every 4th row 2 (3, 4) times, then [every 2nd row once, every 4th row once] 15 times, then from same (left side) edge, bind off (on WS rows) 5 sts once and 4 sts twice.

RIGHT SLEEVE

Work to correspond to left sleeve, reversing decs for raglan cap shaping.

FINISHING

Block cardigan pieces. Sew raglan sleeve caps to raglan armholes. Sew side and sleeve seams.

Facings

(Note: Wind C into double strand balls for working.) With size 4 (3.5mm) needles and 2 strands of C held tog, cast on 242 (266, 290) sts for lower edge facing. Work in k1, p1 rib for 1¼"/3cm. Bind off loosely in rib. Work 2 sleeve facings by casting on 64 (66, 68) sts, and working in rib as for lower edge facing. Work neckband facing by casting on 160 (168, 172) sts, and working in rib as for lower edge facing. Work right front

band facing by casting on 10 sts. Work in rib as for lower edge facing for 6 rows, inc 2 sts at beg of next row. Cont in rib on 12 sts until band measures 16 (17, 18)"/40.5 (43, 45.5)cm from beg. Bind off. Work left front facing in same manner as right front facing, working vertical buttonholes to correspond to buttonholes on left front. (Note: Front facings begin at top of lower edge facing.) With WS tog, pin facings to inside edges of cardigan. From RS, with size E/4 (3.5mm) hook and MC, sc facings to cardigan. Do not fasten off.

Chain edging

Cont with MC, insert hook ½"/1.5cm from outside edge of cardigan and work edging as foll: *[Pull up a lp] twice, yo and through 3 lps, ch 4, skip about 1"/2.5cm and insert hook, rep from * working 2 sc in each corner; at end of rnd, join. Work edging around all edges of cardigan and along lower edge of each sleeve. With matching thread, sew inside edges of facings in place. Sew buttons to WS of right front, opposite buttonholes.

Cording

With CC, make twisted cords for edging as foll: Knot 3 strands cut to specified length tog at each end. Slip one end over a doorknob, slip a pencil or knitting needle through other end. Turn strands clockwise until they are tightly twisted. Keeping strands taut, fold piece in half. Remove pencil and allow the cords to twist onto themselves. For sleeves, cut 3 lengths each 42 (43, 44)"/106.5 (109, 112)cm. For outer edging, cut 3 lengths each 11½ (12½, 13)yd/9.5 (11.5, 12)m. Weave cords in and out of ch edging. Tack ends to WS.

Motifs

Wind A into single strand balls for working. With size 2 (2.75mm) needles and single strand of A, work 19 motifs from charts as foll: Work 1 each of A, C, and G: 2 each of E and F: and 6 each of B and D. Work in rev St st, dec by work-

ing 2 sts tog, inc by casting on at end of last row worked as indicated on charts. Block motifs. With size B/1 (2mm) hook, and single strand of A, work 1 rnd of sc around each motif.

ASSEMBLY
Embroidery and beading

Foll schematics, sew motifs in place with thread, turning under sc edge. Sew on beads and embroider in satin st on motifs as foll:

A Use 2 size 8mm beads for eyes, 2 size 8mm for buttons. Embroider hair with G, belt with H, mouth and hands with J. With D, work 5 French knots along lower edge of body.

B1 and B2 Use 2 size 14mm beads for buttons, 2 size 8mm beads for eyes, 1 small strung bead for nose. Embroider right hand, feet and forehead squiggles with B.

B3 Use 2 size 14mm beads for buttons, 2 size 8mm beads for eyes, red and green bugle beads sewn randomly in groups of 2 for sprinkles. Embroider mouth with H, hair with F.

B4 Use 2 size 14mm beads for buttons, 2 size 10mm beads for eyes, 1 small strung bead for nose. Embroider right hand and feet with B, hair with G.

B5 Use 2 size 10mm beads for buttons, 2 size 8mm beads for eyes. Embroider hair, right hand, right foot with B, mouth with D.

B6 Use 2 size 14mm beads for buttons, 2 size 8mm beads for eyes, 1 small strung bead for nose. Embroider left hand and feet with F.

C Sew green bugle beads just inside star shape edges. Fill in center with red strung beads.

D1 Use 2 size 8mm beads for buttons, 2 size 10mm beads for eyes. Embroider suspenders and shorts with H, mouth with J.

D2 Use 2 size 10mm beads for buttons, 2 size 8mm beads for eyes, blue bugle beads sewn randomly in groups of 2 for sprinkles. Embroider hair with E, mouth with J.

D3 Use 2 size 14mm beads for buttons, 2 size 8mm beads for eyes, 1 small strung bead for nose. Embroider right hand and feet with J, forehead squiggles with E.

D4 Use 2 size 8mm beads for buttons, 2 size 8mm beads for eyes. Embroider suspenders and shorts with F, mouth with J.

D5 Use 2 size 14mm beads for buttons, 2 size 10mm beads for eyes, bugle beads sewn randomly in groups of 2 for sprinkles. Embroider hair with F, mouth with E.

D6 Use 2 size 8mm beads for buttons, 2 size 8mm beads for eyes, 2 bugle beads sewn tog for nose. Embroider

suspenders and shorts with J.

E1 and E2 Use red and green beads for strings of lights, sew bugle beads randomly between strings.

F1 Use 3 size 8mm beads for buttons, 2 size 8mm beads for eyes. Embroider lower edge and hands with B; hat, mouth with J.

F2 Use 3 size 10mm beads for buttons, 2 size 8mm beads for eyes. Embroider lower edge, hands and mouth with B; hat with F, carrot at mouth with H.

G Use 2 size 14mm beads for buttons, 2 size 8mm beads for eyes. Embroider hair and feet with B, mouth with J, and belt with D. ●

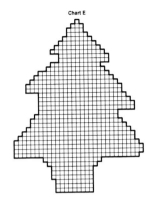

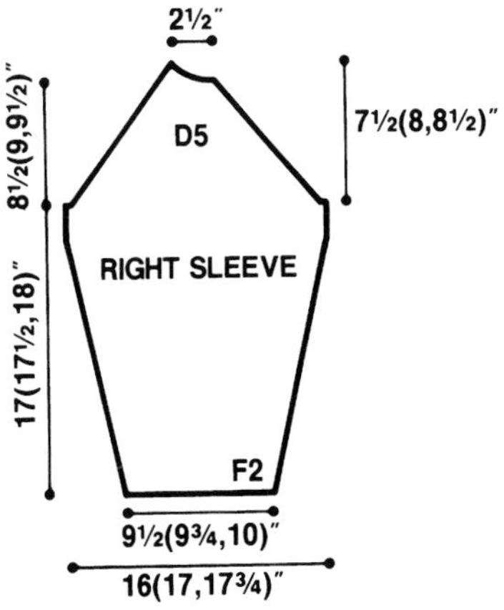

Chart E

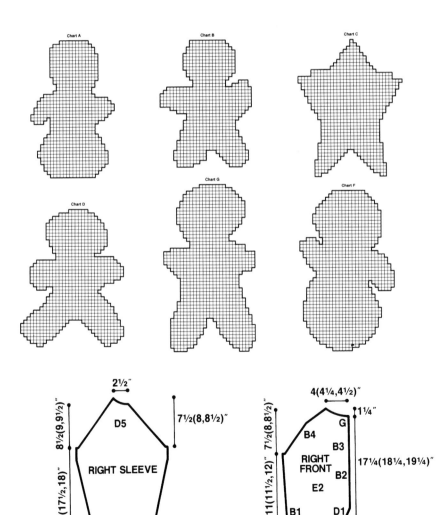

Chart A

Chart B

Chart C

Chart D

Chart G

Chart F

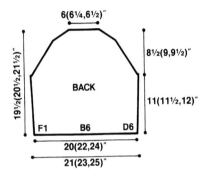

6(6¼,6½)"

8½(9,9½)"

BACK

19½(20½,21½)"

11(11½,12)"

F1   B6   D6

20(22,24)"

21(23,25)"

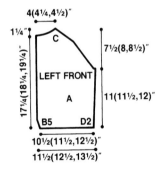

4(4¼,4½)"

1¼"

C

7½(8,8½)"

LEFT FRONT

A

17¼(18¼,19¼)"

11(11½,12)"

B5   D2

10½(11½,12½)"

11½(12½,13½)"

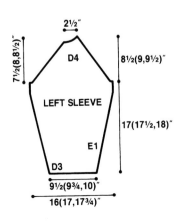

2½"

D5

7½(8,8½)"

8½(9,9½)"

RIGHT SLEEVE

17(17½,18)"

F2

9½(9¾,10)"

16(17,17¾)"

4(4¼,4½)"

1¼"

G

B4

B3

7½(8,8½)"

RIGHT FRONT

B2

E2

17¼(18¼,19¼)"

11(11½,12)"

B1   D1

10½(11½,12½)"

11½(12½,13½)"

2½"

D4

8½(9,9½)"

7½(8,8½)"

LEFT SLEEVE

17(17½,18)"

E1

D3

9½(9¾,10)"

16(17,17¾)"

Nothing's better than a thick, comfy sweater to keep you warm on crisp, cold days. Cynthia Rowley chose a wonderful winter pastel for this classic Aran turtle-neck pullover and hat. Standard fitting; shown in size Medium. The Aran Pullover with Matching Hat first appeared in the Winter '96 issue of *Vogue Knitting*.

Aran Pullover with Matching Hat

FOR INTERMEDIATE KNITTERS

SIZES
To fit Small (Medium, Large). Directions are for smallest size with the larger sizes in parentheses. If there is only one figure it applies to all sizes.

KNITTED MEASUREMENTS
● Bust at underarm 41 (43½, 46)"/104 (110, 117)cm.
● Length 22½ (24, 25½)"/57 (61, 65)cm.
● Sleeve width at upper arm 14½ (15½, 16)"/37 (39.5, 40.5)cm.

MATERIALS
● 15 (16, 17) 3½oz/100g balls (each approx 110yd/100m) of Lane Borgosesia *Knitusa* (wool 5) in #1363 light blue
● One pair each sizes 10 and 10½ (6 and 6.5mm) needles or SIZE TO OBTAIN GAUGE
● One size 10 (6mm) circular needle 16"/40cm long
● Cable needle
● Stitch holder

GAUGE
14 sts and 18 rows to 4"/10cm over St st using size 10½ (6.5mm) needles. FOR PERFECT FIT, TAKE TIME TO CHECK GAUGE.

STITCH GLOSSARY
5-st Bobble K into front, back, front, back and front of st, turn, p5, turn, k2tog, k1, k2tog, turn, sl 1, p2tog, psso, sl st to right-hand needle.
Back Purl Cross (BPC) Sl 1 st to cn and hold in *back*, k2, p1 from cn.
Front Purl Cross (FPC) Sl 2 sts to cn and hold in *front*, p1, k2 from cn.
4-st Back Cable Sl 2 sts to cn and hold in *back*, k2, k2 from cn.
Left Twist (LT) Skip first st and passing behind the st, k 2nd st tbl, k skipped st through front loop, let both sts fall from LH needle.

Side Cable Panel
(Over 10 sts and 4 rows)
Row 1 (RS) LT over 2 sts, p1, 4-st Back Cable, p1, LT over 2 sts.
Row 2 P2, k1, p4, k1, p2.
Row 3 LT over 2 sts, p1, k4, p1, LT over 2 sts.
Row 4 Rep row 2. Rep rows 1-4 for side cable panel.

Honeycomb Panel
(Over 14 sts and 8 rows)
Row 1 (RS) P1, k12, p1.
Rows 2, 4 and 6 K1, p12, k1.
Row 3 P1, (sl 1 st to cn and hold in *front*, k next st, k1 from cn; sl 1 st to cn and hold in *back*, k next st, k1 from cn) 3 times, p1.
Row 5 P1, k12, p1.
Row 7 P1, (sl 1 st to cn and hold in *back*, k next st, k1 from cn; sl 1 st to cn and hold in *front*, k next st, k1 from cn) 3 times, p1.
Row 8 K1, p12, k1. Rep rows 1-8 for honeycomb panel.

Center Cable Panel
(Over 19 sts and 24 rows)
Row 1 (RS) P7, sl 2 sts to cn and hold in *front*, k3, k2 from cn, p7.
Row 2 K7, p2, k1, p2, k7.
Row 3 P6, BPC, k1, FPC, p6.
Row 4 K6, p2, p1, k1, p3, k6.
Row 5 P5, BPC, p1, k1, p1, FPC, p5.
Row 6 K5, p2, (k1, p1) twice, k1, p2, k5.
Row 7 P4, BPC, (k1, p1) twice, k1, FPC, p4.
Row 8 K4, p2, (p1, k1) 3 times, p3, k4.
Row 9 P3, BPC, (p1, k1) 3 times, p1, FPC, p3.
Row 10 K3, p2, (k1, p1) 4 times, k1, p2, k3.
Row 11 P2, BPC, (k1, p1, k1, p1, bobble in next st, p1, k1, p1, k1), FPC, p2.
Row 12 K2, p2, (p1, k1) 5 times, p3, k2.
Row 13 P2, FPC, (k1, p1) 4 times, k1, BPC, p2.
Row 14 K3, p2, (k1, p1) 4 times, k1, p2, k3.
Row 15 P3, FPC, (p1, k1) 3 times, p1, BPC, p3.
Row 16 K4, p2, (p1, k1) 3 times, p3, k4.
Row 17 P4, FPC, (k1, p1) twice, k1, BPC, p4.
Row 18 K5, p2, (k1, p1) twice, k1, p2, k5.
Row 19 P5, FPC, p1, k1, p1, BPC, p5.
Row 20 K6, p2, p1, k1, p3, k6.
Row 21 P6, FPC, k1, BPC, p6.
Row 22 K7, p2, k1, p2, k7.
Row 23 P7, sl 2 sts to cn and hold in *front*, p1, k2, k2 from cn, p7.
Row 24 K7, p4, k8.
Row 25 P7, sl 3 sts to cn and hold in *front*, k2, (p1, k2) from cn, p7.
Row 26 K7, p2, k1, p2, k7. Rep rows 3-26 for center cable panel.

Center Cable Panel for Hat
(15 sts and 20 rows)

Row 1 (RS) P5, sl 2 sts to cn and hold in *front*, k3, k2 from cn, p5.

Row 2 K5, p2, k1, p2, k5.

Row 3 P4, BPC, k1, FPC, p4.

Row 4 K4, p3, k1, p3, k4.

Row 5 P3, BPC, p1, k1, p1, FPC, p3.

Row 6 K3, p2, (k1, p1) twice, k1, p2, k3.

Row 7 P2, BPC, (k1, p1) twice, k1, FPC, p2.

Row 8 K2, p2, (p1, k1) 3 times, p3, k2.

Row 9 P1, BPC, p1, k1, p1, bobble, p1, k1, p1, FPC, p1.

Row 10 K1, p2, (k1, p1) 4 times, k1, p2, k1.

Row 11 P1, FPC, (p1, k1) 3 times, p1, BPC, p1.

Row 12 K2, p2, (p1, k1) 3 times, p3, k2.

Row 13 P2, FPC, (k1, p1) twice, k1, BPC, p2.

Row 14 K3, p2, (k1, p1) twice, k1, p2, k3.

Row 15 P3, FPC, p1, k1, p1, BPC, p3.

Row 16 K4, p3, k1, p3, k4.

Row 17 P4, FPC, k1, BPC, p4.

Row 18 K5, p2, k1, p2, k5.

Row 19 P5, sl 2 sts to cn and hold in *front*, p1, k2, k2 from cn, p5.

Row 20 K5, p4, k6.

BACK

With smaller needles, cast on 99 (103, 107) sts. Work in k1, p1 rib for 3"/7.5cm. Change to larger needles.

Row 1 P2 (4, 6), LT over 2 sts, p2, side cable panel over 10 sts, honeycomb panel over 14 sts, side cable panel over 10 sts, center cable panel over 19 sts, side cable panel over 10 sts, honeycomb panel over 14 sts, side cable panel over 10 sts, p2, LT over 2 sts, p2 (4, 6) sts. Work in est pats until piece measures 13 (14, 15)"/33 (35.5, 38)cm from beg, end with a WS row.

Armhole shaping

Cont pat, bind off 6 sts at beg of next 2 rows.

Row 1 (RS) K1, k2tog, pat to last 3 sts, SKP, k1.

Row 2 P2, pat to last 2 sts, p2. Rep last 2 rows 7 times more—71 (75, 79) sts.

Work even until armhole measures 8 (8½, 9)"/20.5 (21.5, 23)cm, end with a WS row.

Shoulder shaping

Cont in pat, bind off 5 sts at beg of next 6 rows, 5 (6, 7) sts at beg of next 2 rows. Bind off rem 31 (33, 35) sts.

FRONT

Work same as back until armhole measures 6 (6½, 7)"/15 (16.5, 18)cm, end with a WS row.

Shoulder and neck shaping

Next row (RS) Work 26 (27, 28) sts, sl center 19 (21, 23) sts to holder, join second ball of yarn and work rem sts. Working both sides at once, dec 1 st at each neck edge 6 times. When same length as back to shoulders, shape shoulders same as back.

SLEEVES

With smaller needles, cast on 41 sts. Work in k1, p1 rib for 1½"/3.8cm. Change to larger needles.

Row 1 (RS) P1, side cable panel over 10 sts, center cable panel over 19 sts, side cable panel over 10 sts, p1. Work in est pats, inc 1 st each side of next row, then every 6 rows 10 (12, 13) times working added sts in St st—63 (67, 69) sts. Work even until sleeve measures 17½ (18, 18½)"/44.5 (46, 47)cm from beg, end with a WS row.

Cap shaping

Cont pat, bind off 6 sts at beg of next 2 rows, 2 sts at beg of next 16 (18, 18) rows. Bind off rem 19 (19, 21) sts.

FINISHING

Block pieces to measurements. Sew shoulder seams.

Neckband

With RS facing and circular needle, pick up and k74 (78, 82) sts around neck edge. Work around in k1, p1 rib for 8"/20.5cm. Bind off in rib. Sew in sleeves. Sew side and sleeve seams.

HAT

With smaller needles, cast on 72 sts (plus two selvedge stitches which are not counted in following pat and stitch count). Work in k1, p1 rib for 5 rows, increasing 28 st evenly across last row (100 sts). Change to larger needles.

Row 1 (RS) *Side cable panel over 10 sts, center cable panel for hat over 15 sts, rep from * 3 more times. Work in est pats until row 20 of center cable panel has been completed.

Row 21 *Side cable panel over 10 sts as est, p2tog, p4, k4, p5, rep from * 3 more times—96 sts.

Row 22 *Side cable panel over 10 sts as est, k5, p4, k5, rep from * 3 more times.

Row 23 *Side cable panel over 10 sts as est, p2tog, p3, sl 2 sts to cn and hold in *front*, k2, k2 from cn, p3, p2tog, rep from * 3 more times—88 sts.

Row 24 *Side cable panel over 10 sts as est, k4, p4, k4, rep from * 3 more times.

Row 25 *Side cable panel over 10 sts as est, p4, k4, p4, rep from * 3 more times.

Row 26 *Side cable panel over 10 sts as est, k4, p4, k4, rep from * 3 more times.

Row 27 *Side cable panel over 10 sts as est, p4, sl 2 sts to cn and hold in *front*, k2, k2 from cn, p4, rep from * 3 more times.

Row 28 *Side cable panel over 10 sts as est, k4, p4, k4, rep from * 3 more times.

Row 29 *Side cable panel over 10 sts as est, p2tog, p2, k4, p2tog, p2, rep from * 3 more times—80 sts.

Row 30 *Side cable panel over 10 sts as est, k3, p4, k3, rep from * 3 more times.

Row 31 *Side cable panel over 10 sts as est, slip st, p2tog, psso, k4, slip st, p2tog, psso, rep from * 3 more times—72 sts.

Row 32 *K2tog, p1, k2tog, k2tog, p1, k2tog, p1, k2tog, k2tog, p1, rep from * 3 times more—48 sts. Cut yarn, leav-

ing a 12"/30.5cm end. Draw end through rem sts and fasten off. Sew side seam. Make a large pompom and sew to top of hat. ●

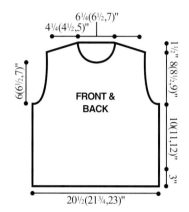

Aran and Bobble Cardigan

Anna Sui incorporates Aran-style cables and bobbles in this curve-enhancing, close-fitting cardigan with raglan yoke, deep rib and round neck. A great design that can go effortlessly from classic to trendy, depending on how you pair and wear it. Shown in size Small. The Aran and Bobble Cardigan first appeared in the Winter '94 issue of *Vogue Knitting*.

Aran and Bobble Cardigan

SIZES
To fit X-Small (Small, Medium, Large). Directions are for smallest size with larger sizes in parentheses. If there is only one figure it applies to all sizes.

KNITTED MEASUREMENTS
● Bust at underarm (buttoned) 32 (34, 36, 38)"/81.5 (86.5, 91.5, 96.5)cm.
● Length 19½ (20, 21, 21½)"/49.5 (51, 53.5, 54.5)cm.
● Sleeve width at upper arm 15 (15½, 16, 16)"/38 (39.5, 41, 41)cm.

MATERIALS
Original Yarn
● 5 (6, 6, 6) 3½oz/100g balls (each approx 137yd/125m) of Classic Elite *Stonington* (wool 5) in #9132 raspberry (A)
● 8 (9, 9, 9) 1¾oz/50g balls (each approx 95yd/86m) of Classic Elite *Tapestry* (wool/mohair 4) in #2232 raspberry (B)
Substitute Yarn
● 6 (7, 7, 7) 3½oz/100g balls (each approx 127yd/125m) of Classic Elite *Artisan* (wool/alpaca 5) in #2334 raspberry (A)
● 8 (9, 9, 9) 1¾oz/50g balls (each approx 95yd/86m) of Classic Elite *Tapestry* (wool/mohair 4) in #2234 raspberry (B)
● Size 9 and 11 (5.5 and 8mm) circular needles 29"/80cm long OR

SIZE TO OBTAIN GAUGE
● Cable needle (cn)
● Stitch holders and markers
● Size F/5 (4.00mm) crochet hook
Note
The original yarn used for this sweater is no longer available. A comparable substitute has been made, which is available at the time of printing. Check gauge of substitute yarns very carefully before beginning.

GAUGE
12 sts and 18 rows to 4"/10cm over St st using 1 strand each A and B held tog and size 11 (8mm) needle.
12 sts to 3"/8cm and 16 rows to 3½"/9cm over cable chart using 1 strand each A and B held tog and size 11 (8mm) needle. FOR PERFECT FIT, TAKE TIME TO CHECK GAUGES.

STITCH GLOSSARY
Right Twist K 2 sts tog, do not sl off needle, k first st; sl both sts off needle.
Left Twist K 2nd st through the back loop, do not sl off needle, k first st; sl both sts off needle.
2-st Front Purl Cross Sl 1 st to cn, hold to *front* of work, p1; k1 from cn.
2-st Back Purl Cross Sl 1 st to cn, hold to *back* of work, k1; p1 from cn.

Rib Pat (even number of sts)
Row 1 *K1, p1; rep from *.
Row 2 *K the purl sts and p the knit sts over first 7 sts*, cont in k1, p1 rib to

last 7 sts, rep between *'s to end. Rep row 2 for rib pat.

Cable Pat (over 6 sts)
Row 1 (RS) P1, k4, p1.
Rows 2 and 4 K1, p4, k1.
Row 3 P1, sl 2 sts to cable needle (cn) and hold to *front* of work, k2; k2 from cn, p1. Rep rows 1-4 for cable pat.

Bobble Pat (over 3 sts)
Row 1 (RS) K3.
Rows 2 and 4 P1, k1, p1.
Row 3 K1, make bobble in next st as foll: [k into front and back of st] 3 times, k into front of st (7 sts made from 1); with tip of LH needle, lift 2nd, 3rd, 4th, 5th and 6th sts over first st on RH needle (bobble complete), k1. Rep rows 1-4 for bobble pat.
Notes
1 Body is worked in one piece to underarm, then joined with sleeves into a yoke.
2 Work with 1 strand each A and B held tog throughout.
3 Sl markers every row.

BODY
With smaller needle and 1 strand each A and B held tog, cast on 116 (122, 128, 134) sts. Placing markers after first 7 and before last 7 sts (front borders), work 5 rows in rib pat.
Next (buttonhole) row (RS) Cont pat, work 2 sts, bind off 3 sts, work to end. On next row, cast on 3 sts over bound-off sts of previous row. Cont rib pat and work buttonholes every

3½"/9cm until piece measures 6½"/16.5cm from beg, ending with a WS row and inc 16 sts evenly across between markers on last row—132 (138, 144, 150) sts. Change to larger needle. Cont to work buttonholes in right front border and beg pats as foll:

Row 1 (RS) Cont 7-st border, k1, work chart sts 7-11, *bobble pat, cable pat, chart sts 1-12*, pm, k6 (9, 12, 15), pm, **chart sts 1-12, cable pat, bobble pat**, chart sts 2-11, rep between *'s once, pm, k6 (9, 12, 15), pm, rep between **'s once, chart sts 2-6, k1, cont 7-st border.

Row 2 (WS) Cont 7-st border, p1, work chart sts 6-2, *bobble pat, cable pat, chart sts 12-1, * p6 (9, 12, 15), **chart sts 12-1, cable pat, bobble pat, ** chart sts 11-2, rep between *'s once, p6 (9, 12, 15), rep between **'s once, chart sts 11-7, p1, cont 7-st border. Cont 7-st front borders, bobble, cable and chart pats as established, working through chart row 16, then cont to rep rows 1-16; work rem 6 (9, 12, 15) sts at underarms and st before and after front borders in St st (k on RS, p on WS). When piece measures 10½ (10½, 11½, 11½)"/27 (27, 29.5, 29.5)cm from beg, end with a WS row, removing all markers on last row. Place sts on holder or spare needle.

SLEEVES

With smaller needle and 1 strand each A and B held tog, cast on 36 sts. Work in k1, p1 rib for 3½"/9cm. Change to larger needle.

Beg pats: Row 1 (RS) K4, pm, work cable pat, bobble pat, chart sts 2-11, bobble pat, cable pat, pm, k4. Working sts before and after markers in St st, cont in pats as established, working through chart row 16, then cont to rep rows 1-16, AT SAME TIME, inc 1 st each side (working inc sts into St st) every 6th row 5 (6, 9, 8) times, every 8th row 3 (3, 1, 2) times—52 (54, 56, 56) sts. Work even until piece measures 17 (17½, 18, 18½)"/43.5 (44.5, 46, 47)cm from beg, removing markers on last row and

end with a WS row. Place sts on holder or spare needle.

YOKE

(Note: On joining row, for sizes small and large only: dec 1 st each side of back for a total of 2 decs; for size medium only, dec 1 st at each sleeve edge for a total of 4 decs.)

Next (joining) row (RS) Cont pats across sts from holders as foll: 36 (37, 38, 39) sts of right front, pm, one sleeve, pm, 60 (64, 68, 72) sts of back (working decs as noted), pm, 2nd sleeve, pm, 36 (37, 38, 39) sts of left front—236 (244, 252, 260) sts. Work 1 row even.

Next (dec) row (RS) *Work to 3 sts before marker, k2tog, k1, sl marker, k1, ssk; rep from * to end—228 (236, 244, 252) sts. Work 1 row even. In same way, dec 1 st before and after each marker every other row 14 (15, 15, 16) times more—116 (116, 124, 124) sts. Cont to rep dec row every other row 4 times more, AT SAME TIME, dec 1 st each sleeve edge on next 2 WS rows—76 (76, 84, 84) sts. Work 1 row even. Yoke measures approx 9 (9½, 9½, 10)"/23 (24, 24, 25.5)cm from joining row. Bind off all sts.

FINISHING

Mark center point of top of each sleeve.

Neckband

With RS facing, smaller needle and 1 strand each A and B held tog, beg at right front and pick up and k19 (19, 21, 21) sts to marker, 39 (39, 40, 40) sts to next marker, 19 (19, 21, 21) sts to left front edge—77 (77, 82, 82) sts.

Next row (WS) P2, *k3, p2; rep from *. Work 2 rows even.

Next row K2, bind off 3 sts, k2, *p1, make bobble in next st, p1, k2; rep from *. On next row, cast on 3 sts over bound-off sts of previous row. Work 2 rows even, binding off in pat on 2nd row. Sew sleeve seams.

Crocheted buttons (make 6)

(Note: Do not turn work after each rnd;

work in spiral fashion. First ch counts as 1 sc.) With crochet hook and B, ch 3. Join with sl st to first ch.

Rnd 1 Ch 1, work sc in same sp, 2 sc in each sc around, sl st to beg ch—6 sc. Rep last rnd once—12 sc.

Rnd 3 Ch 1, sc in each sc around.

Rnd 4 Ch 1, dec by working 2 sc tog around, sl st to beg ch—7 sc. Rep last rnd once—3 sc. Cut yarn, leaving an 8"/20cm strand. Pull through last lp. Stuff button with matching yarn. Thread strand through needle, pick up the outside lp from each sc, gather tog tightly and secure. Sew buttons opposite buttonholes. ●

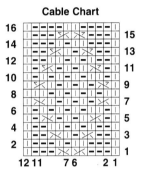

Cable Chart

☐ k on RS, p on WS
⊟ p on RS, k on WS
⧖ Right twist
⧗ Left Twist
⧗ 2-st Back Purl Cross
⧗ 2-st Front Purl Cross

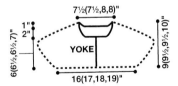

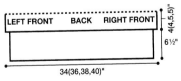

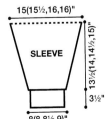

Savor the unexpected—Betty Jackson's modern pony print pullover in exotic black and off-white chenille. The sweater is loose-fitting with square armholes and seed stitch edges. Shown in size Medium. The Pony Print Pullover first appeared in the Fall '92 issue of *Vogue Knitting*.

Pony Print Pullover

FOR INTERMEDIATE KNITTERS

SIZES
To fit Small (Medium, Large). Directions are for smallest size with larger sizes in parentheses. If there is only one figure it applies to all sizes.

KNITTED MEASUREMENTS
● Bust at underarm 40½ (42, 44)"/103 (106.5, 112)cm.
● Length 28"/71cm.
● Sleeve width at upper arm 19"/48.5cm.

MATERIALS
Original Yarn
● 6 (7, 8) 1¾oz/50g balls (each approx 110yd/100m) of Classic Elite/Tiber *Coton-Velours* (cotton 4) in #2111 buff (A)
● 5 (5, 6) balls in #2113 black (B)
Substitute Yarn
● 6 (7, 8) 1¾oz/50g balls (each approx 110yd/100m) of Anny Blatt *Velours* (microfiber 4) in #182 off-white (A)
● 5 (5, 6) balls in #383 black (B)
● One pair each sizes 6 and 7 (4 and 4.5mm) needles OR SIZE TO OBTAIN GAUGE
● Size 6 (4mm) circular needle 16"/ 40cm long
● Bobbins
Note
The original yarn used for this sweater is no longer available. A comparable substitute has been made, which is available at the time of printing. Check gauge of substitute yarns very carefully before beginning.

GAUGE
17 sts and 26 rows to 4"/10cm over St st and chart pat using size 7 (4.5mm) needles. FOR PERFECT FIT, TAKE TIME TO CHECK GAUGE.

STITCH GLOSSARY
Seed St (over even # of sts)
Row 1 *K1, p1; rep from *.
Row 2 Rep row 1. Rep rows 1 and 2 for seed st.

Note
Use bobbins for large blocks of color. When changing colors, twist yarns on WS to prevent holes. To avoid long loose strands, weave or twist yarns not in use around working yarn every 3 or 4 sts.

BACK
With smaller needles and A, cast on 86 (90, 94) sts. Work in seed st for 1"/2.5cm. Change to larger needles and St st. Beg and end as indicated, work chart for back through row 115.

Armhole shaping
Bind off 6 sts at beg of next 2 rows— 74 (78, 82) sts. Work chart through row 174. Bind off.

FRONT
Work as for back, working chart for front through row 148.

Neck shaping
Next row (RS) Work 32 (34, 36) sts, join 2nd ball of yarn and bind off cen-ter 10 sts, work to end. Working both sides at once, bind off from each neck edge 2 sts 4 times, dec 1 st every other row 3 times, 1 st every 4th row 3 times—16 (18, 20) sts rem. When piece measures same length as back to shoulders, bind off rem sts each side.

LEFT SLEEVE
With smaller needles and A, cast on 36 sts. Work in seed st for 1"/2.5cm. Change to larger needles, St st and chart for left sleeve. Work chart for left sleeve, AT SAME TIME, inc 1 st each side (working inc sts into chart pat) every other row 6 times, every 4th row 17 times—82 sts. Cont to work chart through row 105. Bind off all sts.

RIGHT SLEEVE
Work as for left sleeve, working chart for right sleeve.

FINISHING
Block pieces. Sew shoulder seams.

Neckband
With RS facing, circular needle and A, pick up and k98 sts evenly around neck edge. Join.
Rnd 1 *K1, p1; rep from *.
Rnd 2 Purl the k sts and knit the p sts. Rep rnds 1 and 2 for 1"/2.5cm. Bind off in pat. Sew top of sleeves to straight edge of armholes, then sew last 1½"/4cm of sleeve to bound-off armhole sts. Sew side and sleeve seams. ●

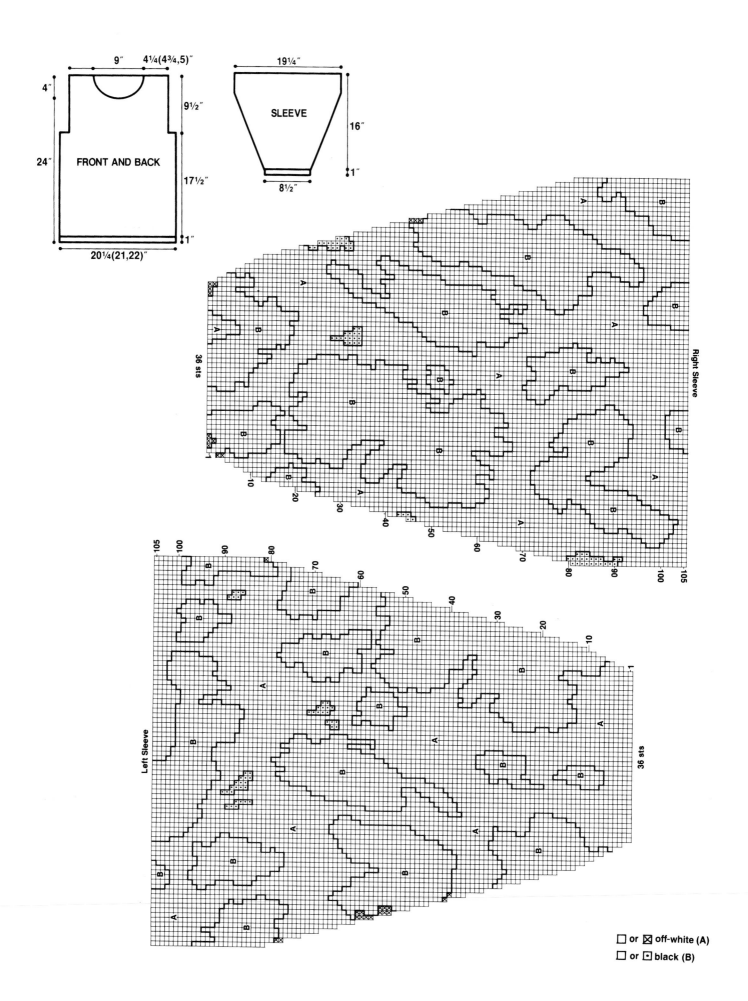

9" 4¼(4¾,5)"

4"

9½"

FRONT AND BACK

24"

17½"

1"

20¼(21,22)"

19¼"

SLEEVE

16"

1"

8½"

36 sts

Right Sleeve

A

B

B

B

B

B

A

A

A

B

B

B

B

B

A

A

A

A

A

B

B

B

A

B

B

B

B

B

A

10

20

30

40

50

60

70

80

90

100

105

105

100

90

80

70

60

50

40

30

20

10

1

B

B

B

B

A

B

A

A

B

A

B

A

B

A

B

A

B

A

B

B

Left Sleeve

36 sts

☐ or ☒ off-white (A)

☐ or ⊡ black (B)

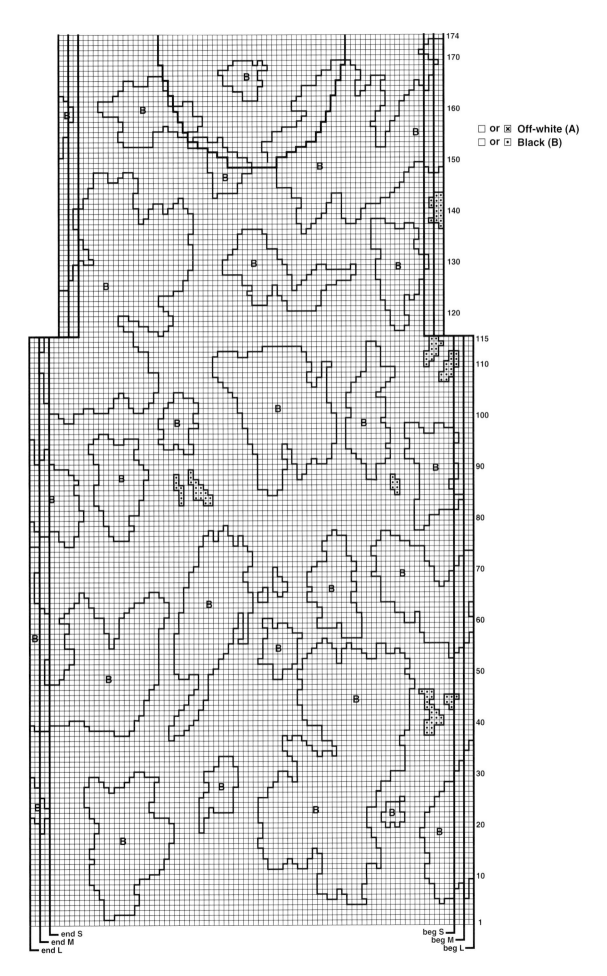

174
170
160
150
140
130
120
115
110
100
90
80
70
60
50
40
30
20
10
1

☐ or ☒ **Off-white (A)**
☐ or ⊡ **Black (B)**

end S
end M
end L

beg S
beg M
beg L

Betty Jackson uses bold diagonals to underscore the contemporary mood of this graphic pullover. The oversized sweater has an intarsia rose motif on the front and a bright diagonal pattern on the back, with drop shoulders, foldover round neck and garter stitch edges. The Rose Tunic first appeared in the Spring/Summer '92 issue of *Vogue Knitting*.

Rose Tunic

FOR INTERMEDIATE KNITTERS

SIZES
One size. To fit 34-42"/86-106cm.

KNITTED MEASUREMENTS
● Bust at underarm 46½"/118cm.
● Length 28"/71cm.
● Sleeve width at upper arm 21"/53.5cm.

MATERIALS
● 17 1¾oz/50g balls (each approx 74yd/68m) of Tahki *Cotton Classic II* (cotton 4) in #2220 ecru (MC)
● 4 balls each in #2002 black (A) and #2995 red (B)
● 2 balls in #2606 green (C)
● One pair each sizes 4 and 6 (3.5 and 4mm) needles OR SIZE TO OBTAIN GAUGE
● Bobbins

GAUGE
20 sts and 27 rows to 4"/10cm over St st using size 6 (4mm) needles.
FOR PERFECT FIT, TAKE TIME TO CHECK GAUGE.

Note
Use separate bobbins for each block of color. When changing colors, twist yarns on WS to prevent holes.

BACK
With smaller needles and MC, cast on 116 sts. Work 4 rows of garter st (2 ridges on RS). Change to larger needles and St st. Beg and end as indicated, work chart #1 through row 186. Bind off.

FRONT
With smaller needles and MC, cast on 116 sts. Work 4 rows of garter st (2 ridges on RS). Change to larger needles and St st. Beg and end as indicated, work chart #2 through row 146. Cont in MC only until piece measures 24½"/62cm from beg, end with a WS row.

Neck shaping
Next row (RS) Work 50 sts, join 2nd ball of yarn and bind off 16 sts, work to end. Working both sides at once, dec 1 st at each neck edge every row 6 times, then every other row 6 times. When same length as back to shoulder, bind off rem 38 sts each side.

SLEEVES
With smaller needles and MC, cast on 50 sts. Work in garter st for 4 rows (2 ridges on RS). Change to larger nee-dles and St st. Beg and end as indicated, work chart through row 22, then cont with MC only, AT SAME TIME, inc 1 st each side (working inc sts into pat) every other row 7 times, then every 4th row 20 times—104 sts. Work even until piece measures 15½"/39.5cm from beg. Bind off.

FINISHING
Block pieces. Sew left shoulder seam.

Neckband
With RS facing, smaller needle, MC and beg at left shoulder edge, pick up and k112 sts evenly around neck edge. Beg at right edge of chart #3, work through row 10. Cont with MC only, knit 5 rows. Cont in St st for 1½"/4cm. Bind off loosely. Sew right shoulder, including neckband seam. Fold neckband in half to WS and sew in place. Place markers 10½"/26.5cm down from shoulders on front and back for armholes. Sew top of sleeves between markers. Sew side and sleeve seams. ●

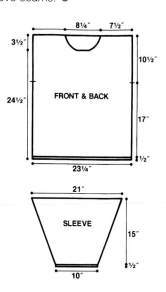

Chart #1

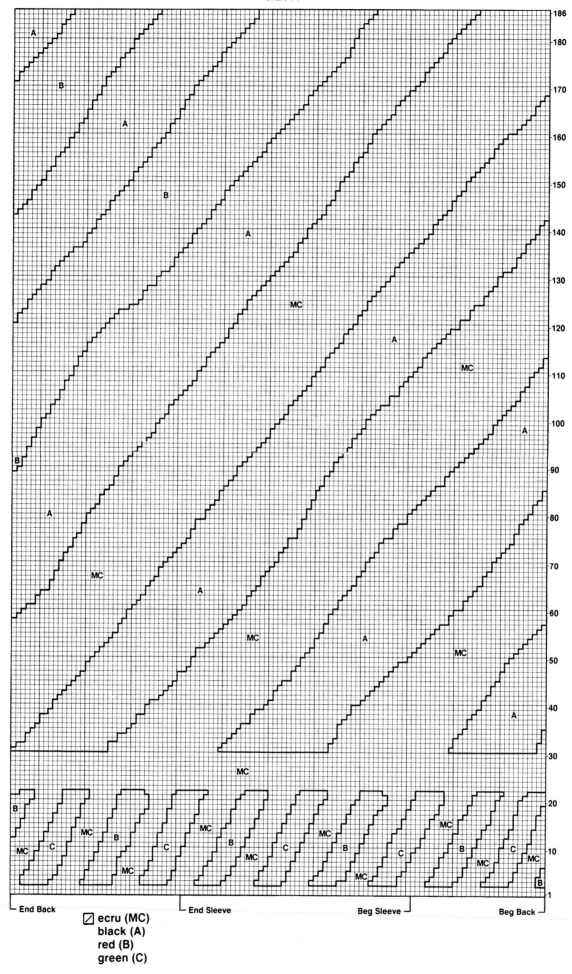

ecru (MC)
black (A)
red (B)
green (C)

End Back   End Sleeve   Beg Sleeve   Beg Back

Chart #2

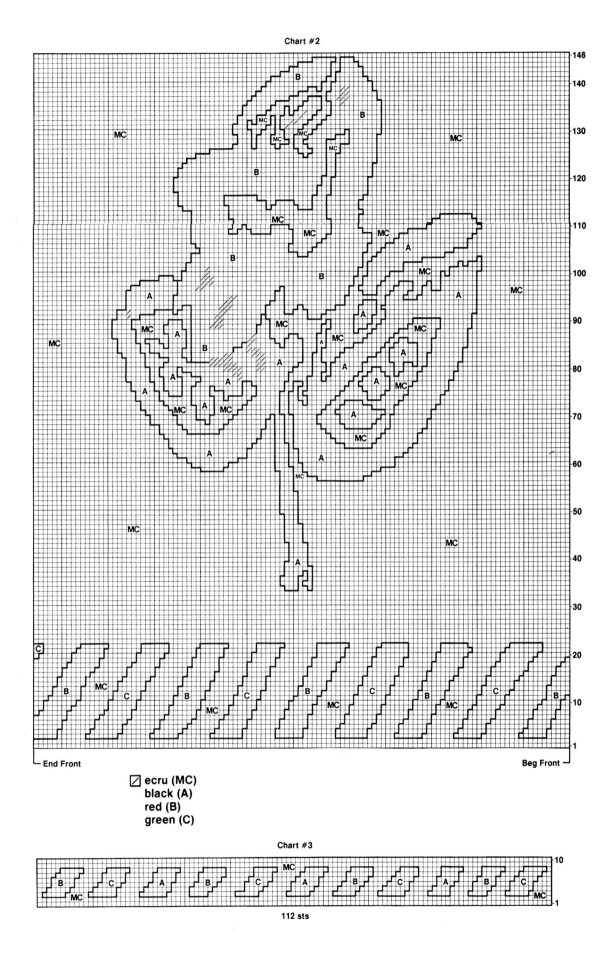

☑ ecru (MC)
black (A)
red (B)
green (C)

Chart #3

112 sts

Todd Oldham

Plush chenille makes an intriguing contrast against flat wool—just the sort of visual excitement that is signature Todd Oldham. His very oversized, striped pullover with set-in sleeves and ribbed highneck can be made micro-cropped or tunic length—but ours just clears the waist to blend easily with wardrobe basics. Shown in size Medium. The Cropped Striped Pullover first appeared in the Fall '94 issue of *Vogue Knitting*.

Cropped Striped Pullover

VERY EASY VERY VOGUE

SIZES
To fit sizes Small (Medium, Large). Directions are for smallest size with larger sizes in parentheses. If there is only one figure it applies to all sizes.

KNITTED MEASUREMENTS
● Bust at underarm 46 (50, 54)"/117 (127, 137)cm.
● Length 15½ (16, 16½)"/39.5 (41, 42)cm.
● Sleeve width at upper arm 14 (15, 16)"/35.5 (38, 41)cm.

MATERIALS
● 2 1¾oz/50g balls (each approx 109yd/99m) of Anny Blatt *Velours* (microfiber 4) in #507 red (D)
● 1 (1, 2) balls each in #382 blue (A), #407 gold (H), and #351 Mer du Sud (F)
● 1 (2, 2) 1¾oz/50g balls (each approx 93yd/85m) of Anny Blatt *No. 5 d'Anny Blatt* (wool 4) in #061 bronze (C)
● 1 (1, 2) balls each in #511 rubis (G), #383 black (E), and #431 paille (B)
● One pair each sizes 5 and 7 (3.5 and 4.5mm) needles, OR SIZE TO OBTAIN GAUGE

Note
Some of the original colors used for this sweater are no longer available. A comparable color substitute has been made, which is available at the time of printing.

GAUGE
19 sts and 26 rows to 4"/10cm over St st using size 7 (4.5mm) needles and C. 19 sts and 32 rows to 4"/10cm over St st using size 5 (3.5mm) needles and A. FOR PERFECT FIT, TAKE TIME TO CHECK GAUGES.

STITCH GLOSSARY
Stripe Pat
Using larger needles when working with B, C, G and E (wool) and smaller needles when working with A, D, H and F (chenille), work 1¾"/4.5cm stripes in foll color sequence: *B, C, D, E, F, G, H, D; rep from *.

BACK
With smaller needles and A, cast on 110 (118, 128) sts.
Row 1 (WS) *K2, p2; rep from*, end k2 (2, 0).
Row 2 (RS) P2 (2, 0), *k2, p2; rep from *. Rep last 2 rows until rib measures 2"/5cm. Change to larger needles and B. Beg with a k row, work in St st (k on RS, p on WS) and stripe pat (changing needle sizes as noted) until piece measures 7"/18cm from beg, end with a WS row.

Armhole shaping
Cont in pat, bind off 5 sts at beg of next 2 rows—100 (108, 118) sts. Cont stripe pat and work even until armhole measures 7 (7½, 8)"/18 (19, 20)cm, end with a WS row.

Neck and shoulder shaping
Bind off 7 (6, 7) sts at beg of next 2

rows—86 (96, 104). Shape neck and shoulder simultaneously as foll: Bind off 6 (7, 8) sts at beg of next 8 rows, AT SAME TIME, bind off center 22 (24, 24) sts and working both sides at once, bind off from each neck edge 4 sts twice.

FRONT
Work as for back until piece measures 13½ (14, 14½)"/34 (35.5, 37)cm, end with a WS row.

Neck and shoulder shaping
Next row (RS) Work 39 (43, 48) sts, join 2nd ball of yarn and bind off 22 sts, work to end. Working both sides at once, bind off from each neck edge 2 sts 3 times, 2 (3, 3) sts once, AT SAME TIME, when armhole measures same as back, shape shoulders as for back.

SLEEVES
With smaller needles and A, cast on 38 (40, 42) sts.
Row 1 (WS) *K2, p2; rep from *, end k2 (0, 2).
Row 2 (RS) P2 (0, 2), *k2, p2; rep from *. Rep last 2 rows until k2, p2 rib measures 2"/5cm. Change to larger needles and B. Work in St st and stripe pat, AT SAME TIME, inc 1 st each side (working inc sts into St st) every 6th row 9 (5, 2) times, every 4th row 5 (11, 15) times—66 (72, 76) sts. When piece measures 13"/33cm from beg, end with a WS row.

Cap shaping
Cont in pat, bind off 5 sts at beg of

next 2 rows—56 (62, 66) sts. Bind off 2 sts at beg of next 24 rows. Bind off rem 8 (14, 18) sts.

FINISHING
Block pieces lightly. Sew left shoulder.

Highneck
With RS facing, larger needles and C, beg at right shoulder, pick up and k36 (38, 40) sts along back neck, 38 (40, 42) sts along front neck—74 (78, 82) sts.

Row 1 (WS) *K2, p2; rep from *, end k2.

Row 2 (RS) P2, *k2, p2; rep from *. Rep last 2 rows until rib measures 2"/5cm, end with a WS row. Change to smaller needles and A.

Next row (RS) Knit.

Next row Rep row 1. Cont to rep rows 1 and 2 until rib measures 4"/10cm from beg. Bind off loosely in rib. Sew right shoulder, including high-neck. Set in sleeves. Sew side and sleeve seams. ●

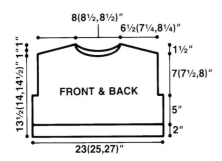

Resources

Write to the yarn companies listed below for yarn purchasing and mail-order information.

ADRIENNE VITTADINI
distributed by JCA
35 Scales Lane
Townsend, MA 01469

ANNY BLATT
7796 Boardwalk
Brighton, MI 48116

BARUFFA
distributed by Lane Borgosesia
PO Box 217
Colorado Springs, CO 80903

BERNAT
distributed by Spinrite Yarns, Ltd.
PO Box 40
Listowel, ON
N4W 3H3 Canada

BERROCO INC.
14 Elmdale Road
PO Box 367
Uxbridge, MA 01569

BROWN SHEEP CO., INC.
100662 County Road 16
Mitchell, NE 69357

CASCADE YARNS, INC.
2401 Utah Ave S., Suite 505
Seattle, WA 98134

CLASSIC ELITE
12 Perkins Street
Lowell, MA 01854

COATS PATONS
1001 Roselawn Ave.
Toronto, Ontario M6B 1B8
UK: Coats Crafts UK
PO Box 22
The Lingfield Estate Darlington
Co Durham DL1 1YQ

CRYSTAL PALACE YARNS
3006 San Pablo Ave.
Berkeley, CA. 94702

DALE OF NORWAY, INC.
N16 W 23390 Stoneridge Dr.,
Suite A
Waukesha, WI 53188

DMC
#10 Port Kearny
South Kearny, NJ 07032
UK: DMC Creative World
Pullman Road
Wigston, Leicestershire LEI8 2DY

FILATURA DI CROSA
distributed by Stacy Charles
1059 Manhattan Ave.
Brooklyn, NY 11222

HAYFIELD
distributed by Cascade Yarns, Inc.
2401 Utah Ave. S., Suite 505
Seattle, WA 98134

JCA
35 Scales Lane
Townsend, MA 01469

LANE BORGOSESIA U.S.A.
PO Box 217
Colorado Springs, CO 80903

LANG
distributed by Berroco Inc.
14 Elmdale Road
PO Box 367
Uxbridge, MA 01569

LION BRAND YARNS
34 West 15th Street
New York, NY 10011

MANOS DEL URUGUAY
distributed by Simpson Southwick
55 Curtiss Place
Maplewood, NJ 07040

MISSONI
distributed by Stacy Charles
1059 Manhattan Ave.
Brooklyn, NY 11222

MUENCH YARNS
118 Ricardo Road
Mill Valley, CA 94941-2461

ORNAGHI FILATI
distributed by Trendsetter Yarns
16742 Stagg St., Suite 104
Van Nuys, CA 91406

PATONS
distributed by Coats Patons
1001 Roselawn Ave.
Toronto, Ontario M6B 1B8
UK: Coats Crafts UK
PO Box 22
The Lingfield Estate Darlington
Co Durham DL1 1YQ

PLYMOUTH YARNS
PO Box 28
Bristol, PA 19007

REYNOLDS
distributed by JCA
35 Scales Lane
Townsend, MA 01469

ROWAN
distributed by Westminster Fibers
5 Northern Blvd.
Amherst, NH 03031
UK: Green Lane Mill
Holmfirth
West Yorkshire HD7 1RW

SESIA
distributed by Lane Borgosesia
PO Box 217
Colorado Springs, CO 80903

SKACEL COLLECTION
PO Box 88110
Seattle, WA 98138-2110
UK: Spring Mill House
Baildon, Shipley
West Yorkshire BD17 6AD

SPINRITE YARNS, LTD.
PO Box 40
Listowel, ON
N4W 3H3 Canada

**STACY CHARLES
COLLECTION**
1059 Manhattan Ave.
Brooklyn, NY 11222

STAHL WOLLE
distributed by Tahki Imports Ltd.
11 Graphic Place
Moonachie, NJ 07074

TAHKI IMPORTS LTD.
11 Graphic Place
Moonachie, NJ 07074

TRENDSETTER YARNS
16742 Stagg St., Suite 104
Van Nuys, CA 91406

UNGER
distributed by JCA
35 Scales Lane
Townsend, MA 01469

**Vogue Knitting
161 Avenue of the Americas
New York, NY 10013-1252
Fax 212-620-2731
www.vogueknitting.com**

**In UK and Europe:
Vogue Knitting
New Lane
Havant Hants PO9 2ND, England
Tel 01705 486221
Fax 01705 492769**

We have made every effort to ensure the accuracy of the contents of this publication. We are not responsible for any human or typographical errors.

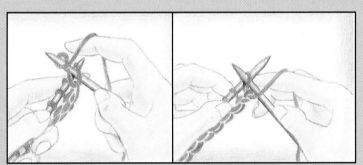

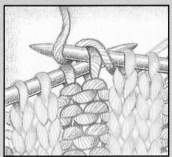
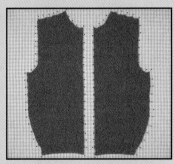
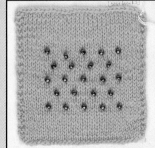
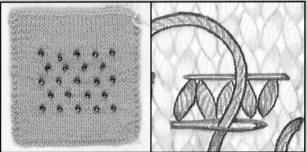

ACKNOWLEDGEMENTS

There are many people who contributed to the making of this book. In particular, and most importantly, we would like to thank the previous editors of *Vogue Knitting* magazine, including Polly Roberts, Marilyn F. Cooperman, Lola Ehrlich, Margaret C. Korn, Meredith Gray Harris, Sonja Bjorklund Dagress, Nancy J. Thomas, Margery Winter, Carla S. Scott, and Gay Bryant, for their vision and impeccable design selections. We would also like to extend our warmest appreciation and gratitude to all of the dedicated and knowledgeable *Vogue Knitting* staff members, past and present, for their skill and countless hours of hard work in bringing the best of knitting to their readers. Special thanks also goes to the tireless knitters and contributing technical experts, without whom the magazine would not be possible.

PHOTO CREDITS

Ruven Afanador (pages 31, 139), Paul Amato (page 95), Eric Boman (pages 13, 93, 111), Jack Deutsch (pages 129, 131), Bob Frame (page 89), Bob Hiemstra (page 29), Hiromasa (pages 35, 57), Barry Hollywood (pages 73, 153), Douglas Keeve (pages 65, 109), Lynn Kolhman (pages 15, 105), Michael O'Brien (pages 19, 87, 115), Danny Sit (pages 99, 103), Wayne Stambler (page 121), Peter Strube (pages 83, 125, 143), Paul Sunday (page 157), Alberto Tolot (page 47), Charles Tracy (pages 45, 51, 61, 67, 79), Diego Uchitel (pages 39, 77, 149), Nick Vaccaro (pages 23, 53, 127, 133, 145), Antoine Verglas (pages 25, 71, 117)